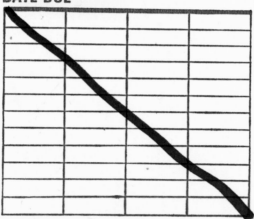

THE CHALLENGE OF JAPAN'S INTERNATIONALIZATION

THE CHALLENGE OF JAPAN'S INTERNATIONALIZATION

ORGANIZATION AND CULTURE

edited by
Hiroshi Mannari and Harumi Befu

Seminar Proceedings
Kwansei Gakuin University, Sengari Seminar House
June 30–July 5, 1981

KWANSEI GAKUIN UNIVERSITY
and
KODANSHA INTERNATIONAL LTD.

Distributed in the United States by Kodansha International/ USA Ltd., through Harper & Row, Publishers, Inc., 10 East 53rd Street, New York, New York 10022. Published by Kwansei Gakuin University, Nishinomiya, Hyōgo, Japan, Kodansha International Ltd., 12-21, Otowa 2-chome, Bunkyo-ku, Tokyo 112 and Kodansha International/USA Ltd., with offices at 10 East 53rd Street, New York, New York 10022 and The Hearst Building, 5 Third Street, Suite 430, San Francisco, California 94103.

Produced by Kodansha International Ltd. Printed in Japan.

ISBN-0-87011-658-4
LCC 83-83097
ISBN 4-7700-1158-X

Dedicated to

KUYAMA YASUSHI
Chancellor, Kwansei Gakuin University

SAJI KEIZŌ
President, Suntory, Ltd. and
Suntory Foundation

CONTENTS

PREFACE

"Internationalization" is one of the most potent and significant words in the contemporary vocabulary of Japanese intellectuals, academicians, politicians and journalists. At first sight, its meaning may seem more inclusive than exact. One can speak of the internationalization of Japanese industry (i.e., investing abroad), the internationalization of Japanese markets (i.e., opening them to foreign competition), and even the internationalization of the Japanese personality system (i.e., enabling the Japanese people to interact with foreigners with greater confidence). The concept therefore seems to have an *organizational* aspect, dealing with technology transfers, institutions of various sorts, and high finance, as well as a *cultural* side, dealing with the symbolic and emotional dimensions of national self-identity.

In a sense, the concerns implied by the term "internationalization" have long been foreshadowed in the history of Japan. Since the close of the Tokugawa period (1868), the Japanese have been actively, but selectively, engaged in absorbing foreign culture and technology. In the past, this process has gone by various names. In its early stages it was known as *bunmei kaika*—civilization and enlightenment. During the Second World War, *Daitōa Kyōeiken* (the Greater East Asia Co-Prosperity Sphere) was the official slogan used by the government to express its militaristic version of "internationalization." After the war, Japan's attention shifted from military expansion in the Far East to the importation of Western values and culture. At that time the term *ōbeika* (Euro-Americanization) became fashionable. In the 1960s, the word "modernization" (*kindaika*) was borrowed from American social science to express the fundamental changes felt to be taking place in Japanese society, culture and personality. It was only in the 1970s and 1980s that the term "internationalization" (*kokusaika*) became popular.

What does the term "internationalization" really mean in the discourse of Japanese opinion-makers? What do they mean when they say that someone is a *kokusaijin* (internationalist)? How does a Japanese acquire *kokusaisei* (internationality)? What kind of firm is it that "goes international" or achieves *kokusaika*?

To answer these questions, various Japanese and Western scholars assembled at Kwansei Gakuin University's Sengari Seminar House near Nishinomiya, Japan, from June 30 to July 5, 1981. The essays included in this volume present the results of their research and deliberations. They point out the importance of internationalization as an historical fact, the rhetorical or ideological distortions of the concept, and its potential usefulness in genuine cultural and social-scientific research. Although no unanimity of views was expected from scholars approaching these questions from many diverse disciplinary and theoretical perspectives, the seminar provided an excellent opportunity to share information and insights. It is our hope that these papers will stimulate further study and thereby contribute to the development of new theories and models of cultural and institutional exchange.

We are indebted to the following persons and organizations, whose moral and financial support made this conference possible.

> Chancellor KUYAMA Yasushi, Kwansei Gakuin University
> President JOZAKI Susumu, Kwansei Gakuin University
> The Japan Foundation, Tokyo
> American Center (United States Information Service), Osaka
> Kansai Electric Power Co., Inc., Osaka
> Osaka Gas Co., Ltd., Osaka
> Suntory, Ltd. and Suntory Foundation, Osaka
> Sumitomo Metal Industries, Ltd., Osaka
> Sumitomo Electric Industries, Ltd., Osaka
> Matsushita Electric Industries Co., Ltd., Osaka
> Matsushita Electric Works, Ltd., Osaka
> Asahi Broadcasting Corporation, Osaka
> Chūbu-Nippon Broadcasting Co., Ltd., Nagoya

The conference was most ably facilitated by the following persons who provided simultaneous translation for effective communication. Our sincere thanks are due them.

Dr. KASHIOKA Tomihide, Assistant Professor, Kansai University of Foreign Studies, Hirakata-shi, Japan

Dr. Jeffrey BROADBENT, Junior Fellow, The Horace H. Rackham School of Graduate Studies, The University of Michigan

Mr. FUJITA Makoto, Director, International Center, Kwansei Gakuin University

Mr. KUNII Toshio, Interpreter, United States International Communication Agency, American Center in Osaka

For publication of the proceedings of the conference, we are indebted to the United States-Japan Foundation, New York, for providing generous subsidies. Finally we wish to thank Mr. Akanoma Yukimori of Kodansha International, Tokyo, and Mrs. Linda Davis for their competently executed editorial work for publication of this volume.

A note on the convention for identifying Japanese names: when a Japanese is identified by both the surname and the given name, the following convention will be used. Both in the text and in the bibliography, Japanese who are active primarily in Japan and whose publications have mostly appeared in Japanese are listed with the family name first, followed without a comma by the given name. On the other hand, when the author is active abroad more than in Japan and has published mostly in non-Japanese sources, his surname in the bibliography is followed by a comma, and then by the given name.

MANNARI Hiroshi
Kwansei Gakuin University
Nishinomiya, Hyōgo, Japan

Harumi BEFU
Stanford University
Stanford, California, U.S.A.

11

CONTRIBUTORS

Koya AZUMI is Professor of Sociology and Department Chairman at Rutgers University (Newark campus). He has done comparative studies of factories and workers in Britain, Japan and Sweden, and is currently engaged in a study of American and Japanese factories.

Harumi BEFU is Professor of Anthropology at Stanford University. He has written on kinship in Japan, gift-giving and social exchange, village structures, political and cultural aspects of Japanese society, and the acculturation of Japanese overseas. He is a past Fulbright-Hays scholar, and the author of *Japan, An Anthropological Introduction* (1971).

Robert N. BELLAH is Ford Professor of Sociology and Comparative Studies and former Chairman of the Sociology Department at the University of California, Berkeley. He is the author of *Tokugawa Religion* (1957), *Beyond Belief: Essays on Religion in a Post-Traditional World* (1970), and *The Broken Covenant: American Civil Religion in Time of Trial* (1975), and various other studies of the sociology of religion and culture.

Winston DAVIS is Professor of Sociology at Kwansei Gakuin University, Japan. He is author of *Toward Modernity: A Developmental Typology of Popular Religious Affiliations in Japan* (1977), *Dojo: Magic and Exorcism in Modern Japan* (1980) and other studies of Japanese religion and society.

W. Mark FRUIN, Professor of History at California State University, Hayward, is currently teaching Japanese business and economic history at the National University of Singapore. His publications include *Kikkōman—Company, Clan, and Community* (1983), from which his contribution to this volume was taken. Currently he is working, with Alfred Chandler, Jr., on a cross-cultural study of the rise of big business.

Jerald HAGE is Professor of Sociology and Department Chairman at the University of Maryland. His most recent book is *Theories of Organizations* (1980).

Geert HOFSTEDE is Director of the Institute for Research on Intercultural Co-operation (IRIC) at Delft, the Netherlands. He has been a teacher and researcher at various institutes throughout Europe, and is the author and editor of numerous books and articles in the areas of management, organization, and culture. His most recent book is *Culture's Consequences: International Differences in Work-Related Values* (1980).

Frank HULL is Assistant Professor of Sociology at the University of Maryland. He is restudying the 110 factories in New Jersey first studied by Peter Blau in 1973.

Chalmers JOHNSON is Professor (and former Department Chairman) of the Political Science Department at the University of California, Berkeley. He has written extensively on Chinese and Japanese politics, including *An Instance of Treason* (translated into Japanese as *Ozaki-Zoruge jiken*), *Conspiracy at Matsukawa,* and *Japan's Public Policy Companies*. His most recent book, a history of the Japanese Ministry of International Trade and Industry, is *MITI and the Japanese Miracle* (1982).

KAMISHIMA Jirō is Professor of Law and Politics at Rikkyō University in Tokyo and President of the Japanese Political Science Association. He is an authority on the political culture of Japan, and has a broad interest in its implications for the other social sciences. Among his publications are *Kindai Nihon no seishin kōzō* (1961) and, more recently, *Nichijyōsei no seijigaku* (1982).

MANNARI Hiroshi is Professor of Sociology at Kwansei Gakuin University, Japan. His areas of interest include social stratification, mobility, and cross-national studies of industrial and other complex organizations. He is the author of *The Japanese Business Leaders* (1974) and various other books and articles in Japanese.

Robert M. MARSH is Professor of Sociology at Brown University. His teaching and research concern complex organizations and societal modernization, with special reference to East Asia. He is author of *Comparative Sociology: A Codification of Cross-Societal Analysis* (1967) and coauthor (with Mannari Hiroshi) of *Modernization and the Japanese Factory* (1976).

Ross E. MOUER is Assistant Professor at the School of Modern Asian Studies at Griffith University, Australia. He has organized, with Yoshio Sugimoto, a symposium on Alternative Models for Understanding Japanese Society, and an International Colloquium for the Comparative Study of Japanese Society. He is coauthor with Sugimoto of the monograph "Japanese Society: Stereotypes and Realities" and the book *Nihonjin wa "Nihonteki" ka* (1983).

Herbert PASSIN, Professor and former Department Chairman of the Sociology Department at Columbia University, has written widely on modern Japanese culture, education, and the role of intellectuals in society. His books include *Society and Education in Japan* (1965) and *Japanese and the Japanese* (1980). He is a member of the East Asia Institute, Columbia University.

Yoshio SUGIMOTO is Professor of Sociology and former Department Chairman at La Trobe University, Australia. He was the first Director of the Japanese Studies Center in Melbourne. His collaboration with Ross Mouer includes numerous articles and the jointly edited volume *Nihonjinron ni kansuru junisho* (1982). A volume jointly authored with Ross Mouer, *Images of Japanese Society: A Study in the Social Construction of Reality,* is forthcoming.

WAGATSUMA Hiroshi is Professor of Behavioral Sciences and Cross-cultural Studies at the University of Tsukuba in Japan. He is a specialist on the psychology of the Japanese, with a special interest in Japanese attitudes toward foreigners, overseas Japanese and other areas with international implications. He has published numerous books and articles in Japanese, English and German in the field of psychological anthropology, and coauthored (with George DeVos) *Japan's Invisible Race: Caste in Culture and Personality* (1967).

Four other participants presented papers at the conference, but did not submit final papers for publication: KANAI Minori, Agency of Industrial Science and Technology, Ministry of International Trade and Industry; WATANUKI Jōji, Sophia University; HOSHINO Akira, International Christian University; and SATŌ Seizaburō, Tokyo University.

OVERVIEW:
THE INTERNATIONALIZATION OF JAPAN—
SOME REFLECTIONS

Herbert Passin

I

Internationalization, we are reminded by Harumi Befu, means if not all things to all men, then at least many different things to many men (see his paper in this volume). As currently used in Japan, it refers to several different aspects of the interrelations between the country and the larger international society: opening up of the Japanese economy, improving Japan's ability to participate in the world economic and political order, and becoming more like the rest of the advanced industrial societies.

On any of the usual measures brought to mind by the word "internationalization" Japan would appear to rank quite high. It has a very extensive involvement in the world. Its world trade is booming, its overseas capital investment is expanding, and its manufacturers—such as Sony, Matsushita, Toyota, Kawasaki—have become household words throughout the world. Every year more than four million Japanese go abroad for business, study, or tourism, and close to two million foreigners visit Japan. Several hundreds of thousands live abroad, working or studying. The Japanese tourist has almost replaced the American tourist of an earlier day as the symbol of the rich materialistic provincials. A great deal of attention is given to foreign languages: English is a required subject in junior high school, and even if not formally required, it is virtually so in senior high school and university. All Japanese can therefore be said to have studied, or at least had some exposure to English for at least six years. And beyond formal schooling, English language education has by now become a major industry.

Almost all American and European books of any importance are translated and published in Japan, some for the benefit of specialized

15

audiences such as scientists, scholars and engineers, most for the large general reading public. Japanese media give extensive coverage to foreign events; Japan has more media representatives in Washington than any other nation. Why then, one might well wonder, has "internationalization" become such an important issue recently?

Moreover, the process has been under way for a long time; "internationalization" is a perennial theme in modern Japanese history. One of the archetypal historical experiences of Japanese internationalization is embodied in the famous lines written by Sakuma Shōzan (quoting from Confucius' *Analects*, II, 4) in the year 1854 when he was sitting in prison, about as isolated from the rest of the world as he could be:

> At twenty I realized I had a part to play
> in the life of my state.
> At thirty I realized I had a part to play
> in the life of the entire nation.
> At forty I realized I had a part to play
> in the life of the entire world.

Shōzan recounts his personal movement from a narrow parochial loyalty to a progressively wider sense of involvement, ultimately embracing the entire world.

Some seventy years later Uchimura Kanzō described another archetypal Japanese progression (1925: 599–600), in the form of an inscription for his own tombstone, this time in an idiom that is perhaps more appropriate to the Christian institution where this symposium on internationalization was held:

> I for Japan;
> Japan for the world;
> The world for Christ;
> And all for God.

The theme of internationalization has been around at least since the late eighteenth century, when Japan first began to feel threatened by the spread of Western power. Japan must remodel at least some of its institutions along Western lines in order to be able to stand up to the West and to be competitive in the world. As the awareness of European power pressed in upon isolated Japan, the concern with internationalization grew, and by Meiji it reached its first great climax.

Since then it has remained a constant theme in Japan's modern history. And because the Meiji conception of internationalization was essentially of a self-transformation along Western lines, it inevitably carried in its train the problem of identity—What does it mean to be Japanese? Are we "Eastern" or are we "Western"? How can one be both modern and Japanese? Is a westernized Japanese a true Japanese? Are we not selling out our traditional heritage for a mess of Western pottage?[1]

In the past few years, however, internationalization has become not only a national preoccupation, but a popular, perhaps even a pop issue. The Japanese market is flooded with books on the subject: the international man, the conditions of internationalization, what it takes to be international, how to beat foreigners in an argument, how to debate Western style, how to assert yourself, international responsibilities, international manners and behavior, Japan's place in the international order, Japan's standing on a variety of international measures, and the internationalization of the economy.

II

The concurrent interest in Japanese culture—*Nihonjinron,* or *Nihon bunkaron*—is not so much a contrary current as the other side of the coin. Its general thrust is that Japanese culture is unique and therefore, by implication, incomprehensible to the outside world. Western stereotypes about the inscrutability of the Japanese have no difficulty finding an echo in Japan itself. One possible conclusion from the notion of Japanese exceptionalism is that Japanese culture is so unique that the bearers of that culture, that is, the Japanese people, can never become truly international. The conclusion comes in two versions: that internationalization is necessary but that Japanese culture is a hindrance; or, contrariwise, that internationalization is not necessary for the Japanese to be successful. But an equally plausible conclusion from this same thesis of Japanese exceptionalism is that it is precisely by holding on to their cultural identity—their unique qualities and cultural traditions—that Japanese will succeed and will make their independent contribution to international society.

Whatever position one takes, however, what is clear is that the concern with identity and with internationalization is at a very high level in Japan. This contrasts vividly with the lack of comparable concern in most of the other advanced industrial societies. One would not be

17

surprised to find it in the newly developing nations, especially those that have only recently acquired their independence or are still struggling for a higher degree of autonomy.[2] But in a country that has been "developing" for more than 100 years now, the preoccupation is, if not surprising, at least different from what we observe among the other advanced countries.

All countries have their own traditions of uniqueness and theories of exceptionalism. American history has no shortage of concern with our unique historical mission, our manifest destiny, our distinctiveness from our European ancestors. "The genius of American democracy," writes historian Daniel Boorstin (1958), "comes from a peculiar and unrepeatable combination of historical circumstances. . . I argue in a word, that American democracy is unique. It possesses a 'genius' all its own." And Richard Hofstadter (1968: 445) following de Tocqueville, speaks of the "ineluctable singularity of American development." In 1929, when the Executive Committee of the Communist International set out to expel the then leadership of the American Communist Party, one of its gravest charges was that of "American exceptionalism." Jay Lovestone, Benjamin Gitlow, and the rest of the majority of the Central Committee of the CPUSA were accused of right-wing Bukharinist deviation in arguing that American conditions were different from European and that therefore American revolutionary strategy and tactics had to be different (Wolfe, 1981: chapters 31, 32, 33).

It would be instructive, therefore, to raise the same questions in the United States, or indeed in any of the other advanced industrial nations, that are being raised today in Japan. Is the United States internationalized? How international is it? How do Americans rate on whatever scales of comparative internationalization that can be devised: foreign language ability, knowledge of foreign cultures and societies, foreign tastes, openness to ideas of foreign origin, willingness to try new experiences, food habits, openness of markets, ability to function in foreign settings, convergence of organizational forms and behavioral patterns to those of other industrial societies, ability to get along with local people, ability to melt into foreign settings, ability to empathize with the feelings and points of view of people of different societies. And once we are able to answer these questions, let us then ask them of, say, the USSR. These modest experiments may help to place the problem of Japan's internationalization in a clearer perspective.

III

The present concern with internationalization shows some similarities to the earlier concern, but it also has some new features. In the nineteenth century, Japan was a "backward" industrializing country struggling to be accepted by the Powers, in current jargon, a developing country, even an LDC. One of the primary reasons for the formulation of law codes based upon Western models was the widespread conviction that the unequal treaties, and particularly the humiliating extraterritoriality could be eliminated only by convincing the Powers that Japanese law was as civilized and modern as their own. Meiji Japan was also forced, by the pressure of the growing economic and political interdependence, to think about keeping up with the world and doing business with foreign countries. To do this, it was necessary to internationalize—that is, to "modernize" its organizational forms, institutions, practices, and behavior along lines that would facilitate interaction with the outside world. This meant essentially to westernize. On a political level, there was constant concern about getting along with other nations—being respected, being liked—and with international responsibilities.

The concern with making some contribution to the world starts at an early point. Ideas of "cultural exchange," vague though they might be, were not far behind. At first, this was a passive process. Japanese acquired foreign knowledge and ideas—an elite by foreign travel and study, the rest through reading translations. Generally, understanding Western civilization was thought of simply as a necessity for Japan's own development. But for many, Western ideas became ideals against which Japanese development was to be measured: the closer Japan approaches these ideals, the more "modern" it is, the farther away it is the less modern. The distance from Western ideals was a measure of the distance Japan had to go to become modern.

Increasingly, however, cultural exchange came to be conceived as a more active process, one in which Japan had something to give as well as to receive. The issue thereupon arose of what, if any, aspects of Japanese culture could be exported. The growth of the Empire provided some outlets for this impulse. In Korea, Taiwan, and then later in parts of China and of Southeast Asia, Japanese culture was exported,

19

language schools were established, modern Japanese institutions were put into place where appropriate, and Japanese styles and forms encouraged. World War II brought all of this to an end.

Japan was defeated, and the defeat attainted confidence in Japanese culture. Psychologically, Japanese were driven back to a condition approximating the Meiji period: a lack of confidence in themselves, doubts about their traditional culture, extreme dependence on the outside world, and a great need for acceptance.

Three decades or more later, Japan is again one of the Powers. Nevertheless some of the same issues remain. This time, however, Japan must create an acceptable international role for itself at a much higher level of interdependence. Internationalization remains as urgent a national issue as it has ever been in modern times.

IV

Internationalization may be seen today on at least four different levels: first, national, that is, Japan's participation as a nation in international society economically, politically, and socially; second, organizational, that is, the adjustments Japanese organizations, particularly those involved in the process of international association, must make in order to be able to take part effectively; third, cultural, that is, the adaptation of Japanese culture to the exigencies of increased international interdependency; and fourth, individual, that is, on the one hand, the changes that internationalization brings to the individual and, on the other hand, the changes that must take place if individuals are to participate more fully in international activities.

The changes at the national level are the ones that engage the greatest public attention these days. For the outside world, this often reduces itself to the question of the opening up of the Japanese economy (see Johnson's paper in this volume). By that measure Japan is less international than the United States in many respects, but more international than most European countries, not to mention the developing and communist countries. Japan still has a long way to go, but then so do many other countries. Much attention has been and is being directed to the question of how far along the road of internationalization Japan has come, what obstacles stand in the way, and how these obstacles can be overcome.

Economic internationalization involves another set of considerations, which were broadly examined in the symposium: the internationalization of business activities (see in this volume the papers by Fruin; Azumi, Hull and Hage; and Marsh and Mannari). These concern structural changes within corporations, adjustments of individual behavior, and styles of training appropriate to international participation.

Another range of issues that developed in our discussions had to do with international cooperation and international understanding. These can be viewed both as a necessity for living in a highly interdependent world or as something inherently desirable in and of itself. But from whichever viewpoint one wishes to regard them, cooperation and understanding are important.

Internationalization also involves the notion of being in step with the world, *sekai-nami* in Japanese: we must keep up with the world. "The world" here obviously means the advanced industrial societies (or the "civilized world," as they were referred to in an earlier age, or the "enlightened nations," or "the Powers"); nobody is likely to think that Japan should be in step with the less developed countries. Related is the concept of being competitive, being up-to-date, being up on the latest state-of-the-art technology.

Internationalization also implies some behavioral considerations: learning how to get along with other peoples, however different they may be; enjoying foreign culture; being able to associate with and even live with foreigners; and learning to be liked. All of these involve both moral and pragmatic considerations.

V

One can detect here several paradigms, or frameworks, that underlie these different concepts of internationalization. The most prominent is the modernization paradigm. Much of the contemporary discussion about internationalization would fit quite comfortably into the tradition-to-modernization continuum (this is implied in the Azumi, Hull and Hage paper and in Marsh and Mannari's contribution). Closely connected is the idea that internationalization is somehow related to "democratization" (see, for example, Fruin's paper in this volume; the Mouer and Sugimoto paper, however, comes close to seeing an inverse relation, at least between democratization and talk about internationalization as national policy).

There is also a more narrowly conceived version of the modernization paradigm—westernization, an old theme in Japan. Spencerian evolutionism, the notion that the world is all going in one direction and that the future first came to Europe and the United States, is deeply entrenched in Japan. Marx's formulation, that the "backward peoples" look at the advanced countries and see the image of their future, is widely accepted, at least implicitly, in spite of sincere efforts to escape it.

This notion of unilineal evolution is strongly related to, even though conceptually distinguishable from, convergence theory. I do not here intend to discuss convergence theories per se but only to point out that they cling stubbornly to our thinking about internationalization. We often measure internationalization in terms of degree of similarity to what are considered to be basically Western organizational characteristics. Organizational (or other) typologies usually imply historical sequence. The more, for example, Japanese firms approach the generalized characteristics of Western organizations in their own fields, whether multinationals or other kinds of corporations, the more internationalized they are rated to be. The theoretical end point, that is, "complete internationalization," would be reached when Japanese organizations show 100 percent of the same characteristics as the relevant Western organizations in the same field. Our symposium discussions managed to avoid commitment to the extreme position.

Quite obviously many of the questions that arise here are generic to modernization theory in general, or at least to the more traditional forms of tradition-modernization dichotomies. This is not to say that the evolution, modernization and Western paradigms have nothing of value to contribute to our understanding. There are some kinds of progression that cannot be denied. Nor can it be denied that the perceived practices or organizational forms in what a company or a society may regard as the more advanced societies may have an important effect on what they do. But whether one can generalize that subjective intention or perception into a principle of social change, or evolution, or internationalization is a different question.

VI

My own preference would be to define internationalization without any implication of unilateral direction, as the awareness of interdependence, the process of adjusting to the involvement that arises from it, and the conditions that facilitate or impede the capacity to engage in these interactions.

One thing this clearly involves is the ability to communicate with the outside world. If everybody in the world, or at least everybody with whom contact was necessary, spoke Japanese, there would be no problem. But this is not the case. Japanese—or at least some Japanese— must be able to handle foreign languages, and certainly English, which has become the international language. The question that arises is how many Japanese must be able to handle what languages to what degree? Must all Japanese speak some foreign language at a high level of proficiency, or is it sufficient that specialists and those professionally engaged in international activities do so? How broad a base of foreign language ability does Japan need in order to function effectively on the international scene? Obviously this will vary with the nature of the needs and the scale of activities. Foreign language skill, however, is not a free good. It comes at high social cost, and therefore the question of how many at what level of proficiency cannot be disregarded.

International participation requires many different kinds of knowledge. Here, even ordinary Japanese people appear to have an impressively high level of information about many parts of the world. Japanese media and publishing give much attention to the outside world. And in Japanese government, business, academia, and journalism the level of detailed knowledge is very high indeed. The question still remains, however, of how much knowledge is enough. How many American specialists does Japan have to have in order to understand the United States? How many experts in the American parliamentary process, or local politics, or industrial relations do there have to be for Japan to have sufficient "understanding" to deal with the United States? How many specialists on China, the Soviet Union, England, France, Germany, India, or Saudi Arabia are needed?

The process of adjusting to international involvement requires not only organizational change, a subject that was discussed extensively in some of the symposium papers, but also value changes. These value adjustments must be made both by institutions and by individuals. A high degree of behavioral adjustment may be required of people who are directly involved in international activities. They may have to learn how to give up some Japanese behavioral modes in order to be able to interact with foreigners. Such changes are potentially capable of affecting the inner core of the personality (see the papers by Befu and Wagatsuma in this volume for discussion of these issues).

The suggestion emerged in the symposium that some of these behavioral adjustments may have negative consequences for the individual's capacity to function in a purely Japanese environment. One is reminded here of the ever-recurrent theme of the overseas sojourner returning to live in Japan—*Nihon kaiki,* the return to Japan, to use poet Hagiwara Sakutaro's phrase (*Nihon e no kaiki—waga hitori utaeru uta*). Many years ago, Bennett and I (1958) tried to describe this experience reported to us by many respondents by the metaphor squeezing back into the tight shoes one used to wear in an earlier period of one's life. Once you have removed the tight Japanese shoes, it is very hard to step back into them. Many of the returnees had grown through their foreign experience, and they could no longer fit the older mold.

If, as was suggested, international experience often makes it difficult for people to fit back into a traditional Japanese environment, is there not, Wagatsuma asks in his paper in this volume, danger of a "polarization of the Japanese into the group-oriented, non-internationalized majority and the individualistically-oriented internationalized minority?" Conversely, there seems to be some persuasive evidence that Japanese personality characteristics interfere with internationalization. In that case it may be that the international "cultural brokers" (in Wagatsuma's phrase), those on the front lines of international activity, might have to be somewhat deviant personality types, thus once again entraining the danger of polarization.

As Hofstede points out, although a "strong Uncertainty Avoider (a type he finds common in Japan) is not the best foreign representative . . . it is possible to select those with a relatively high tolerance for uncertainty . . . for working abroad." However, "they may have a problem communicating with their home base. . . . A strongly Uncertainty Avoiding society does not treat with kindness its sons and daughters who return with foreign ideas. . ." (see Hofstede's paper in this volume).

Foreign experience creates some problems of re-entry into the home society for individuals and institutions, but it can also be seen as a very valuable national asset (see Wagatsuma's contribution). Nevertheless, Japan still has difficulty making use of it. Younger people who have had a significant part of their schooling and socialization abroad often have difficulty fitting into Japanese schools, and if they have had their higher education abroad, without having gone through a Japanese university, they may have difficulties finding a place for themselves in mainline Japanese institutions.

Historically, where the overseas experience has been sponsored—that is, when people go abroad on leave, as it were, from their company or university and then later return to it—they are able to fit back into the formal and informal organizational structures reasonably well. But when they are self-sponsored or otherwise go abroad without this kind of sponsorship or base, they often have a great deal of difficulty.

It is gratifying to note, however, that many efforts are under way to create institutions or channels of adjustment that would allow better utilization of this valuable resource. Special schools or programs within schools have been set up for the readjustment of young people who have had a good part of their schooling abroad. Many companies and universities make a special point of trying to integrate individuals with unique educational and work experience abroad into their structures. But the process is a slow one; Japan still lags far behind the other advanced industrial democracies. In spite of Japan's anxious concern for greater internationalization, it is ironic that international experience still remains for many a disadvantage rather than the advantage one would expect it to be.

VII

It is clear that on one level internationalization is a process of adjustment to the outside world. Historically this has always meant learning from the outside, borrowing from the West, and self-transformation towards Western modes. The reverse of Japan's capacity to adjust to the world is the capacity of the world to adjust to Japanese culture, practices, and organizational styles, or, looking at it from the opposite side, the exportability of Japanese culture.

On this, Japanese intellectual opinion has been sharply divided ever since Perry forced the opening of the country in 1854. The "yes" side has in general been associated with a more nationalistic emphasis. In the extreme case it inspired the ultra-nationalistic notions of Japan's unique mission in the world. In Japan's colonial empire, this was the operative position, and Japanese culture was imposed on the Koreans,

Taiwanese, and later the other peoples who came under the control of the imperial forces.

But the "no" answer has been, if anything, an even more powerful motif in modern Japanese history. The non-exportability of Japanese culture has long been argued from two opposite points of view. One states that Japanese culture is inherently inferior and therefore had nothing to offer. "No aspect of Japanese culture," as Taguchi Ukichi argued in 1888, "could be superior to Western culture" (see Pyle, 1969: 91). The other side, however, argued that it was not any inferiority, but rather the unique ineffable character of Japanese culture that made it impossible for non-Japanese to comprehend.

To take a very homely example, there is the question of Japanese food. It is a settled conviction among many Japanese people that foreigners cannot possibly like real Japanese food. Sashimi, sushi, or *nattō*, they are sure, must all be too inwardly Japanese for any non-Japanese palate to appreciate. How wrong this judgment has turned out to be can be appreciated when we contemplate the extraordinary boom in Japanese cuisine that has swept the United States and is spreading throughout Europe as well. Before World War II, there were exactly 3 Japanese restaurants in New York City; today there are about 500, including among them every variety or cuisine from sushi to *kaiseki ryōri* to rāmen, and every major regional type. On a recent walk down a street in midtown Manhattan, I ran across Akita, Fukushima, and Kyoto cuisine within the space of one block. Clearly, this aspect of Japanese culture, which so many Japanese have tended to think of as incommunicable, turns out to be very communicable indeed.

In fact, much more of Japanese culture has been exported to the West than is generally realized. A few examples will suffice. A very obvious one nowadays is the martial arts. Judo, for example, has become an Olympic sport, and it even happens that non-Japanese win titles in it. All over the United States you will find *dōjō* for judo or karate or even *aikidō*, and often in small towns you will hear the thumping of young bodies on tatami and see high-school age boys walking around in their judo constumes. Elvis Presley himself used to be proud of his *gi*, as he called his own judo costume. There would appear to be no difficulty about exportability there.

Already in the mid-nineteenth century, soon after Perry's arrival in Japan, the French impressionists' contact with Japanese art, particularly the *ukiyoe*, was having enormous effects. Through its influence on Van Gogh, Toulouse-Lautrec, Manet, Dégas, Munch, Beardsley, and other painters of the late nineteenth century, ukiyoe had a transforming effect on Western aesthetic concepts of space, perspective, and color. And in the twentieth century, Japanese conceptions of space, calligraphic design, and "modulated line" profoundly influenced many of the main modern trends in world art (see Svanascini, 1973: 647).

Japanese pottery has also had enormous influence in the West, since at least the late sixteenth century. Dutch Delft or English Crown Derby are essentially based upon the Hirado modifications of late Ming dynasty styles. Today, there is almost no pottery in the advanced industrial societies that has not been profoundly influenced by Japanese pottery, especially *mingei*, and almost no potter who is not acquainted with the names and works of the great modern Japanese ceramic masters.

Architecture is another area that comes to mind. Japanese architecture has had a very important influence on the West. One might even make the case that Japanese architectural concepts are today much more alive in the West than in Japan itself. In new domestic construction, better traditional style Japanese style houses are built on the West Coast of the United States than in Japan.

Another interesting Japanese cultural export is Zen Buddhism, which attracts rather considerable interest among some sectors of anti-establishment youth in the United States and, to a lesser extent, in Europe. It may very well be that Zen is more popular among young Americans than among young Japanese these days. Aside from its cultic and technical philosophical aspects, it has seeped deeply into many forms of pop culture and even its vocabulary. It seems to me unlikely, however, to become as generally popular as instant soba has become. But then, that is true in Japan as well.

One final consideration about the internationalization of culture. Earlier, I have argued against the extreme form of convergence theory. Nevertheless, it must be acknowledged that in the field of culture there is a process under way in the world that is suggestive of convergence. We might perhaps better characterize it as homogenization, or the development of international, as distinct from the traditional separate national, styles. Some might even wish to see this as a harbinger of a kind of world culture yet to come.

The clearest example may perhaps be seen in the arts. In music, for example, the most significant developments no longer have a specific national home. Composers are distinguished by the musical schools they adhere to—dodecaphony, *musique concrète,* electronic music—rather than by their national origins. The international styles have adherents from all countries, and there is no way to tell from the music itself whether the composer is German, French, American, Greek, or Japanese. The international musical styles are the result of the vast increase in communications that has opened musical styles formerly unknown or considered exotic to the inspection of all, the development of new technologies, and growing familiarity with diverse musical forms. Composers whose experience now includes Indian ragas, Javanese gamelan, African drums, Middle Eastern modes, and Japanese *gagaku,* can no longer compose in the traditional styles of their countries with the single-mindedness, even naiveté, they might have done had they never heard these other musics. And now with the stimuli coming from the new technologies and the harnessing of the computer this becomes even more difficult.

In painting and sculpture, one sees the same tendency. Although some artists continue to pursue purely traditional forms, most belong to abstract expressionism, action painting, pop art, or one of the other fashionable schools of modern art. In the past, one could look at a painting and see immediately that it was French, Chinese, Indian, or Japanese. One might even guess that it was painted in Paris or New York. Today, this is no longer possible. Paintings by modern Japanese painters are not differentiable from those of modern French, German, American, Korean, or Indian painters. The artist's national origin is less important than the aesthetic concepts he works with and the theory he identifies himself with.

One can see this same development of an international style in architecture, hotel styles, clothing styles, hair styles, furniture styles, food, sports, and automobiles. Japanese no longer simply copy the modes of the outside world; they now participate actively in the development of international styles in all of these fields.

It should be remembered, however, that the homogenization of styles does not necessarily entrain a homogenization of the forms of social organization that underlie them. Japanese and American factories both produce automobiles, for example, but they are organized very differently. There is organized professional baseball in both countries, and one can see many similarities in the way they are played, the uniforms they wear, and in the culture of baseball in general. And yet in spite of the fact that they both produce the same product—baseball games—the social organization of the production is different (for a very illuminating analysis see Whiting, 1977). In other words, there are many alternative possible structural forms that are compatible with particular outcomes, whether these be music, paintings, sculptures, modern clothing, or automobiles.

Whatever the case may be with regard to convergence at the social structural level, it is clear that Japan is in no way behindhand with regard to the development of homogenized international styles. Its enthusiastic participation here is one measure of how far it has come along the path of internationalization.

NOTES

1. It is interesting to observe the belated popularity of the English word "identity" these days in Japan. In 1953 and 1954, John Bennett and I used the term to describe what we considered to be the central dynamic in the experience of Japanese studying abroad (Bennett et al., 1958). We thought we had invented the term— neither of us had as yet read Erik Erikson. It came as a great shock when some years later, after a long period of residence outside the United States, I came across Helen Lynd's *On Shame and the Search for Identity* on a shelf in a bookstore and for the first time learned about Erikson. Obviously the term was part of the *zeitgeist* in the United States at the time and Bennett and I had not so much independently invented it as plucked it out of the air. For some 25 years or so after Bennett and I thought we had invented the term, it was almost impossible to use it in Japan: nobody could understand it, and it did not translate well—*shutaisei, shōmei, jidōsei, dōitsusei, shozokusei*. But recently, it has quietly slipped into intellectual discourse as *aidentetei* (or *aidenchitei*), and it is used with about the same range of vagueness as it is in English.
2. Anwar Sadat, for example, gave his last book the title *Search for Identity*.

REFERENCES

Bennett, John W., Herbert Passin, and Robert McKnight
    1958   *In Search of Identity—The Japanese Overseas Scholar in America and Japan.*
            Minneapolis: The University of Minnesota Press.
Boorstin, Daniel
    1958   *The Genius of American Politics.* Chicago: University of Chicago Press.
Hofstadter, Richard
    1968   *The Progressive Historians.* New York: Knopf.

Pyle, Kenneth
  1969   *The New Generation in Meiji Japan—Problems of Cultural Identity, 1885–1895*. Stanford: Stanford University Press.
Svanascini, Osvaldo
  1973   "Influence of Japanese Art on Twentieth Century Western Art." In Japan Pen Club (ed.), *Studies on Japanese Culture,* 2. Tokyo.
Uchimura Kanzō
  1925   "To Be Inscribed Upon My Tomb." Originally composed in English and quoted from his *Zenshū*, 15.
Whiting, Robert
  1977   *The Chrysanthemum and the Bat*. New York: Dodd, Mead and Co.
Wolfe, Bertram
  1981   *A Life in Two Centuries*. New York: Stein and Day.

THE INTERNATIONALIZATION
OF THE JAPANESE ECONOMY

Chalmers Johnson

During the late 1970s and early 1980s, to judge from official statements, declarations of international economic conferences, and the preoccupations of the world's commercial and financial newspapers, many people both in and outside of Japan believed that Japan was faced with a pressing need to internationalize (*kokusaika*) its economy. Thus, for example, the semi-official journal *Business America,* published by the U.S. Department of Commerce, devoted its May 1980 issue to the subject "Japan: Is the Market Open?" (pp. 3–19). The official Japanese *White Paper on International Trade* for 1980, written by the Ministry of International Trade and Industry, proclaimed that the "internationalization of Japan" had become prerequisite to the nation's continued economic prosperity, indeed to its very economic viability in the face of protectionist trends appearing in various parts of the world (pp. 1, 62). And the report of the so-called Wisemen, a group of senior economic statesmen appointed by former Prime Minister Ōhira and former President Carter to look into the problems of the bilateral economic relationship between Japan and the United States, said that "both Japan and the United States need to develop new international roles and to 'internationalize' their societies" (*Report of the Japan-United States Economic Relations Group,* 1981: iv).

In contrast to these statements calling for positive reform, some observers have assumed that Japan's insularity and its alleged lack of internationalization will remain as unalterable givens, and they have proposed various ways in which other nations might respond to this. For example, Leslie Fielding, an official of the European Common Market concerned with Japanese trade, has asserted that because of "a number of typical Japanese behavioristic and cultural reasons," Japan's market is much more difficult to penetrate than those of the other advanced industrial democracies. He therefore proposes that economic relations be equalized through the imposition of a handicap on Japan, similar to those assigned to golfers or mountaineers. Doing business with Japan "is as difficult as the north face of the Eiger, compared to a walk up Mount Fuji," he writes, and should be so handicapped. In Fielding's view, Japan enjoys a "natural advantage" in the global economy, and it is this quality that allegedly justifies such proposed discriminatory treatment (*Japan Economic Journal,* December 9, 1980).

But why is selling to the Japanese market as difficult as the north face of the Eiger while selling in America is no harder than a walk up Mount Fuji? And how does a lack of internationalization bestow some "natural advantage" on Japan? What do calls for internationalization actually mean? Serious answers to these questions are harder to come by than might appear on initial reflection. The concept of internationalization is anything but clear, and it is by no means obvious that Japanese society is any less international than those of North America or Western Europe. As I shall try to make clear later in this article, it is doubtful that the alleged lack of internationalization in Japan has any bearing on the difficulties that foreigners encounter in trying to market their products there. A strong possibility exists that the calls for internationalization are misconceived and that conscious efforts to promote it would have little effect on the current trade imbalances between Japan and some of its international commercial partners.

The problems of the internationalization of the Japanese are both conceptual—What does internationalization mean?—and concrete—What in Japan should be internationalized? An equally important question, from a Japanese perspective, is: What are the likely consequences for Japan of internationalization, however the concept is understood?

In my view, the term "internationalization" is merely the latest code word or jargon expression for a much longer standing tradition of intellectual discourse about Japan. I am referring to the basic values/ societal consensus/national character school of Japanology, an approach to the explanation of Japanese behavior that goes back at least to the work of Ruth Benedict and that is rooted in the cultural contact and processes of acculturation that began in the mid-nineteenth century between Japan and Western societies. This approach stressed Japan's fundamental cultural differences from all other societies, particularly from those of the West, but also including the societies of the Sinitic cultural area from which parts of Japanese culture were derived. Many Japanese themselves have taken up this theme, using it first to attempt to legitimize Japan's prewar imperial ideology, and more recently as a basis for arguing that Japan should be exempted from international comparisons or standards when these standards seem to conflict with the developmental goals of the Japanese government. One result of this tradition has been that until very recent times analytic social science in Japan was almost exclusively the preserve of academic Marxists. Most non-Marxist social scientists and thinkers had no interest in integrating the Japanese "case" into a universal social science; instead, they wanted to discover and display Japan's uniqueness.

Many Japanese also find the unique-national-character school a flattering alternative to the work of domestic social and political critics and a convenient rationalization for the sometimes strained social fabric they had to endure during the early postwar period. The Japanese popular enthusiasm for national character explanations of their economic success was revealed in the *Nihonjinron* ("on the Japanese") publishing boom of the late 1970s and early 1980s—for example, in the extraordinary sale of Ezra Vogel's *Japan as Number One* in Japan, as opposed to the slight interest evinced in the United States.

This stress on Japan's cultural singularity reached its high point during the Pacific War, when it was used within Japan to foster solidarity in the face of the rigors of total war and by Japan's opponents as a form of propaganda to justify and reinforce their war effort against Japan (see S. Johnson, 1975: 4–10; and Minear, 1980: 36–59). However, it did not die out with the end of the war. During the 1960s, with the first international acknowledgements of the Japanese economic "miracle," the search for the causes of Japan's astonishing high-speed economic growth began. And once again the theme of Japan's cultural eccentricity reappeared. In essence, the national character explanation of the Japanese economic miracle holds that high-speed growth occurred because the Japanese possess a unique, culturally derived capacity to cooperate with each other. The most important

33

contribution of the culture to economic life is said to be Japan's famous "consensus," meaning virtual agreement among the government, the ruling political party, the leaders of industry, and the people on the primacy of economic objectives for the society as a whole and on the means to achieve those objectives. Some of the terms invented to refer to this cultural capability are "rolling consensus" (Halloran, 1970: 72), "private collectivism" (Hadley, 1970: 87), "inbred collectivism" (*The Economist, Consider Japan,* 1963: 16), "spiderless cobweb" (Hitani, 1976: 181), and "Japan, Inc." (Kaplan, 1972: 14).

Despite extensive economic and political research in Japan and abroad on the actual causes of the Japanese economic miracle—particularly on the government-business relationship that developed in Japan during the Korean War and after the end of the Allied Occupation in 1952—the idea that the "Japanese behave like Japanese because they are Japanese" took strong root in the Western mass mind and among foreign journalists. Its attractions lay in its simplicity, its stress on Japan's exotic quality, and its function in relieving Japan's foreign competitors from the need to assess their own performances (if the Japanese are literally unique, to be understood as more like a force of nature or the north face of the Eiger, then comparisons with them become meaningless).

Two recent examples of the foreign preference for cultural explanations of Japan's economic performance illustrate this longstanding tradition of discourse. In the United States, in a feature article entitled "How Japan Does It, the World's Toughest Customer," the editors of *Time* magazine (March 30, 1981) argue that "much of [Japan's] success traces back to cultural traits as old as Japan itself," these cultural traits being "emulation, consensus, futurism, quality, and competition." In Europe, during 1979, in a much less friendly recitation of Japan's cultural orientations, a commission of the European Common Market concluded that Japan was "un pays de maniaques du travail, qui vivent dans ce que les Occidentaux ne considereraint guere mieux que des clapiers, ou les cadres abandonnent leur droit aux vacances parçe qu'ils estiment que leur entreprise a besoin de leurs efforts" (*Le Monde,* March 31, 1979) ("a country of workaholics who live in what Westerners would regard as little better than rabbit hutches, and where workers give up their rights to vacations because they believe their enterprises need their efforts").

It is not my intention here to dismiss the entire field of explanations of social behavior in terms of culture, modal personality, or societal values; but a small parenthesis on the subject is necessary before proceeding to a discussion of what I think the calls for internationalization of the Japanese economy are all about. National character has had a long and controversial history as an explanatory variable in political research. Hannah Arendt's famous work *The Origins of Totalitarianism* (1951) was addressed in part to those individuals, particularly in Anglo-American countries, who believed that German cultural traditions were a sufficient explanation for the phenomenon of Nazism. She was at pains to show that fascism was a possible political outcome, under specific pressures and circumstances, in any social system. This perennial argument has erupted again in recent times in a debate between Richard Pipes, who wants to locate the roots of Soviet behavior in Russian national character, and Alexander Solzhenitsyn, who believes that a sufficient explanation can be found in the specific institutions of Leninism.

There are several objections to be leveled at national character studies from the point of view of social science. One is logical. "National character" is so poorly conceptualized that its use for any serious analytical purpose leads only to obfuscation. As Ralf Dahrendorf has put it:

> Prehistoric national characters have a status somewhat similar to that of instinct theories: they repeat an observed state of affairs in terms that are removed from the control of intersubjective experience, and thus manage to add nothing to the original observations except a mystical air of obscurity (Dahrendorf, 1967: 25).

It is one thing to observe, for example, that Japanese in the postwar world have achieved the highest rates of savings out of personal disposable income of any capitalist society in peacetime, but it is quite another to assert that this savings was due to some innate frugality imparted to the Japanese by their culture. Such assertions cut off research into whether the Japanese have always been so frugal, whether there were positive incentives for them to save, and whether their behavior resulted from rational calculations or from some alleged cultural predisposition. To the extent that explanations rest on national character, they inhibit concrete research: no further inquiry is necessary, even though precious little has actually been explained.[1]

A second objection to national character explanations in the case of Japan is that they tend to be merely an artifact of the Western scholarly traditions of "Orientalism," or of "area studies" (*Regional-wissenschaften*), or of what one scholar has called the "orchid sciences" (Park, 1980–81: 5). Western arguments about the alleged singularity of Japanese values or the need for Japan to internationalize may tell us more about Western scholarly proclivities than they do about Japan. The organization of scholarship around a particular country or civilization—as in Indology, Egyptology, Sinology, or Japanology—inevitably emphasizes the unique elements in the society being studied rather than the universal ones. By their very nature such scholarly orientations are inhospitable to comparisons. Their achievements in the study of ancient and medieval history and in the elucidation of classical languages are not to be denied, but when the assumptions of the "orchid sciences" (to the orchid lover, the unusual or unique blossom is the most prized) are extended to the areas of economics, politics, and the state, the lack of theoretical or conceptual rigor immediately becomes a serious handicap. Professor Sung-jo Park (Free University of Berlin) contends that the traditions of Japanology in Europe have contributed directly to the contemporary conflicts between the European Community and Japan because of their failure to make Japan's problems and policies comprehensible within a universal framework. Needless to add, the orchid sciences are not to be found exclusively in the study of exotic cultures; their attitudes also flourish in the domestic study of one's own society—for example, in the study of America by Americans.

In my own view, the study and analysis of cultural traits and basic values of social systems are, of course, valid and important disciplines, but they must be used with care in assessing the purposive or intentional behavior of adult actors in a modern society. While there is surely a "kernel of truth" to the concept of modal personality, the concept should be reserved for the final analysis, for the irreducible residual of behavior that cannot be explained in cognitive or other more economical ways. It should never be used as the first tool of social explanation, since it is much more likely to obscure interesting institutions or social relationships than illuminate them. This is particularly the case when the official stewards of the institutions being studied would much prefer that their activities not be scrutinized or that their own explanations of their behavior be accepted without question. Such is almost invariably true when one is dealing with state bureaucrats, politicians, or economic managers.

Let me now try to relate this discussion of the various perceptions of Japanese culture to the problem of the internationalization of the Japanese economy. First, are Japanese attitudes toward economic activities more parochial or culture-bound than in other societies? There is almost no evidence to make one think so. Setō Sumihiko of JETRO comments on the "once generally favorable image of all imported goods" held by Japanese consumers. He acknowledges that these attitudes have become much more discriminating in recent times, but this is due to the greater sophistication, even international-ization, of Japanese consumers, and not because of some rise in a nationalistic antipathy to foreign goods (Setō, 1980: 13). One might also note that Japan has long been known as a paradise for foreign artists, entertainers, and musicians. It is one of the few places on earth where they can command top ticket prices and normally still expect sold-out houses. Tickets for concerts rarely go for less than ¥5,000, and when the Vienna State Opera performed in Tokyo during October 1980, tickets at more than $100 each were impossible to obtain several months before the performances began. By contrast, one can think of several large American cities (Houston, for example) where tickets to major cultural or musical events are normally available right up to curtain time. This may not prove much, but it does suggest that the Japanese consumer is not lacking in international taste or interest.

Similarly, on measures such as foreign travel, Japanese have shown no reluctance to go abroad. Whenever the government lets them go and permits them to take their money with them, they have done so in great numbers and have spent their cash freely. During the first nine months of 1980, the normal Japanese deficit on the travel account dropped somewhat from $3.3 billion during the same period of 1979, to $3 billion, but this was largely because of a relatively weak yen, air fare increases, and political turmoil in South Korea (the most popular destination), and not because Japanese tourists had lost any of their wanderlust. To take another indicator, Japanese television advertising is notorious for its use of Western actors and actresses to signify approval or to attest to the quality of a product being offered, including domestically manufactured products. Again, none of this may prove that the Japanese are unusually cosmopolitan, but it does raise doubts that Japanese society is in serious need of internationalization.

In my view, the object of internationalization in Japan has been misplaced. The internationalization of the Japanese economy does not concern cultural mores to any greater degree than in other open capitalist countries with active, free mass media of communications. Japan's problem of internationalization concerns governmental policy. This is a problem no less difficult to solve than societal internationalization, but it is one of an entirely different intellectual and conceptual order. The term *sakoku* (closed country) in Japan does not refer to a cultural trait but to a political policy. As is well known, Japan was a politically closed country during the two and a half centuries of the Tokugawa *bakufu*. What is perhaps less well known is that, economically, from about 1935 to 1975, Japan was again a sakoku. As Robert Ozaki has argued:

> It is important to note that before the 1930s Japan had, by and large, practiced free trade. Only after the mid-1930s did quantitative as well as qualitative restrictions on imports and control of foreign capital come into being and add to the notoriety of postwar Japan (Ozaki, 1978: 264).

During this century, Japan has not always been a closed country and its closure for about 40 years in mid-century had very little to do with culture and everything to do with politics. In fact, one might generalize and say that the problem of internationalization in a country like the United States is one of the need to internationalize the society, state policy being comparatively open (ease of trade, travel, immigration, capital transfers, purchases of assets by foreigners, etc.), whereas the problem in a country like Japan is one of the need to internationalize state policy, the society being already comparatively cosmopolitan (because of extensive education, dependence on trade, awareness of Japan's economic vulnerability). This is not particularly surprising. Japan and the United States have different starting points for their government-business relationships and their economic relations with the rest of the world; these factors directly affect the problems of internationalization they face under the circumstances of the 1980s.

The problem appears strange only because of the lack of foreign understanding of Japan's state policy and the long habit among foreigners of regarding Japan's culture as a form of "non-tariff barrier" to all sorts of international relationships.

Japan's state economic policy is not simply a variant of that prevailing in the Anglo-American capitalist democracies. It is a different type altogether. One element of internationalization that *is* needed in the English-speaking world is recognition that there are other forms of capitalism than that found in the United States, just as there are other forms of socialism than that found in the Soviet Union. For almost a century, the functions of the state in American capitalism have been overwhelmingly regulatory (with the notable exception of the national defense sector), whereas the functions of the state in Japanese capitalism have been overwhelmingly developmental. Japan's developmental orientation of course began with the Meiji Restoration, when the state proclaimed the goal of "rich country, strong military" (*fukoku kyōhei*) as the overarching goal of the new Japanese nation. That goal, and the state's role in achieving it, were dictated by Japan's late development, its perceived vulnerability to foreign imperialism, and the terms of the unequal treaties imposed on it by the Western powers (Japan did not regain full tariff autonomy until 1911).

This history is well known. What is less well understood abroad is that from approximately the time of the first Sino-Japanese War (1894–95), the Japanese state began progressively to withdraw from active intervention in the domestic economy (as distinct from Japan's colonies). A period of more or less orthodox laissez faire existed in Japan from approximately the turn of the century down to the mid-1930s. Then, in a context of global economic depression and political crisis, the Japanese state again assumed primary responsibility for supporting and guiding Japanese economic growth. This role of the state reached its zenith not during the 1930s or the Pacific War but during the Allied Occupation and the 1950s period of high-speed growth. It was dictated by several factors: Japan's loss of its empire and the political transformation of its traditional main trading partners (China and Southeast Asia), the extensive war damage to the domestic economy combined with a rise in population due to the repatriation of Japanese living and serving abroad, a devastating inflation that left all Japanese equally poor, the weakening of the leading elements of the old private sector (the *zaibatsu*) because of Allied policy, dependence on the United States for a good part of Japan's basic sustenance, domestic technological backwardness as a result of the international isolation of the 1940s, and perhaps most important of all, an acute shortage, even dearth, of capital within the Japanese economy.

Under these circumstances the official economic bureaucracy, led by the Ministries of Finance and International Trade and Industry, assumed draconian economic control powers, and state economic policy became the core of Japanese politics. Speaking of the transfer in 1949 of economic powers from the Occupation authorities to the Japanese government, Leon Hollerman concludes:

> In liquidating the Occupation by "handing back" operational control to the Japanese, SCAP [Supreme Commander for the Allied Powers] naively presided not only over the transfer of its own authority, but also over the institutionalization of the most restrictive foreign trade and foreign exchange control system ever devised by a major free nation (Hollerman, 1979: 719).

This new, government-imposed Japanese sakoku lasted for a long time and undoubtedly had an effect on contemporary political attitudes. As Satō Kiichirō, the late chairman of the Mitsui Bank, once remarked, "During and after the war, Japan's economy was controlled until it has become second nature with us to uphold a planned, controlled economy" (Shiba and Nozue, 1971: 32). In fact, the historically unique and remarkably long-lived postwar period has caused many observers to lose sight of the origins of its institutional features in the aftermath of the Pacific War and the development of the Cold War. Lacking historical perspective, they have concluded that these institutional features are immutable elements of culture rather than artifacts of recent history and politics.

Throughout the 1950s the Japanese government operated and perfected what is recognized today as a model of the state-guided capitalist developmental system. During the 1960s and 1970s, such high-growth economies as South Korea, Taiwan, and Singapore began to emulate and adapt this model. Its basic ingredients are, first, a marked separation in the political system between reigning and ruling— the politicians, i.e., the Liberal Democratic Party in Japan, reign, while an elite state bureaucracy actually rules. Second, there is a commitment by the state to use market-conforming methods of intervention in the economy, thereby gaining the advantages of competition and private initiative while avoiding the disadvantages of state mobilization of resources that afflict the Soviet type command economies. And third, the government guides the economy through extensive tax incentives, state economic institutions such as the Fiscal Investment and Loan Plan (*zaisei tōyūshi keikaku*) and the Japan Development Bank, state sponsorship of well over a hundred public corporations, and permanent institutions for governmental consultation and coordination with the private sector, e.g., *shingikai,* the posting of government officials at Keidanren headquarters, the re-employment of retired government bureaucrats by big business, the creation of innumerable auxiliary organs and trade associations (*gaikaku dantai*) as buffers between the government and industry, etc. (see C. Johnson, 1978).

This system worked phenomenally well in Japan. It led to the successful second stage (i.e., capital intensive, as distinct from first stage labor intensive) industrialization of Japan and to some of the highest rates of capital formation ever achieved by any economy. The Japanese people supported the system—and also tolerated its undesirable side effects (lack of access to the government for low priority interests, recurring corruption scandals, industrial pollution problems, and so forth)—because of their recognition of Japan's extremely dependent and vulnerable economic position in the world, because the benefits of high-speed growth were distributed more or less equitably, and because of the attractions of material prosperity after the devastation of the 1940s. A national consensus over the economic goals of the nation and the means to achieve them came into being and lasted approximately from the time of the Korean War until the so-called Pollution Diet of 1970. (Incidentally, those who believe that consensus is a permanent feature of Japanese decision making contributed by the culture would have to explain the conspicuous absence of consensus from Japanese society during the 1930s, the Occupation era, and the period after the first "oil shock.")

During the mid-1960s, as the Japanese economy forged well past the levels it had attained before the war and as people around the world began to recognize a Japanese economic "miracle," Japan's allies and trading partners began to apply pressure on Japan to open up its highly protected (some called it a "hothouse") domestic economy. The Japanese government resisted stubbornly, still believing that Japan's vulnerabilities greatly outweighed its newly achieved strengths and also because some elements in the state and society had inevitably developed vested interests in the high-growth system as it was then constituted. In 1964, the government liberalized to a significant degree its control over foreign trade and over conversion of yen into foreign currencies. Until then a Japanese student going abroad, for example, could take out of the country a maximum of $30. State control of foreign exchange and foreign trade had lasted without interruption from 1933 and 1937 respectively.

After the achievement of trade and exchange liberalization (a step the European nations had taken in 1958), the Japanese government was forced to act on foreign demands for capital liberalization. This was a much more serious change, since it involved opening up the Japanese economy to foreign ownership, something that the government felt was clearly incompatible with the *uchiwa* ("all in the family") government-business relationship on which high-speed growth was based. In 1967, with great fanfare, the Japanese government proclaimed the first round of capital liberalization. It did not allow foreigners to purchase a controlling interest in Japanese companies (they still cannot do so easily today), but it did open Japan's doors to foreign manufacture and sale of such items as *geta,* sake, motorcycles, and cornflakes—that is, to industries in which foreign competition was negligible or for which there was virtually no domestic market. Despite this initially cosmetic liberalization, Japan has progressively lightened the weight of controls over capital transfers into and out of Japan. As of 1981, great progress had been made, but as we shall see, the complete liberalization of neither trade nor capital was achieved.

In talking about the internationalization of the Japanese economy, we are thus actually discussing the dismantling of the government-business relationship of the high-speed growth era (1955–73). When the problem of the internationalization of the Japanese economy is posed in this manner, several new and important policy questions arise. How far can or should Japan go toward fully internationalizing its governmental controls over the economy, given Japan's foreign trade and energy dependencies and its need for some central supervision of that most implacable of economic constraints, the international balance of payments? Should Japan's allies continue to press for more Japanese economic internationalization, or should they instead attempt to emulate Japan's developmental relationship between the state and the privately owned economy? Is Japanese economic liberalization necessary for the sake of the newly industrializing economies of East Asia, including mainland China, even more than for the benefit of Japan's other trading partners? Is Japan carrying its weight in terms of contributions to the common defense and the need to recycle the funds paid to the Arab petroleum cartel? These are the sorts of questions posed by the subject of Japan's economic internationalization when it is seen in its political rather than in its cultural dimension.

Some answers to these questions can be found by examining the actual state of Japanese internationalization in three areas: finance, trade, and defense. On the financial front, the key to the twentieth-century *sakoku* (closed country) economic system was the Foreign Exchange and Foreign Trade Control Law of December 1, 1949. It was enacted with the full approval of the Occupation authorities in order to continue and reinforce the then current policy of concentrating all foreign receipts earned from exports into a government account and disbursing them in accordance with a government-created and -supervised foreign exchange budget. This budget was one of MITI's prime tools for promoting Japan's rapid economic recovery and for its industrial modernization campaign in order to achieve economic independence from American aid. SCAP also approved the law as a way of transferring its own authority and the powers that it had been exercising over foreign trade to the Japanese government in anticipation of a Japanese-American peace treaty. The system created by the law was the one described earlier by Hollerman as "the most restrictive foreign trade and foreign exchange control system ever devised by a major free nation."

SCAP believed that the Foreign Exchange and Foreign Trade Control Law was merely temporary. As it wrote in one of its official histories:

> This broad enabling act authorized the Government to maintain a unified system of control over foreign exchange and foreign trade transactions only to the extent necessary to safeguard the balance of international payments, and in effect transferred to the Government certain responsibilities which had been exercised by

SCAP since the beginning of the Occupation. The restrictions in the law were to be gradually relaxed by cabinet orders and ministerial ordinances as the need for them subsided (Supreme Commander for the Allied Powers 1951: 110).

But in the eyes of the Japanese economic bureaucracy, the need for such restrictions never subsided. The law was still on the books during 1981 as Japan's most important piece of economic legislation. Of course, the law had been modified and amended numerous times, beginning with trade liberalization in 1964, when the government-controlled foreign currency budget had to be abandoned, and most decisively in 1979, when the law was rewritten. But it has never been abolished (it has, in fact, been used for some purposes that were never anticipated in 1949—for example, in the indictments against Kodama Yoshio and the other defendants in the Lockheed case who are charged with violations of the Foreign Exchange and Foreign Trade Control Law).

In 1977, Prime Minister Fukuda initiated the basic revision of the law that the Diet enacted on November 11, 1979, and that came into effect on December 1, 1980. Fukuda believed that the most objectionable restrictions in the law had already been abolished through ordinances of the Ministry of Finance, but the system that had resulted from these ad hoc modifications was extremely complex; and the stated purposes of the original law still struck many foreigners as symbolic of Japan's closed economic status. This was highly embarrassing to Japan during the years 1976–78, when its bilateral trade surplus with the United States was growing from $5.4 billion to $8 billion to $11.6 billion and its worldwide trade surplus was increasing from $3.7 billion to $10.9 billion to $16.5 billion. Fukuda thus created a blue-ribbon deliberation council, headed by Nagano Shigeo, president of the Japanese Chamber of Commerce and Industry, to recommend changes in the law. Based on the Nagano council's report, Fukuda introduced his reform legislation in the 87th to 89th Diets before the 90th finally passed it. The *Financial Times* of London (December 3, 1980) hailed the coming into effect of the new law on December 1 as signifying Japan's first genuine steps toward capital liberalization and concluded that the reform had ushered in a "forced march toward internationalization."

The most important change in the law is conceptual. Under various articles of the old version, all external economic transactions between Japan and the rest of the world were "prohibited in principle," foreign trade thus being legally permitted by the government only in the form of an exception to the law. Under the new version the objectives of the law are changed so that "foreign exchange, foreign trade, and other external transactions will be conducted freely," subject only to the emergency restrictions that the government is authorized to impose.[2] This change from "prohibition in principle" to "freedom in principle" has been cited by Japanese commentators as one of Japan's most important acts of liberalization, even though some foreigners feel that it was about 15 years overdue.

Regardless of the principle, the restrictions in the new version still leave Japan a considerably less open country than most of its leading trading partners. The most important of these restrictions concerns foreign takeover bids to acquire established Japanese companies. Under the rules that surrounded the old law, foreigners were prohibited from acquiring more than a 25 percent ownership share of an established Japanese company, unless the company had been exempted from this provision by the Ministry of Finance (Sony, for example, was exempt); and an individual foreigner was limited to no more than a 10 percent share in any single company and then only as portfolio investment (that is, in order to earn dividends or capital gains, but not to name a member of the board of directors or otherwise gain a controlling influence over the company). The new regulations continue the 10 percent limit on individual foreign ownership of an established company; but in place of the old 25 percent limit on all foreign investment, the Minister of Finance can now intervene and limit foreign investment to 25 percent of a particular company or industry only if he designates them to be vital to the national interest, so that foreign control will interfere with the "smooth management of the Japanese economy." Otherwise, foreign purchases of Japanese companies are, in principle, unrestricted.

This provision of the new law distinguishes Japan from countries like the United States, where foreigners face no legal restrictions on the purchase of American firms or banks. As the *Japan Economic Journal* (February 10, 1981) noted:

> The number of cases of American firms purchased by Japanese enterprises is increasing sharply. This is because takeovers of

firms in the U.S. involve far less risk than starting out from scratch and because the Japanese enterprises can secure a stabilized business and sales share in that country more effectively and quickly.

This, of course, could also work in reverse. Until now, American firms entering Japan have had to do so on their own or in a joint venture; they could not acquire an established Japanese firm. This has undoubtedly contributed to the 90 percent failure rate of American firms trying to sell to the Japanese market (see Mikuriya, 1980: 17). However, the availability of the new takeover route depends on how the Ministry of Finance uses its authority to designate enterprises or firms as economically strategic and therefore exempt from foreign takeovers.

So far, in the few months since the new law came into effect, the Ministry of Finance has designated as exceptions such industries as atomic power, defense, oil, mining, and agriculture. There is nothing surprising about this; these are the traditionally protected sectors in many countries, and ample precedents exist abroad for similar restrictions. But there are several more disturbing trends. The ministry has established certain criteria calling for the use of its emergency intervention powers, and these include the prevention of volatile changes in exchange rates, the need to offset balance of payments problems (either large deficits or surpluses), and the avoidance of domestic economic disruptions that could affect the financial markets. Meanwhile, it has actually designated as exceptions such companies as Hitachi, Ltd., which did not (publicly) ask for special treatment even though Arab investors were pouring money into it, and Fujitsū Fanuc, the big computer manufacturer that forms the core of MITI's plan to foster a Japanese competitor to IBM. It is doubtful that foreign investment in either of these companies would have any negative effect on (much less cause a disruption of) the financial markets.

One of the most interesting cases suggests that the Ministry of Finance may be responding to political pressure; this case has already ended up in the Japanese courts. It concerns Katakura Industries Company (Katakura Kōgyō K.K.), a textile company that the Ministry of Finance made exempt from foreign takeover not because it was of strategic importance but because of alleged past attempts by foreign speculators to acquire large chunks of its equity capital. The facts, to the extent that they have been uncovered by the economic press, are these: Katakura is a second-rate textile manufacturer and silk-egg producer that also happens to be located on some prime real estate in the vicinity of Tokyo. Wang Hsiang-tsang, a prominent Hong Kong investor and chairman of Newpis Hong Kong, Ltd., together with a group of his associates, had acquired some 23 percent of Katakura's shares before the Ministry of Finance stepped in and designated the company as strategic. The Ministry of Finance was backed up by the Ministry of Agriculture, which claimed that Katakura's output had a significant bearing on the well-being of the nation's silk farmers, and that it feared that if Wang acquired the company he would develop the land for other, admittedly more profitable, uses. Wang replied that "Japan's economic integrity or national security is hardly at stake in this matter."

Well-informed Japanese observers note that farmers are among the prime electoral backers of the Liberal Democratic Party. They also recall that a few years ago Wang and his associates bought about ten percent of the shares of the Ōji Paper Company. Suddenly and in perfect unison, all Japanese securities companies refused to accept any further orders from Wang for Ōji shares. When Wang sought an explanation, it never came. Rumors suggested that the government had intervened. This time, in light of the new law, Wang filed suit against the Minister of Finance in Tokyo District Court. Concerning this case, the *Japan Economic Journal* (March 3, 1981) wrote, "Not a few Japanese in industry and the stock market support Wang's questioning of the Japanese Government's designation of Katakura as a restricted company. If there is an easy recourse to hiding behind the Government's protection against foreign ownership, what is the meaning of the liberalization of foreign exchange and other external transactions under the new foreign exchange law?" (see pp. 1, 10, 15). The answer will have to come from another branch of the Japanese government, the courts, but given the legal system's past performance and its notorious delays, the outlook is not encouraging.

An issue that always comes up in cases of this sort is who in Japan is the real protectionist, the government itself or private industrial clients of the government who influence it through political pressure? The evidence on this score is contradictory. In the case of MITI, foreign and domestic observers agree that since 1966, the leaders of the ministry have been drawn from its international faction and they have successfully eradicated the old protectionist orientation that prevailed during the 1950s and early 1960s (see C. Johnson, 1977: 227–79). For example, the authors of one of the background papers for the Wisemen conclude:

> In the textile case MITI took a strong stand in defense of domestic industry, and it did not cooperate in the more conciliatory and internationalist policies pursued by the Ministry of Foreign Affairs. However, over the years MITI has become much more internationalist, in the sense that it is now more willing to accommodate the interests of Japan's major trading partners instead of trying to defend the narrow and immediate interests of the industries under its jurisdiction. The auto situation was proof of this generalization, for MITI took the lead in dealing with this problem on the Japanese side, and its position on the issues negotiated was generally receptive to the concerns advanced by the Carter administration (Winham and Kabashima, 1980: 62).

In the case of the Ministry of Finance, however, I believe the evidence supports the opposite point of view—namely, that private business interests are considerably more internationalized than the ministry itself, which is doing its best to preserve the old order. Many Japanese industrial and financial leaders have made the point that since they can buy foreign firms and invest in foreign countries, there is no good reason why foreigners should not be able to invest in Japan. For example, in the highly volatile Nippon Telephone and Telegraph Company case, Kōmoto Toshio, a prominent industrialist, former minister of MITI, and chairman of the LDP's Research Council, said that "since we can bid on orders anywhere in the world, foreigners should be allowed to bid in Japan" (Curran, 1980: 61). These sentiments echo those of the leaders of the Japanese steel industry.

It is the Finance Ministry that seems to be unwilling to see key structural features of the Japanese high-growth system either disturbed or abandoned. These features include the high savings rate, the channeling of small savers' deposits directly into government accounts through the postal savings system, the practice of financing industry through loans from the city banks (which the ministry controls), the use of the distribution system to absorb labor during economic down-turns in lieu of a more extensive unemployment insurance system, and the higher reliance on subcontracting in Japan than in other countries, which provides a key buffer for the semi-lifetime employment system. The Ministry of Finance fears that these institutions cannot prevail in the face of widespread foreign participation in the Japanese domestic economy.

Part of the ministry's concern reflects a desire to maintain its own bureaucratic jurisdiction, but another part is its genuine and under-standable belief that Japan as an overpopulated, highly industrialized, resource-deficient nation cannot be expected to operate exactly like continental-sized countries with low trade and energy dependencies. The ministry noted with alarm how quickly Japan's huge balance of payments surpluses turned into deficits following the second oil shock of 1979. It also observes that whereas the highly publicized American governmental budget deficit amounts to about 9 percent of total governmental spending, Japan's deficit amounts to about 30 percent. Under these circumstances the ministry wants to keep the Japanese economy under its control.

These are some of the reasons why the Ministry of Finance has persistently discriminated against foreign banks in Japan, even though Japanese banks operate freely in the United States and until recently purchases of American banks were the most common form of Japanese capital acquisition in the United States. An American purchase of a Japanese bank is unthinkable under current conditions. It is also the reason why the foreign stake in the shares traded on the Tokyo Stock Exchange during 1980 amounted to no more than three percent of the total, less than before the first oil shock of 1973. Nonetheless, the pressure on the Ministry of Finance to change is there and will grow. Extensive foreign involvement in the economies of Taiwan and Korea has not prevented them from growing at rates even higher than Japan's, and these countries have also escaped some of the protectionist pressures now being applied against Japan. Moreover, if the ministry should persist in using its powers to protect firms such as Katakura, it can anticipate countervailing trade restrictions to protect industries such as American automobiles. This becomes clear from a considera-tion of the internationalization of Japan's trade.

According to one of Japan's leading officials concerned with international trade, Awaya Tadashi, chief of the Imports Section of MITI: "As far as I am concerned, Japan is in regard to trade the most liberal nation in the world—more liberal even than America." Sawano Hiroshi, a director of JETRO and a former official of the Ministry of Finance, adds, "After all, what other nation can you name which has public and private bodies allocating funds to help increase the exports of their trading partners?" (*The Wheel Extended* 7, 1980: 2, 7). Any fair-minded observer must acknowledge the accuracy of these statements, even though the conditions described are quite recent. Japan today has very few tariff barriers, has worked hard to lower non-tariff barriers, and has sent missions abroad to try to encourage sales *to* Japan. All these measures came about because of the huge trade surpluses that Japan earned during the second half of the 1970s and that threatened to cause its foreign trading partners to reduce drastically Japan's access to their own markets.

Why are Japan's trading relations with the rest of the world (except for the OPEC petroleum exporters) chronically unbalanced in Japan's favor? One possible answer is that they are not. It is only with respect to certain highly visible merchandise that Japan enjoys a favorable balance. When the measurement is broadened to include services and invisibles (insurance, freight, capital transfers, etc.), Japan's overall balance of payments slides into the red. During 1980, Japan spent more abroad than it took in. It is because Japan's expenditures for imported raw materials, particularly energy, are so high that it must compensate for them with large surpluses in its exports.

This pattern cannot be avoided in Japan's case, so long as the country is to remain economically viable, and Japan's allies would be wise frequently to remind themselves of that fact. Japan itself could reduce the tensions this pattern generates if it would spread its exports across a broader spectrum of merchandise than just a few products that often flood a foreign market. For example, during 1980, American imports of one Japanese product—automobiles—were worth around $8 billion, more than the total of all imports from any other American non-OPEC trading partner except Canada. Even those of Japan's allies who appreciate that Japan's trade balance must be seen in a global rather than a strictly bilateral perspective cannot be indifferent to the effect of a torrent of Japanese imports on their domestic levels of employment. The problem of unemployment is in any case the real concern underlying most trade disputes, as the Japanese well understand. They themselves certainly did not tolerate the near bankruptcy of Tōyō Kōgyō Motors when it overinvested in the rotary engine (see *Wall Street Journal,* March 24, 1975), and it is impossible to imagine Japan accepting the levels of unemployment or the damage to the tax bases of several states that the United States has sustained in the face of Japanese automobile imports.

However, so long as imbalances such as those in automobiles result from genuine competition and not from structural barriers to trade, they should be accepted and protectionism rejected. Such competition benefits all consumers and achieves a more productive allocation of resources. An American policy of protecting its own, often inefficient, auto industry would probably cost the American economy more in imported petroleum for less fuel-efficient cars and in inflation than the value of the jobs saved. This is the primary reason that American protectionist policies have so far been avoided, at least through the first quarter of 1981.

Another reason why Japan's trading relations often seem unbalanced in its favor is the comparatively low level of Japanese imports of merchandise. Even if it is unreasonable to expect a balance in any manufacturing nation's merchandise account with Japan, the question still remains whether the merchandise account should be as drastically unbalanced as it is. What prevents foreign manufacturers from selling more than they do in Japan? As we have already seen, the Japanese government believes that formal barriers to such sales are nonexistent, although some foreigners believe that the culture itself is a kind of non-tariff barrier. The actual answer seems to lie between these two poles.

One official Japanese view of this matter is that foreigners simply should try harder to sell in Japan—at least as hard as Japanese do in foreign countries. Too often foreign sales organizations in Japan have not committed themselves to a long-term strategy of market penetration and have given up when short-term profits were not immediately forthcoming. Those companies that have persisted—for example, Coca-Cola and Johnson and Johnson—have done very well indeed.

But persistence alone cannot be the answer. During 1979, Japan had a favorable balance of trade with some 88 nations. Even if American businessmen are not as persistent as Japanese businessmen, it seems unlikely that all the world's businessmen (except for the oil sheiks) are lazier than the Japanese. The Taiwanese, for example, do not think that their problem is due to a lack of effort. Given a $3.18 billion trade deficit with Japan during 1980 (a deficit that offset its combined surpluses from trade with the United States and Western Europe), Taiwan promulgated rules requiring governmental approval of any proposed import worth more than $200,000. In such cases the government advises the importer to obtain his product from any other country than Japan. The "Jones Committee" of the U.S. Congress concluded that

> unlike some, we are not sure that American businessmen as a general classification should be criticized for not trying "hard enough" to sell in Japan. There have been inadequate opportunities, and rewards have not been commensurate with the risks and difficulties (U.S. House of Representatives, 1979: 17).

What are some of the risks and difficulties of selling in the Japanese market? One semi-official American government answer is that "even when a foreign firm does become established in Japan, particularly if it appears to threaten a Japanese industry's ability to compete, the Japanese Government will potentially take action to limit that firm's market growth" (Weil and Glick, 1980: 5). The current list of alleged impediments to access to the Japanese market includes the following: customs procedures, product approval procedures, governmental procurement procedures, administrative guidance, and the Japanese distribution system.

There are no legal customs procedures that restrict imports, but foreign businessmen maintain that they are treated in a discriminatory manner when it comes to actually passing goods through the customs houses. The conviction in March 1979 of Steven H. Rempell, an American businessman, by the Yokohama District Court did nothing to relieve foreign anxieties on this score. Rempell was importing foreign liquor at prices lower than the Ministry of Finance said he should be charging, and it sued him for the customs duties lost to the state. The *Japan Times Weekly* (March 3, 1979) declared that Rempell was "a victim of Japan, Inc." and noted that his conviction would mean higher prices for Japanese consumers. The Rempell case is on appeal to a higher court.

Product approval procedures refer to the import inspection regulations contained in the Electrical Appliances Law, the Drugs, Cosmetics, and Medical Instruments Law, and similar statutes. Weil (former Assistant Secretary of Commerce for Industry and Trade) and Glick (staff director of the U.S.-Japan Trade Facilitation Committee, U.S. Dept. of Commerce) maintain that "Japanese product approval procedures appear import-restrictive in theory as well as in practice" (1980: 5). Among the many complaints on this score are that a product certified as safe by Japanese testing authorities may be imported into the United States without a retest, but a product certified by Underwriters Laboratories of the United States must still be retested in Japan; Underwriters Laboratories maintains facilities to conduct tests in Japan, but Japan will not go abroad to issue its JIS (Japan Industrial Standards) seal at the point of manufacture; Japanese product approval requirements are based on design rather than performance characteristics, meaning that foreign goods with performance characteristics superior to approved Japanese products may still not be approved because of differences in design (differences that may account for the improved performance); foreigners are excluded from Japanese standard-setting deliberations; and the Japanese approval process often requires the submission of proprietary information about a product, which is not the case in most other countries. Many of these obstacles are currently being removed as a result of Japan's efforts to internationalize its economy, but the process is slow.

Governmental procurement procedures concern the fairly large proportion of the Japanese economy that is controlled by governmental corporations. The problem here is not so much explicit "buy Japan" policies as longstanding arrangements between the corporations and the domestic suppliers, arrangements that both sides are loathe to give up, often for political reasons. President Akigusa Tokuji of Nippon Telephone and Telegraph was intransigent on the subject, remarking that "the only thing NTT would buy from the United States is mops and buckets," despite Japan's having signed the 1979 GATT treaty opening up the governmental sector of the industrialized democracies to foreign participation (Curran, 1980: 26). Since this issue concerns governmental procedures, it is probably best dealt with not through negotiations but through automatic retaliatory measures when reciprocity is not forthcoming from one side or the other. Japan, for example, might find that all its advertising for automobiles in the

United States would have to be conducted in the Japanese language so long as the Ministry of Finance continues to restrict advertising in Japan of imported tobacco to English-language media. Similarly, the United States might find the landing rights for its airliners in Japan curtailed to exactly the same number as Japan is allowed in the United States. This is the quickest way to achieve reciprocity among governments, as has long been true, for example, in the treatment of diplomats.

Administrative guidance by the Japanese government is defined by Weil and Glick as "a flexible technique for maintaining 'harmony' in the economy through the use of temporary measures that avoid the need for legislative action." It is clearly a practice left over from the recent sakoku era. However, actions by the Japanese Fair Trade Commission seem destined to limit its use in the future to cases of genuine national emergency. There is no question that in the past administrative guidance was a non-tariff barrier to trade, but it appears today to be of much less significance largely because many sectors of Japanese industry and commerce have become resistant to governmental interference of this sort. Administrative guidance began to decline in 1969, when Mitsubishi Heavy Industries defied MITI and went ahead with a joint venture with Chrysler to manufacture automobiles in Japan. The success of the Mitsubishi revolt meant that the government had to become much more circumspect in giving orders to industry.

With regard to the domestic distribution system, the Japanese rightly resent foreigners describing it as a barrier to trade. Japanese customers like the numerous small retail outlets available to them—about 1.61 million, compared to 1.55 million in the United States, a country with a population twice the size of Japan's. The Japanese distribution system conforms to the needs and scale of Japanese housing and commuting; it makes the streets safer because of the high levels of activity it generates; it gives work to seven times as many wholesalers as in Great Britain, even though Japan's population is only twice as large as Britain's; and it is not a governmental barrier to trade because no governmental policy is involved.

The distribution system has seemed to be a barrier to trade because, much to their own disadvantage, foreigners have tended to favor large scale Japanese outlets, such as department stores and supermarkets. They have been ignorant of or insensitive to the longstanding political conflict between medium- and small-scale retailers and the financially (sometimes politically) powerful department stores. Because of such foreign myopia, some wholesalers for the small retailers have come to distrust foreign products, seeing their manufacturers as potential allies of Japanese big business and as a threat to their small retailers' existence. They have been known to sabotage foreign sales campaigns. These problems could be alleviated by greater knowledge on the part of foreign sales organizations, more candor on the part of Japanese concerning these same realities, and foreign acquisitions of Japanese firms. To the extent that the Ministry of Finance permits such foreign takeovers under the new Foreign Exchange and Foreign Trade Control Law, foreigners would obtain more capable and reliable partners than they have enjoyed in the past. The result should be a considerable boon to Japanese consumers, who for many years have not had genuine access to the same benefits of international competition that are commonplace in other industrialized countries.

Japan is making tremendous progress in internationalizing its trade. Before concluding this discussion, however, one further matter must be mentioned because it is inextricably involved in the threat of protectionism faced by the world today. This is the defense issue. Nothing has done more to prolong the postwar period for more than 40 years than the strategic contest between the United States and the Soviet Union. When the United States first assumed primary responsibility for the defense of its Japanese and Western European allies, it also accounted for about 40 to 45 percent of all goods and services produced on the planet. Japan's share at the time was either negative or negligible. By 1978, America's share of the world's gross national product had fallen to 21.8 percent and Japan's had risen to 10 percent. It is this huge shift in productive power that today demands a new division of labor among the democratic allies concerning political and military responsibilities.

Even if Japan should succeed in fully internationalizing its economy, if it fails to reach agreement on a new political and military division of labor with its allies, the whole economic liberalization effort could be in vain. The United States, as Japan's most important market, will be unable politically both to continue to provide the primary strategic defenses of the allies and to accept permanently unfavorable balances of trade with them. This problem is not particularly acute, since it is recognized by all sides, and the trend of developments is toward a reallocation of security tasks. When that reallocation has been achieved, then the postwar world will finally have come to an end. If it is not achieved, then the postwar world is likely to end in a much less satisfactory way.

Although the internationalization of Japan is difficult both to conceptualize and to implement, its occurrence is not really in doubt. Japan today is one of the world's richest nations. More important, a generational change of profound significance is occurring in Japan. Young Japanese, born in the 1950s and 1960s, are just now achieving responsible positions in government and private industry. They differ from all other Japanese born in this century in their ready familiarity with peace and prosperity. They do not have the experiences or the priorities that led their fathers and grandfathers in the 1950s to work as hard as they did—or to tolerate the conditions of sakoku that prevailed then. They can be expected to persist with the internationalization of the economy since it has become fundamental to Japan's continued prosperity. The internationalization of Japanese society has already been largely achieved. The continuing process of the internationalization of Japan's economic institutions and norms is well started but not yet completed.

NOTES
1. As an example of the misplaced cultural explanation in the economic field, note the following: "Neither profitability nor common financing or trading activities explain the grouping of firms along the *keiretsu* lineage. The basic motivation for the grouping of keiretsu firms lies in sociological factors. The tendency to form a group is an inherent part of Japan's cultural tradition" (Haitani, 1976: 124). But the creation of banking keiretsu during and following the Dodge Line deflation of 1949 is easily explained by the intense shortage of capital in the Japanese economy, the reliance on bank "overloans" guaranteed by the Bank of Japan, and the policies of Ichimada Naoto, then governor of the Bank of Japan, and Ikeda Hayato, then minister of finance (see C. Johnson, 1982: 201–211).
2. For the text of the new law and an analysis of it, see *Look Japan,* 1980: 12–13.

REFERENCES
Anon.
    1980   " 'Prohibition Principle' Amended to be Free." *Look Japan*, 25.
Curran, Timothy J.
    1980   *Politics and High Technology: U.S.-Japan Negotiations over the Nippon*

Telephone and Telegraph Company, 1978–1979. Washington, D.C.: U.S.-Japan Economic Relations Group (typescript).

Dahrendorf, Ralf
1967 *Society and Democracy in Germany.* Garden City, N.Y.: Doubleday.

The Economist, Consider Japan
1963 London: Duckworth.

Hadley, Eleanor M.
1970 *Antitrust in Japan.* Princeton, N.J.: Princeton University Press.

Haitani, Kanji
1976 *The Japanese Economic System, an Institutional Overview.* Lexington, Mass.: D. C. Heath.

Halloran, Richard
1970 *Japan: Images and Realities.* New York: Knopf.

Hollerman, Leon
1979 "International Economic Controls in Occupied Japan." *Journal of Asian Studies,* 38, 4, 707–19.

Johnson, Chalmers
1977 "MITI and Japanese International Economic Policy." Robert A. Scalapino (ed.). *The Foreign Policy of Modern Japan.* Berkeley and Los Angeles: University of California Press.
1978 *Japan's Public Policy Companies.* Washington, D.C.: American Enterprise Institute.
1982 *MITI and the Japanese Miracle.* Stanford: Stanford University Press.

Johnson, Sheila K.
1975 *American Attitudes Toward Japan, 1941–1975.* Washington, D.C.: American Enterprise Institute.

Kaplan, Eugene J.
1972 *Japan: The Government-Business Relationship.* Washington, D.C.: Government Printing Office.

Mikuriya Fumio
1980 "Distribution: The Key to Success in the Japanese Market." *The Wheel Extended,* 10 (Summer).

Minear, Richard H.
1980 "The Wartime Studies of Japanese National Character." *The Japan Interpreter* (Summer).

Ministry of International Trade and Industry
1980 *White Paper on International Trade 1980.* Tokyo: Tsūshō Sangyō-shō.

Ozaki, Robert S.
1978 *The Japanese: A Cultural Portrait.* Tokyo: Tuttle.

Park Sung-jo
1980–81 "Social Science-centered Japanese Studies in West Germany, Japanology as an 'Orchild Science.' " *The Japan Foundation Newsletter,* 8 (December–January).

Report of the Japan-United States Economic Relations Group
1981 Washington, D.C.

Setō Sumihiko
1980 "Manufactured Imports and Their Marketing Promotion Strategies." *The Wheel Extended,* 10 (Summer).

57

Shiba Kimpei, and Nozue Kenzō
　　1971　*What Makes Japan Tick?* Tokyo: Asahi Evening News Co.
Supreme Commander for the Allied Powers
　　1951　"Foreign Trade" (monograph 50), *History of the Non-military Activities of the Occupation of Japan, 1945–1951.* Washington, D.C.: National Archives.
U. S. Congress. House.
　　1979　*Task Force Report on United States-Japan Trade.* Subcommittee on Trade of the Committee on Ways and Means. 95th Cong., 2d sess. Washington, D.C.: Government Printing Office.
Weil, Frank A., and Norman D. Glick
　　1980　"Japan: Is the Market Open?" *Business America,* 3 (May 5).
The Wheel Extended
　　1980　"A Round Table Discussion: Japan Moves to Encourage Manufactured Imports." Special Supplement, no. 7 (Summer).
Winham, Gilbert R., and Kabashima Ikuo
　　1980　*The Politics of United States-Japan Auto Trade.* Washington D.C.: U.S.-Japan Economic Relations Group. Typescript.

THE INTERNATIONALIZATION
OF MANAGEMENT
IN JAPANESE MULTINATIONALS

Robert M. Marsh
Mannari Hiroshi

The multinational corporation (hereafter, MNC) is a phenomenon that invites study. At the macro-level it poses such problems as the relative power of MNCs and the nation-state; the effect of MNCs on local capital formation, oligopolies, and economic development in general in Third World societies; and the relationships between MNCs and power, class structure and stratification in host countries (Kumar, 1980). At the micro-level there is a broad range of problems concerning the internal structure of the MNC as an organization, the relation between its managerial strategy and organizational structure, the cultural distance between foreign managers and their local employees, and the interaction between the MNC's organization and its host country environment (Evans, 1981).

This paper focuses on Japanese MNCs, defined as manufacturing or mining firms that have at least one manufacturing or mining operation abroad. The extent to which Japan's economy and its firms have become internationalized can be measured along several dimensions: the export of Japanese goods and services; the importing of foreign raw materials, goods and services into Japan; the export of Japanese capital in the form of direct investment in firms in other countries; the import of foreign capital into Japan; and the liberalization of foreign exchange controls. As Japan becomes more internationalized in its production, trade and financial systems, it is worth asking if there is a parallel process by which Japanese MNCs also become "internationalized" in their organization structure and management practices. We shall seek answers to this question within the "strategy and structure" theoretical framework developed by Alfred Chandler (1962) and

Oliver Williamson (1970). An organization's *strategy* is its operative goal or policy for survival and growth at a given time. Organizational strategies are the application of theories—which reflect past experiences and ways of thinking in the organization—to perceived opportunities or problems. Strategy is constantly interacting with structure. When management formulates a strategy—e.g., product diversification —it may find that its existing organizational *structure* is inadequate to the task of effectively implementing the strategy. The strategy can only be realized by structural changes in the organization.

This leads to an important hypothesis: Correctly matching strategy to opportunities and structure to strategy increases a firm's performance (profit, market share) and also increases the efficiency with which society's resources are used (Caves, 1980: 79).

Thus, we ask, to what extent can a Japanese MNC export a "made in Japan" management and organization to its foreign subsidiaries? American firms, which became multinationalized earlier than Japanese firms, made certain adaptations of their organizational and management structures to their multinational strategies. To what extent do these originally American structures comprise an "international style" of MNC management which, under optimality constraints, Japanese latecomer MNCs must imitate? Are the adaptations of a Ford or a General Electric universal, or should we expect a Tōyō Kōgyō or a Sanyō to make different organizational adaptations to multinational strategy?

The derived hypothesis we shall test is that in matching strategy to opportunity and structure to strategy, there are universals such that (1) the extent of "made in Japan" management and organizational structure declines over time as multinational strategies are played out by Japanese MNC subsidiaries abroad; and (2) Japanese MNCs come to resemble Western MNCs in their structure more than they resemble Japanese firms that produce their output wholly within Japan.

Our paper draws heavily on recent Japanese publications of the Workshop for the Study of Japanese Multinationals (Takokuseki kigyō kenkyūkai). The chairman of the workshop Kobayashi Takenori stated, "The most important problem for multinationalization of Japanese enterprises in the 1980s is internationalization of management. This . . . means, first, to invest directly in overseas business; second, to operate overseas production; and third, to develop with the host societies a global management" (Kobayashi, 1980: 1). This raises the question, does "global management" mean something other than "distinctively Japanese style management," and if so, what?

Historical Trends in Japanese Management

We begin with a historical perspective provided by Ono Toyoaki's book *Organizational Strategies in Japanese Corporations* (Nihon no kigyō no soshiki senryaku, 1979). Ono sees three stages in the development of Japanese corporate structure from 1945 to the present.

1. *Ringi* management and corporate organization, 1945–55.
2. Modernization of management and corporate organization, 1956–65.
3. Strategic management and corporate organization, 1966–.

Until 1955, the prevailing management pattern in Japan was an extension of the prewar ringi system. Top management consisted of one-man control coupled with an informal Board of Directors (*jyūyaku-kai*). Management at the factory level was under the centralized control of company headquarters. The ringi system is usually described as a procedure for the "bottom-up" initiation of managerial policy planning. As the written proposal is read by successively higher managerial levels, there is widespread input into whatever form the proposal takes, and consensus is built up.

While the general features of the ringi system have often been described, Ono draws out some of its implications that may be less well understood. First, the ringi system has a direct control function, but it is one in which the chief executive decides items on a case-by-case basis. Such a mode of decision making deviates from the modern rational-legal bureaucratic form of administration, since it is not derived from the application of systematic, abstract general rules to particular cases (Weber, 1946). Second, although the ringi system is a participative management system, it does not mean that *control* is decentralized. The superior retains the right to reject his subordinates' collective recommendations. Third, in fact the ringi system presupposes the *centralization* of decision-making authority in headquarters and the functional, rather than divisional organization of the firm (a point to which we shall return below).

Ono describes stage 1 as one in which management functions were relatively undifferentiated. The authority of each position was not clearly defined. Organizational units were not differentiated beyond two—headquarters and factory shop(s). The relationship between headquarters and the factory was one of functional, line authority. The case-by-case decision making was essentially management without plan; it worked at that time for the following reasons: even in large scale firms the abilities required of executives were relatively simple; direct control by the chief executive through the ringi system was effective; men with strong leadership personalities were at the top; and Japanese management emphasized competent persons more than organization.

Stage 2, the modernization of management and organization, was initiated by the influence of the United States in the Allied Occupation period. Top management was reformed. The New Commercial Law of 1952 set up the Board of Directors (*torishimari-yakukai*). The ringi system and centralized, direct control by the chief executive were replaced by the council of managing directors (*jōmukai*), which was established as the supreme group decision-making body in the firm (cf. Tsurumi, 1976: 239). The introduction of the controller system contributed to budget control, cost control, and internal checking by indirect and system methods.

Modernization of management and organization brought about the replacement of the status hierarchy (*mibun seido*) by the work role (*shokunō*) or functional hierarchy. The chief executive was given a general staff to assist him; the professional and service staff people became more specialized and expert. In short, a line and staff organization developed. The authority and responsibility of managerial positions were defined more clearly. Rationalization and functional differentiation were extended to both office and factory work, as illustrated by the shift from the *soroban* to the electronic computer and the development of industrial engineering.

Stage 3 was initiated by the need for organizational innovation after 1965, to adapt to changes both outside and within the organization. Environmental changes included a multiplication of interest groups, an increasingly international scale of operations and the need to recognize foreign management, and the emergence of employee-oriented management in an affluent society with a more highly educated labor force. While the management cycle had been thought of as a closed system—consisting of "make a plan, carry it out, check it"—the new pressures gave rise to management theories that viewed the firm as a dynamic, open system.

Ono's discussion of stage 3 changes in Japanese organizational innovation closely parallels Oliver Williamson's (1970) theory of the shift from unitary (U-form) to multidivisional (M-form) structures in American firms. Before the invention of the multidivisional form, organizations tended to have a unitary form, in which the principal operating parts are functional divisions, e.g., manufacturing, sales, finance, and engineering (see Figure 1). As a firm continues to expand in scale and

FIGURE 1
Unitary and Multidivisional Forms of Organization

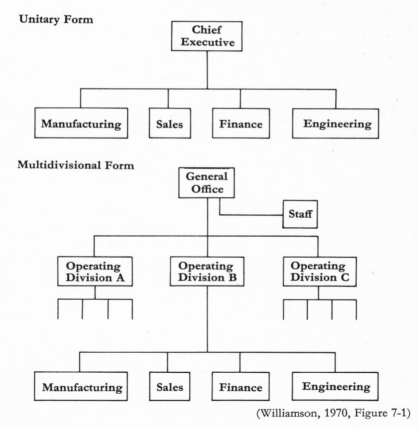

(Williamson, 1970, Figure 7-1)

product diversification *within* the U-form structure, the following problems emerge. Given finite spans of control at each hierarchic level, expansion of the firm leads to an increase in the number of hierarchic levels. This in turn leads to loss of control, through incomplete or inaccurate transmission of information and instructions moving up and down the longer hierarchy. The chief executive, the office of peak coordinator, must perform two disparate kinds of functions, day-to-day operational coordination of the functional departments and long-range strategic planning. As the organization expands, the chief executive is overburdened in attempting to discharge both of these demanding responsibilities. He brings in the heads of his functional departments to share these peak coordination tasks with him, but finds that they tend to advocate the partisan interests of their own department. This impedes overall long-range planning.

In the United States, as Chandler (1962) showed, these problems led DuPont and General Motors in the early 1920s to develop a quite new form of organization, the multidivisional form. Here, the principal operating parts are semiautonomous operating divisions, rather than functional departments. Each division is organized along product and/or geographical lines. The office of chief executive is replaced by a general office whose executives concentrate on company-wide, long-range entrepreneurial functions, while the manager of each fairly self-contained operating division handles the day-to-day operational activities of that division. Each division has complete jurisdiction over its functional departments—manufacturing, sales, etc.—but the division manager has the responsibility for achieving performance goals. The top team of generalists in the general office, assisted by their elite staff, are relieved of operating duties and tactical decisions, and are less likely to reflect the partisan interests of one part of the organization. The partisanship problem is less likely to affect strategic planning since division managers are not involved in strategic planning.

It should be noted that M-form organization does not abandon U-form structure; instead, it harnesses the latter solution to the division of labor problems *within* each product/geographic division. Figure 1 makes clear that within each operating division of M-form organizations the U-form is reproduced. The benefits of U-form are preserved, while its undesirable control loss and partisan sub-goal pursuit problems are held in check by the new M-form. As Chandler and Williamson have shown, the superiority of M-form over U-form with regard to long-range strategic goal formation and internal efficiency accounts for why large, product-diversified firms tend to undergo reorganization along M-form lines. Ono's work makes it abundantly clear that M-form structure has been adopted by Japanese firms having the requisite structural characteristics, overcoming cultural boundaries.

One credits Peter Drucker's account (1946) of General Motors as the source of the diffusion of the M-form system to Japan. The largest Japanese firms adopted this divisional system (*jig yōbu seido*) around 1960. The division head runs his division as a profit center. In the *jig yō-honbu* system, company headquarters controls one or more *groups* of related individual divisions. This reduces the span of control of the company chief executive officer(s).

In stage 3, organizations became more dynamic by establishing project teams (task force, or matrix organization) and top executive teams (*shūdan shidō seido,* collective leadership system). The section (*ka*) is eliminated as a unit, in order to reduce "sectionalism." The staff becomes more professionalized than in stage 2 and is given a larger role. Groups of workers are formed into zero-defects groups, quality control circles, etc.

Given the divisionalization of a firm on a geographic basis within Japan, the stage was set for divisionalization of MNCs beyond Japan's borders. It was not until October 1969 that the foreign exchange law made it possible for Japanese firms to make direct investments in foreign countries. After 1965, Japan's largest firms expanded to include a general staff for the planning and control of overseas subsidiaries. Facing a dynamic environment, top management and general staff thoroughly displaced the slow, bottom-up ringi system in the conduct of planning. Ono states that there is still a so-called ringi system in many firms, but, despite the title, its substance has changed to rational, scientific decision making.

The defining characteristic of stage 3 for Ono is strategic decision making in an environment of uncertainty and internationalization. Strategic decision making is distinguished from two other kinds of decision making, decisions concerning daily work and managerial decision making, and is defined as "the decisions in which firms adapt to environmental change, alter management objectives, satisfy customers' needs, optimize economic resources, and secure the maintenance and development of the firm" (Ono, 1979: 260). However, Ono points out that even among large Japanese firms, two-thirds probably remain in stage 2, with functional (line and staff) rather than multidivisional structures.

Stages in the Internationalization of Management

Kobayashi's work (1980) is another attempt to specify stages in a universal process by which management becomes internationalized as firms become multinational. His stage theory is based on the earlier experiences of American and European MNCs. The five stages have two dimensions, which are shown in Table 1. One dimension is the way a firm's foreign business is organized, and proceeds from (1) functional, or what Figure 1, following Williamson, calls Unitary or U-form organization to (2) product segmentation (M-form) to (3) geographical segmentation (also M-form) to (4) a matrix system that combines types (1) through (3), and then to (5) a regional headquarters for each major world region in which the MNC operates.

The second dimension's five stages outline a different set of successive structural adaptations. Most Japanese manufacturing firms entered foreign manufacturing activities almost by accident (Yoshino, 1976: 127). In the beginning (stage A) an export division of the manufacturing firm handled all export operations through its own sales subsidiaries abroad, or through one or more Japanese trading companies. The major initial impetus for direct foreign investment was to protect the firm's export market: when host countries adopted a policy of import substitution, Japanese firms saw new investment opportunities in the establishment of new foreign *manufacturing* (rather than sales) subsidiaries. In stage A, the firm's export division continued to handle all foreign operations, both manufacturing and sales. However, the export division could not respond well to the new needs of the local subsidiaries, so the international staff of the export division sought, and obtained, an independent status as the parent company's international division (stage B). Tensions then developed between the powerful export division and the new international division (cf. Tsurumi, 1976: 231–42 for a parallel discussion of the international division, the *kaigai jigyōbu*). Although the latter division was strengthened, the continuing importance of exports meant that the export division could not be superceded by the international division. To coordinate the operations of the MNC's foreign subsidiaries, there was a centralization of decision making within the international division; the coordination of the export and the international divisions was achieved by having the heads of both divisions report to the same managing director (Yoshino, 1976: 142). Thus, Kobayashi characterized stage C as one in which a corporate officer, in charge of all foreign operations control, coordinates all foreign business. Stage D is when independent subsidiaries are incorporated to conduct international business, and stage E involves the setting up of a global organization to achieve unified control of both domestic and foreign business. Kobayashi collected data from 80 (out of a sample of 100) Japanese MNCs, and compared this with responses of managers in 23 (out of a sample of 40) American and European MNCs. The respondents were asked both what their present overseas management organization was and what they expected their future organization to be. This allows us to specify perceived changes, the most important of which are as follows. Consider first the column marginals in Table 1. Stage C—a corporate officer in charge of all foreign operations—is the most common type both now (62 firms) and in the future (63 firms). The earliest two stages—(A) export division and (B) international division—are both expected to decline, from 5 firms to 0 and from 8 firms to 5, respectively. A slight increase from 3 to 7 firms is expected for stage D, incorporating independent subsidiaries to conduct international business. The most advanced stage, E, a global organization controlling both domestic and foreign business, characterizes only 2 firms and is not seen as increasingly common in the future.

Examining next the row marginals, we see that these MNC managers perceive a very significant decline in functional or U-form organization—from 61 firms now to only 18 in the future. Functional organization will be replaced by a matrix system (26 firms), regional headquarters for each major world region in which the MNC operates (18 firms), and by the two sub-types of multidivisional (M-form) structure: geographical (11) and product (4). While these perceptions of future changes are not a strict test, they provide a lead for testing the American-based hypothesis that since many MNCs are diversified both in terms of product and geographic markets, they must therefore move beyond a simple multidivisional (M-form) structure to a "matrix" structure (Davis and Lawrence, 1977, quoted in Evans, 1981: 216).

TABLE 1

PRESENT AND FUTURE PERCEIVED MANAGEMENT ORGANIZATION OF JAPANESE MULTINATIONAL CORPORATIONS

	A Export division handles foreign operations	B International division deals comprehensively with foreign business	C Corporate officer coordinates and controls all foreign business	D Incorporate independent company for international business	E Global organization to control both domestic and foreign business	Total
1. Organize foreign business functionally	3 firms	8 2	50 16			61 18
2. Organize foreign business according to product segmentation	2	1	9 2	2	1	13 4
3. Organize foreign business according to geographic segmentation			2 –	4	2	4 11
4. Adopt a matrix organization, combining 1, 2 and 3		1	1 23	1 1	1	2 26
5. Develop regional headquarters for each major region		1	15	2		18
Total now Total future	5 0	8 5	62 63	3 7	2 2	80 77

Upper number in each cell is number of firms that at present have the given characteristics; lower number refers to number of firms perceived to have given characteristics in the future. Sample = 89 firms; 9 did not answer "present" and 12 did not answer "future" characteristics, so totals are 80 and 77, respectively.
(Adapted from Kobayashi, 1980, Tables 1-1-23 and 1-1-27.)

Overall, we see in Table 1 much more perceived change in the 1 to 5 dimension—from U-form to M-form organization and toward delegation of authority from company headquarters to regional headquarters abroad—than in the A to E dimension, where there is a shift from coordination by the export division to a global organization that controls both domestic and foreign business.

Kobayashi depicts the trends in modal Japanese and Western MNCs in terms of these two dimensions. The modal Japanese MNC is perceived to change from state 1C (50 firms) to 4C (23 firms); i.e., both now and in the perceived future the modal MNC will have a corporate officer in charge of all foreign operations, but at present those operations are organized along functional or unitary form lines, while in the future, operations will be organized along matrix lines. Western MNCs are seen by Kobayashi as already in stage 4E or 5E, where there is a global organization that controls domestic and foreign business in a unified way, and the organization has either a matrix form or a regional headquarters in each major region where the company operates. Thus, although the net change perceived by the Japanese managers is in a modern direction, toward Western MNCs, Kobayashi stresses the fact that Japanese MNCs are generally still in a less developed stage of internationalization. Specifically, Japanese MNCs are less developed in recruiting personnel from host countries, in production procurement, marketing, research and development, and financial management. On Kobayashi's five-point scales for these elements (0 = least developed, 5 = most developed stage of internationalization), the mean score is 2.72 for the Japanese and 4.09 for the Western MNCs. Kobayashi finds the Western MNCs satisfied with their organizational strategy-structure mix, while half of the Japanese MNCs consider their organization inadequate for their strategic needs.

Corporate Planning

Yoshino (1976) studied a sample of 25 Japanese MNC subsidiaries in Thailand engaged in such industries as metal fabrication, synthetic fiber, home appliances, consumer electronics, automobiles, and chemicals. Like the other writers we have discussed, Yoshino views "Japan's distinctive managerial system, which was nurtured in the home environment and proved effective in that setting" as "an important factor inhibiting the growth of Japanese multinational enterprise" (Yoshino,

1976: 161). He asserts that Japanese MNCs will converge toward the American system with regard to strategy and structure, but not with regard to management practices. Chief among these practices are the ringi system, which presupposes the traditional Japanese reliance on "implicit, unspoken understanding between individuals" which makes for "an aversion to explicit definition of organizational goals" (Yoshino, 1976: 165).

Hayashi Kichiro (1979) surveyed 19 Japanese corporations representing multinational enterprises in a variety of industries.[1] He argues that there are conflicts between the socio-cultural characteristics of Japanese management and the basic premises of corporate planning as presented in American management texts. American corporate planning begins by setting objectives, especially long-range objectives. It then selects means, i.e., a corporate program designed to achieve these objectives. In the case of MNCs, this involves selecting the appropriate countries and locations for the realization of the objectives. Then comes the execution of the plan, through directing, informing, leading and motivating, monitoring and evaluating.

Hayashi reviews the work of those scholars who have stressed the "Japaneseness" of Japanese organizations, such as Nakane (1967: 14) and Hazama (1971). If they are right, Hayashi reasons, Japanese MNC management should find it difficult to become "internationalized" or "global." Hayashi then analyzes areas of conflict: setting objectives, program design and excution of plans.

Conflicts in setting objectives. Paternalistic leaders in Japanese MNCs are selected for their social skills rather than their strategic decision-making ability. Despite her emphasis on verticality in Japanese society and organizations, Nakane (1967: 136) reports a lack of communication between top executives and their middle or lower managerial subordinates. Top executives achieve their positions after lengthy careers as subordinates, which does not prepare them for the independence required to make long-range strategic objectives. The larger the firm, the older top executives tend to be; this shortens their time horizons and tends to make them less flexible about management innovation.

Like Yoshino (1976) and Ono (1979), Hayashi describes the ringi system of bottom-up decision making as fragmented and done on a case-by-case basis. As such, it is better suited to short-term problem solving than to medium- or long-term strategic planning. While 15 of the 19 MNCs Hayashi studied have medium-range strategic plans, only 5 of these 15 have concrete strategic programs to achieve these plans, according to the managerial respondents. Moreover, these few strategic programs are not set by top management, but formulated by lower managerial ranks. By contrast, American medium- and long-range strategic planning is based on top management initiative. By depending on the ringi system, Japanese corporate planning is too piecemeal, and lacks a total framework of top management strategy. This makes for difficulties in fitting individual projects into an organic system (Hayashi, 1979: 52).

Conflicts in program design. Hayashi cites Nakane's argument that Japanese management is stronger in vertical (*tate*) than in horizontal relationships. Modern management has a rational, contractual basis whereas Japanese management is semi-*gemeinschaftliche* and this characteristic may be in conflict with the management objective of maximizing profit. The strategic program to achieve long range objectives may require changes in the existing organizational equilibrium, and these changes may be blocked by tate, gemeinschaftliche human relations among managers.

Conflicts in the execution of plans. Japanese management is more group- than individualistically-oriented. There is more respect for men than for impersonal rules. There is inconsistency between a manager's own opinion (*honne*) and his public rationalizations (*tatemae*). Firms do not monitor the execution of their medium- and long-range plans: a feedback system has not yet been established. One reason for this is that management strategic objectives lack a specific program by which the objectives are to be realized, and without a specific program there is no way meaningfully to monitor progress toward objectives. Finally, the translation of strategic plans into concrete organizational arrangements is facilitated when the firm is job-centric; Japanese firms, however, tend to be man-centric. These characteristics are hypothesized by Hayashi to be in conflict with the execution of strategic plans.

Strategy and Management in Japanese and American MNCs

To return to Kobayashi Takenori's *Japanese Multinational Corporations* (*Nihon no takokuseki kigyō*, 1980), the Japanese MNC executives he interviewed gave the following description of the "Japanese pattern of MNCs" (in contrast to Western MNCs).

1. Japanese management gives higher priority to long-term expansion of market share than to short-term profits.
2. They tend to make fewer demands on their host country.
3. They engage in more joint ventures with Japanese trading companies (*sōgō shosha*).
4. They seldom buy local firms in host countries.
5. They enter joint ventures with host country firms rather than seek 100 percent ownership (Tsurumi, 1976: 202).
6. They are very dependent on company headquarters[2] and on the Japanese government.
7. Their operations are concentrated in developing countries, whereas American MNCs are concentrated in the most advanced countries.
8. They are concentrated in the area of procurement of resources (raw materials).
9. They tend to be in labor- rather than capital-intensive industries.
10. They have a strong "Japanese consciousness."
11. They have distinctive management practices, e.g., lifetime commitment, paternalism, bottom-up decision making, and provide fewer promotion chances to employees from the host country.[3]

Table 2 indicates which of these strategies or managerial patterns are perceived by Japanese managers of MNCs as likely either to continue or change in the future. Arranged according to the ratio of "will continue" to "will not continue" responses, we see that the more enduring patterns are joint ventures with host country firms[4] and with Japanese trading companies; giving higher priority to market share than to profits; procurement of raw materials abroad; paternalism and lifetime commitment. At the other extreme, respondents are more likely to perceive the following patterns as changing in the future. They believe Japanese MNCs will reduce their dependence on company headquarters. Yoshino has shown that in the early phase of Japanese firms' manufacturing abroad, "day-to-day operations of the subsidiaries had to be closely controlled by the export division of the parent company . . . Managers of local subsidiaries had only limited discretion over major decisions . . ." (Yoshino, 1976: 132). In contrast, the managers of local

TABLE 2

PERCEPTIONS OF MANAGERS IN JAPANESE MULTINATIONAL FIRMS:
WHICH JAPANESE PATTERNS WILL CONTINUE IN THE FUTURE

Japanese Managerial Pattern in MNCs	Ratio of $\left\{\dfrac{\text{Will continue}}{\text{Will not continue}}\right.$
1. Joint ventures with host country firms	51/ 4 = 12.8
2. Market share more important than profits	37/ 5 = 7.4
3. Joint ventures with trading companies (*sogo shosha*)	37/11 = 3.4
4. Procurement of raw materials	30/ 9 = 3.3
5. Paternalism	11/ 5 = 2.2
6. Lifetime commitment	10/ 5 = 2.0
7. Bottom-up (*ringi*) decision making	7/ 4 = 1.8
8. Japanese consciousness	40/47 = 1.5
9. Dependence on company headquarters	25/33 = 0.8
10. Concentrated in developing countries	20/33 = 0.6
11. Seldom buy local firms in host countries	6/11 = 0.5
12. In labor- rather than capital- or technology-intensive industries	12/32 = 0.4
13. Dependence on the Japanese government	9/25 = 0.4
14. Promote few host country employees	5/21 = 0.2
15. Little self-assertion toward the host country	4/20 = 0.2

Number of sample firms = 89. Totals for each item are less than 89 because the items were multiple choice and respondents were not forced to answer each item.

Source: Adapted from Kobayashi, 1980: p. 99, Table 1-1-14; p. 100, Table 1-1-15; and p. 104, Table 1-1-18.

subsidiaries of American MNCs at a comparably early stage in overseas operations had much more autonomy. Japanese MNC managers clearly see convergence toward American patterns on this point. Table 2 also indicates that Japanese MNCs will reduce their dependence on the Japanese government, reduce their concentration on developing countries and invest more in the advanced industrial countries, invest in more capital-intensive industries, promote more host country employees, and be more self-assertive toward host countries (*genchi kankeisha ni taishite jiko shuchō ga sukunai*). These perceptions are one basis for predicting the ways in which the management of Japanese MNCs will become more internationalized, and the respects in which they will continue to use Japanese management styles abroad.

Conclusion

Summary of findings. As in our earlier writing (Marsh and Mannari, 1976), we have posed the question of convergence in this paper. As Japanese firms adopt a multinational strategy, do they adapt their "made in Japan" organizational structure and management practices to this strategy such that they come more to resemble Western multinational firms? Drawing upon recent empirical investigations by Japanese scholars, we have seen that in a number of ways this does occur. Both Ono and Kobayashi show that actual changes and perceived future changes in Japanese MNCs are from functional or unitary-form to multidivisional and matrix organization, a transition that has already taken place in diversified American MNCs. Some Japanese management practices—e.g., the ringi system—are viewed as dysfunctional to effective internationalization (Hayashi, 1979; Yoshino, 1976) and as being displaced by a dynamic top management and their general staff (Ono, 1979). Kobayashi finds other instances of convergence in the perception by Japanese MNCs that in the future they will promote more host country employees to responsible positions, and in the fact that Japanese managers in MNCs that are less modern than typical Western MNCs are less satisfied that their organization and management practices are adequate to their multinational strategy.

There is also evidence that some "made in Japan" management practices will persist—e.g., paternalism and lifetime commitment (Kobayashi, 1980). In the main, however, our Japanese authors clearly see convergence as the dominant trend. Thus, our hypothesis that "made in Japan" organizational structure and management decline over time and that a convergence toward Western forms occurs as multinational strategies are played out by Japanese MNC subsidiaries must be regarded as provisionally confirmed.

Future research. At the theoretical level, we have seen that the Chandler-Williamson strategy and structure framework is a useful tool for analyzing Japanese MNCs. The early strategy of Japanese firms was to undertake manufacturing abroad in order to protect their export markets from import substitution policies. The flaw in this strategy was, however, that the Japanese joint ventures abroad tended to be in standard, mature industries which local firms could imitate relatively easily. Such industries had fewer barriers to entry. As local competitor firms entered the market, price competition resulted and the profits of the Japanese MNCs declined. To cope with this problem, Japanese MNCs adopted new strategies, e.g., vertical integration and moving upstream in the production process, where barriers to entry by local firms were greater (Yoshino, 1976). The first type of research needed is on the specific structural changes these latter strategies brought about in Japanese MNCs, as well as on future structural changes that will become necessary as these firms embark on still newer strategies, e.g., developing new technologies that can be translated into commercially feasible products in new industries.

Second, in assessing the extent of convergence between Japanese and Western MNCs, we need to take into account the variables known to cause variations in organizational structure and management practices, such as size and industry. Insofar as MNCs from different home countries will differ as a function of firm size, the fact that more small Japanese firms than American firms have embarked on direct foreign investment means that firm size should be controlled when comparing Japanese and American MNCs. It is less likely that small Japanese MNCs will converge toward American patterns than that large Japanese MNCs will. By the same reasoning, we should expect "divergence" as a result of industry differences: American MNCs are in industries that emphasize capital intensiveness and skilled manpower, whereas Japanese MNCs are found more in industries with standard, mature products, more labor-intensive, and requiring less skilled manpower. More research is needed, then, on the effect of strategy on structure and management in Japanese and Western MNCs controlling for firm size, industry, and other parameters known to influence structure and management.

A third area of research is needed to clarify what at present appear to be conflicting findings. On the one hand, Ono, Kobayashi, and Hayashi suggest that Japanese MNCs are not yet as modern or mature as American MNCs in their formal organizational structures, and that this hinders long-range strategic planning. Against this picture of the shortcomings of Japanese MNCs, we are told by other writers of the success with which Japanese style management has been introduced into Japanese subsidiaries in the United States. Johnson and Ouchi (1974) claim that Sony's plant in San Diego had an absenteeism rate 25 to 50 percent lower than other American-managed electronic firms in the area. The point is that at the micro-level of manager-worker interaction, Japanese style management appears to be quite successful. Specifically, managers communicate the feeling that they *care* about their employees as people. When recession threatens, instead of laying employees off, the Japanese MNC reduce paychecks and bonuses for both the Japanese managers and the host country employees. Ouchi (1981) has now enshrined these success stories in his Theory Z, a kind of Japanese version of human relations theory. Vogel (1979) and Dore (1973: 20) also see Japanese management style as a model to be adopted by Western firms, rather than as a tradition-bound hindrance to effective functioning.

Although Japanese style "Theory Z" management may have proved successful in the United States, there is evidence that it has not worked well in some Southeast Asian countries. Japanese MNCs in Indonesia tried to encourage Indonesian plant managers or chief engineers to mingle with the Indonesian workers and get to know them personally. Such mingling went against the more elitist strain in Indonesian culture (Tsurumi, 1976: 265). Japanese managers feared that their ignorance of Indonesian customs and manners might inadvertently cause negative reactions from workers, and to avoid this, preferred to mechanize operations. Nor could Japanese managerial skills handle the militancy of Thai workers, and again, the strategy of substituting machines for workers was followed.

MacLeod (1979) also found that it is difficult for Japanese to work harmoniously with Thais in the office or factory environment because of their different cultural backgrounds. She observed as signs of this mismatch a lack of friendship between Japanese and Thais, complaints of irresponsibility, misunderstandings over what makes for an acceptable work atmosphere, and divergent notions of loyalty. She suggests a possible explanation for the greater success of Japanese management in the United States than in Thailand: "Japanese-Thai relations lack a viable 'third culture' context in which common verbal and nonverbal cues have evolved and been agreed upon" (MacLeod, 1979, abstract).

As for Hayashi's view that "made in Japan" management hinders long-range planning, here again there is conflicting evidence. Tsurumi (1976: 31–32) argues that Japanese MNCs have been quite effective in the strategy of riding an international product cycle. This strategy is based on the fact that there is a time lag in market demand, in which a new, advanced product like the zigzag sewing machine or color television will hit peak demand first in the United States, later in Japan, and still later in the developing nations. A given MNC can capitalize on this international product cycle by marketing the product first in the United States, where it is fine-tuned and streamlined, then in Japan, and finally in the less developed countries. What we need to know is whether Japanese MNCs that exploited this long-range planning strategy differed in their organizational structure—e.g., used centralized top management and staff, rather than ringi-type decision making—from Japanese MNCs that have been less successful in long-range strategic planning.

It is clear, then, that we need much more research which (1) specifies particular aspects of Japanese MNCs—all the way from the formal or macro-level (e.g., unitary and multidivisional organization) to the informal, micro-level of "human relations" between managers and workers; and which then (2) seeks to discover systematically which of these aspects of structure or management function well or badly in which specific host countries, and why. This kind of research should help us to develop a theory of the internationalization of management in Japanese MNCs. Considering the volatility of the international environment in which Japanese MNCs must operate, these tasks of research and theory construction are bound to provide us with lively challenges for a long time to come.

NOTES

1. Three firms are in the textile industry, 3 in electrical machinery, 3 in general machinery, 2 in chemicals, 1 each in transportation, machinery, and food, and 6 are general trading companies (*sōgō shōsha*). Dividing the 19 MNCs into the 13 manufacturing firms and the 6 trading companies, their average characteristics as of March 1973 were as follows (Hayashi, 1979):

	Manufacturing	Trading
1. Export rates as % of total sales	19%	40%
2. Overseas production rates	5%	2.8%
3. Overseas investments (assets) ($ million)	2,400	126
4. Years experience in overseas investment	17 yrs.	14 yrs.
5. Number of overseas subsidiary manufacturing firms owned	14	

2. Yoshino, 1976: 169–70 agrees.
3. Yoshino suggests that the reason Japanese nationals occupy most key positions in foreign subsidiaries is that if the Japanese managerial system is to work at all, there must be a minimum density of managers socialized in Japanese society and its organizations and management practices. To promote local people is to under-

mine this "critical mass in the number of Japanese managers" (Yoshino, 1976: 168). Even Japanese employees recruited in the host country "become, in effect, more functionaries and interpreters, regardless of seniority or experience" (Yoshino, 1976: 174).

4. Yoshino (1976: 156) predicts joint ventures will decline and majority control to 100 percent ownership of manufacturing and raw materials-acquisitions subsidiaries will increase in the future. Tsurumi (1976: 208–211) explains why this shift occurs.

REFERENCES

Caves, Richard E.
1980 "Industrial Organization, Corporate Strategy and Structure." *Journal of Economic Literature*, 18 (March): 64–92.

Chandler, Alfred D.
1962 *Strategy and Structure*. Cambridge, Mass.: MIT Press.

Davis, Stanley M., and Paul R. Lawrence
1977 *Matrix*. Reading, Mass.: Addison-Wesley.

Dore, Ronald P.
1973 *British Factory: Japanese Factory*. Berkeley: University of California Press.

Drucker, Peter F.
1946 *The Concept of the Corporation*. New York: Day.

Evans, Peter B.
1981 "Recent Research on Multinational Corporations." *Annual Review of Sociology*, 7: 199–223.

Hayashi Kichiro
1979 "Japanese Management and Corporate Planning." 41–59. In *Takokuseki kigyō kenkyūkai* (Workshop for the Study of Japanese Multinational Corporations) (ed.), *Nihonteki takokuseki kigyō ron no tenkai* (The Evolution of Japanese Multinational Corporations). Kyoto: Hōritsu Bunkasha.

Hazama Hiroshi
1971 *Nihonteki keiei* (Japanese Style Management). Tokyo: Nihon Keizai Shimbunsha.

Johnson, Richard T., and William G. Ouchi
1974 "Made in America (Under Japanese Management)." *Harvard Business Review*, 52 (September–October): 61–70.

Kobayashi Takenori
1980 *Nihon no takokuseki kigyō* (Japan's Multinational Corporations). Tokyo: Chūō Keizaisha.

Kumar, Krishna (ed.)
1980 *Transnational Enterprises: Their Impact on Third World Societies and Cultures*. Boulder, Colorado: Westview Press.

MacLeod, Margo W.
1979 "Ethnicity and Class in Multinational Corporations: The Japanese-Thai Case." Paper presented at American Sociological Society meetings.

Marsh, Robert M., and Mannari Hiroshi
  1976   *Modernization and the Japanese Factory*. Princeton, N.J.: Princeton University Press.
Nakane Chie
  1967   *Tate shakai no ningen kankei* (Human Relations in a Vertical Society). Tokyo: Kōdansha.
Ono Toyoaki
  1979   *Nihon no kigyō no soshiki senryaku* (Organizational Strategies in Japanese Corporations). Tokyo: Management-sha.
Ouchi, William G.
  1981   *Theory Z*. Reading, Mass.: Addison-Wesley.
Tsurumi, Yoshi
  1976   *The Japanese are Coming: A Multinational Interaction of Firms and Politics*. Cambridge, Mass.: Ballinger.
Vogel, Ezra F.
  1979   *Japan as Number One: Lessons for America*. Cambridge, Mass.: Harvard University Press.
Weber, Max
  1946   *From Max Weber: Essays in Sociology*. New York: Oxford University Press.
Williamson, Oliver E.
  1970   *Corporate Control and Business Behavior, an Inquiry into the Effects of Organization Form on Enterprise Behavior*. Englewood Cliffs, N.J.: Prentice-Hall.
Yoshino, Michael Y.
  1976   *Japan's Multinational Enterprises*. Cambridge, Mass.: Harvard University Press.

THE TASTE OF SUCCESS:
THE DEMOCRATIZATION AND INTERNATIONALIZATION OF THE KIKKOMAN CORPORATION

W. Mark Fruin

This essay examines the way the macropolicies of the Allied Occupation of Japan (1945–52) affected the strategy and structure of the Noda Shōyu Company (later, the Kikkoman Shōyu Company and, still later, the Kikkoman Corporation). Among the major policies of the Occupation—land reform, demilitarization, economic deconcentration, and democratization—one factor, democratization, had a major effect and another, economic deconcentration, a minor effect on the company. The apparent impact of these—principally, democratization—proved to be so great that Kikkoman was noticeably transformed as a result.

The Course of Democratization

The transformation of business under the Occupation did not occur suddenly, since what constituted democratic behavior was not always apparent to the Japanese or, even more surprisingly, to the victorious Allies. Especially after the so-called reverse-course was inaugurated in 1947–48, Occupation authorities overturned so much of their previous handiwork that a set of consistent and coherent policies was hard to discern. As a result of this vacillation as well as a wholly understandable reticence on the part of the Japanese, the impact of democratization was not immediately or openly apparent.

It was in the process of institutionalizing democracy, rather than in the rhetoric or ideology of democracy itself, that democratization would have such a considerable effect on the Kikkoman Corporation. Yet as the full effects of any process require time to take hold, it would be some years—indeed, not until after the Occupation period officially ended in 1952—before the full force of democratization of Kikkoman would be felt. Further, the process of institutionalizing democracy, it must be kept in mind, was not an isolated action but was telescoped within a visibly greater force for change in postwar Japan, namely, the internationalization of business planning and activities. Thus, the changes introduced by the Occupation, rather than representing a rupture with past practices, advanced a number of interrelated developments which appeared long before the Occupation and which continue to affect the course of Kikkoman's development even today.

Democratization affected the company structure in three areas. First, it altered the legal definition of the family in Japan and, as a result, refined the concept and utility of the family form as it was employed for business purposes among the soy sauce brewers of Noda. Democratization changed the family from an institution designed to control business activities in a variety of ways to an institution that was separate and distinct from, and increasingly subordinate to, the firm in the control and manipulation of assets. Secondly, the Occupation inspired a Western style labor union movement which finally gained momentum in Noda City (home of Kikkoman) during the 1950s, resulting first in labor strikes and the rise of an autonomous and active labor union movement that was beyond the company's control, and then in the labor union's support of the election of a series of Socialist party representatives to the county, prefectural, and national assemblies as well as to the mayoral office in Noda. All of this had the effect of severing the close ties that had been maintained between Kikkoman and the town of Noda for half a century. The third effect of democratization came in the form of antimonopoly hearings that were called to investigate the reasons for Kikkoman's overwhelmingly large share of the soy sauce market, its price-fixing and market-sharing agreements with other manufacturers, and certain of its selling arrangements with wholesalers and retailers. These hearings prompted the company to reorganize its sales and marketing practices, internationalize its operations, and diversify its product line. Thus, in all these areas—ownership and management of the firm, relations between company and union as well as between company and community, and the product and market strategy of the firm—the primary force for change in the postwar period appears to have been the Occupation policy of democratization. How democratization affected family, community relations (both inside and outside the factories), and business strategy in Noda after World

War II, will be discussed in the succeeding sections of this essay.

Democratization of the Family

The Japanese stem family, or *ie*, is a patrilineal household organized for perpetuity around common property, genealogy, and ceremony, such as the veneration of ancestors and other household-focused ritual. Stem families were encouraged legally in Japan by repeated government pronouncements, beginning in 1675, as a preventative measure against land fragmentation (Tamaki, 1956: 14–15); the result was that lineages based on the access, use, and preservation of common resources became frequent after the seventeenth century. Common ownership of resources meant realistically that the main or head household controlled most of the land, tools, and technology required for farming or for other property-based endeavors and that branch households, when they were permitted to form, were allowed some degree of access to and use of the lineage's "common" resources.

The Allies, which meant primarily the Americans, sought to undo the absolute legal authority of the household head and the age-related as well as sex-related biases that went along with the prewar family system. In the Occupation view of Japanese culture, the ie (stem family) allowed household heads an unwarranted amount of civil and moral authority over their children, other household members, and relatives. Moreover, just as this authority tended to be absolute within a lineage group organized around a system of common property, so too the same authority was extended to the emperor of Japan in his assertions of headship over all Japanese. The emperor's claims were based upon the nationalization of land that occurred in the name of the emperor after the Meiji Restoration of 1868. The entire country, as a result, was united under the emperor, who was both landowner and householder over everything and everyone. Propaganda in schools and in the military constantly inculcated a belief in the common identity of all Japanese in turn, based in part on theories of racial superiority and in part on assertions of common household origin emanating from the imperial headship. Hence the foundations of the imperial state in prewar Japan hinged on ideological as well as organizational claims of family-oneness that united all Japanese.

The use, by analogy, of such family-based symbols of authority within the industrial enterprises of prewar Japan was common. At

82

Kikkoman, after the Great Noda Strike of 1927–28, the company practiced a family-like management ideology and style. Indeed, the domination of the top positions in the firm by members of the Mogi-Takanashi families helps account for this emphasis. But even more important than this organizational rationale for family authority were the efforts of the Mogi-Takanashi themselves to articulate consciously an ideological function for the company within the overarching imperial mission. In the end, such a family-owned and -operated enterprise as Kikkoman could expect and receive outstanding performance from its workers and managers in large measure because of the close conjunction of company structure and ideology based on the family model.

The Occupation changed all that by making equality and not hierarchy the basis of society. The individual and not the household became the focus of legal responsibility. Male-centered inheritance and family headship were eliminated, and this removed much of the institutional inequality in the status and rights of women. Finally, by abrogating the household-centered ideology of the previous three-quarters of a century, an end could be brought to the provision of successors to households (conceived as enduring corporate structures) through such practices as *inkyo* and *yōshi*,[1] rather than via the transfer of property to individuals (most often one's natural descendants). In these ways, the absolute power of the household head was eliminated and in its place parental obligation and a much reduced civil authority of parent over child were substituted. In short, Occupation authorities essentially legislated a transition from what might be called the institutional-imperial family of prewar Japan to the companionate family of the postwar period (Kawashima, 1957: 13–15). Hereafter, only a few spheres of family life would be regulated by law.

In the case of Kikkoman as it operated before the war, the family system provided not only heirs and successors for the management of corporate resources (90 percent of which were closely held either by the Mogi-Takanashi families directly or by these same families indirectly through a holding company), but it also allowed for the patriarchal and paternalistic supervision of the company's employees by top management. The democratization of the family, however, changed this in three principal ways. First, holding companies were outlawed. In the case of the Senshusha holding company, which controlled a majority of the assets of Kikkoman before the war, Imperial Edict 567 of 1946 froze and eventually forced the liquidation of its two-thirds share in the company while new family inheritance and successor laws interdicted the undivided accumulation of the remaining one-third share by the designated heirs of the Mogi-Takanashi families. Imperial Edict 567 required those enterprises designated as "restricted concerns"—all companies with a capitalization of ¥5 million and above—to divest themselves of shares in other companies (Hadley, 1970: 73–74).

Also, the aspirations and actions of members of the Mogi-Takanashi families changed as a result of the Occupation policy of democratization. The lineage and household heads no longer enjoyed the unquestioning obedience they had previously commanded. They could no longer determine the career choices, marriage partners, and patterns of succession to be followed by their offspring. They could no longer pass on an undivided estate to just one heir in the interest of preserving and concentrating capital nor could they exclude women from issues of inheritance and succession. They could, in short, do little of what they had done previously to husband the family's resources and manage them as if the family were a firm—a corporate entity in which property counted for more than people.

The declining ability of a household head to wield family resources was matched in importance by the changing values of family members, especially by their rising sense of egalitarianism. In particular, younger family members, those educated after the war and not socialized into the traditional family system, were reluctant to accept the dominance and submission that it demanded. Not surprisingly, the frequency of interlineage marriage and adoptions, by which the Mogi-Takanashi families had been able to control succession and maintain the continuity of management personnel and power within the lineage system, dropped remarkably in the postwar period. Only 2 cases of interfamily marriage or adoption have been recorded in the postwar period, in contrast with 46 such events which transpired between 1738 and 1938 (1 every four and one-third years). The sharp break with past practice is indisputable. In the new era of the democratic family, the kinship system has been directed away from the promotion of social and economic solidarily, the protection of property, and the continuity of family enterprise—the primary concerns of the stem family during most of the prewar years.

Yet the demise of the stem family and the rise of the egalitarian family have not signalled, at least in the one short generation since 1945, a loss of managerial talent flowing from the Mogi-Takanashi families to Kikkoman. Because the Mogi-Takanashi families still retain one-quarter share ownership in the firm (shares which were held separately from the Senshusha) and because a fast-track career within Kikkoman is more attractive than an otherwise slow promotion into Japan's geriatric leadership, the scions of the Mogi-Takanashi families in Noda still enter Kikkoman in reliable fashion. By virtue of birth alone, their chances for success within the firm are good. Not content with such odds, however, most of these sons (daughters are still excluded from significant managerial careers outside of the family) add a graduate education in business or economics at the best Japanese and American universities to their already impressive undergraduate educations in Japan. Due to the large number of Mogi-Takanashi families connected with the firm—nine families joined together in 1918 to establish the company, although three of the nine in particular wield exceptional political and economic influence within the coalition—achievement must be added to the lineal status of sons in order to ensure them an opportunity for a top position within the firm. In this way, the combination of ascription and achievement has resulted in rapid promotion for the continuity of family management at Kikkoman in spite of the greatly reduced degree of family ownership since the war.

Finally, another way in which democratization of the family in postwar Japan has affected management policies lies in the ideological revolution it induced regarding the motivation and supervision of employees of large enterprises. Obedience to hierarchy and a quiet dedication to productivity were hallmarks of employee performance at Kikkoman from 1930 to 1945. But these were predicated on patriotic zeal in view of the ideological connection between work in the breweries of Kikkoman and Japan's imperial mission in East Asia. Loyalty to the company was equated with loyalty to country.

Since the war, however, the entire ideological scaffolding on which the country's remarkable prewar performance was based has been dismantled. Demythologizing the emperor has removed the final and essential element in a national hierarchy of loyal Japanese. The household head, be he the emperor, the corporate chief executive officer, or the patriarch of a lineage association, no longer claims or exerts legal and moral authority over those beneath him. Although patriarchal attitudes (and policies) may not have disappeared altogether, the absolutistic basis for such behavior has been removed and an egalitarian ethic has been relentlessly replacing it. The best example of this process comes from the second major area in which democratization has affected Kikkoman, namely, in the appearance of an increasingly powerful, militant, and autonomous labor union movement.

Community Relations—Within and Without the Factory

The first labor unions formed at Kikkoman after the war were instituted in January 1946 at the Kansai plant in western Japan and in the following month at the Noda plants in the hinterland of Tokyo. Neither union, in the beginning, was aligned with the other nor identified with any larger union movement. In October 1949, a liaison committee between the two unions was finally formed, and ultimately in 1957 a single unified union was forged representing soy sauce workers in all the Kikkoman plants.

The top-down democratization of Japan encouraged the labor union movement, among other programs, to open up economic opportunity and to liberalize the economic structure. In 1946, with the encouragement of the Supreme Commander of the Allied Powers (SCAP), the Japanese government passed three laws that provided a powerful legal basis for the formation and function of unions: the Labor Union Law, the Labor Standards Law, and the Labor Mediation Law. Under such patronage, the early union movement flourished, as did the Socialist and Communist parties.

The two most powerful unions were the General Federation of Labor, or Sōdōmei, a revival of the prewar Yūaikai-Sōdōmei under Matsuoka Komakichi, which had ties to the right-leaning Social Democratic Party, and the National Congress of Industrial Labor Unions, or Sanbetsu (Zen-Nippon Sangyōbetsu Rōdō Kumiai Kaigi), which had an association with the Communist party. The Kikkoman unions were unaffiliated with either the Sōdōmei or Sanbetsu at first, although by August 1947 they had joined the Sōdōmei. The Sōdōmei's strength was in prefectural union associations and in light industry, while Sanbetsu was strongest with government workers, miners, and laborers in heavy industry.

When the Noda Shōyu Labor Union was formed on February 9,

1946, it claimed 1,813 members or 80 percent of the blue-collar work force. Within two weeks of its establishment, the union negotiated and won major concessions on ten demands concentrated in three areas: wages, participation in management, and union prerogatives in matters of hiring, firing, and work conditions. By these negotiations, wages were immediately increased by 45 percent, with an additional 8.33 percent salary increment for food, and two labor-management committees were formed—one for sharing information relating to economic and business conditions and one for mutually resolving matters of work conditions. The latter included an agreement that required the union's consent for layoffs and dismissals (Editorial Committee of Kikkoman Labor Union, 1977: 31–32).

In spite of these impressive gains, however, the union's leadership in the formative period of the union movement can hardly be described as typical. Umeda Isao, the first leader of the local, held a Ph.D. in Agricultural Sciences and was director of the corporation's research and development laboratory. Okada Shirō, his almost immediate successor, lacked a university education but had been plant manager of several of the soy sauce breweries in Noda. Under Okada, the Noda local avoided Sanbetsu efforts to organize the Noda labor association as an industry-based union within the national foods industry. Yet even as Noda turned away from the overtures to national politics offered by Sanbetsu, the Noda local garnered its first political victory by having one of the candidates it backed win a seat on the prefectural assembly, 7 more on the Noda City Council, and 16 out of 20 in the Regional Township Association. In spite of these successes, it was not until June 1949 and the election of Yokozeni Jukichi to the headship of the Noda union that the atypical character of the union's leadership was remedied. Barely a graduate of elementary school, Yokozeni possessed a political savvy and skill that any politico would envy.

Yokozeni worked quickly not only to consolidate his control over the union but also to solidify the place of the Kikkoman union within the larger political arena. In February 1949, he had joined the Socialist party and by March had been elected as one of that party's representatives to the Prefectural Assembly. In August 1949, the Association of Labor Unions in Chiba Prefecture was formed and Yokozeni was elected its deputy head. In the same month, membership criteria in the Noda Shōyu Labor Union were clarified; section heads and assistant section heads in offices and factory foremen and assistant factory foremen in the breweries were excluded from membership. This decidedly swung the balance of power within the union to non-supervisory personnel for the first time. In October, the union associations representing Kikkoman employees in eastern and western Japan merged with Yokozeni as the head of the amalgamated association. Finally, in November 1949, Yokozeni was appointed as the head representative of the Sōdōmei in Chiba Prefecture. In less than a year, Yokozeni had been elected to the Prefectural Assembly, had taken over the Noda Shōyu Workers Union, had become the second-in-charge of the Consolidated Labor Union Association of Chiba Prefecture, had organized the All Kikkoman Workers Union and then become its head, and had been appointed the chief representative in the prefecture of the largest federation of combined unions in the country. And, in the course of the next year (1950–51), Yokozeni successfully led a campaign for the equal treatment of union and nonunion regular employees in matters of wages and fringe benefits. This campaign, called "Shakō Ipponka" (Normalization of White- and Blue-Collar Employment), exerted pressure on the company to pay all employees according to a combination of seniority and experience and to equalize health, retirement, and fringe benefits for everyone. The campaign at Kikkoman coincided generally in timing and in content with similar union efforts nationwide that resulted in significant gains for unions throughout the country.

Even for a man of Yokozeni's ambition and talents it would take some time to digest these gains, and it was not until 1953 that he again actively pursued new offices. In that year, the union advanced him as a candidate for the National Assembly (a bid that eventually failed, due for the most part to the lackluster support he received from the Socialist party in Chiba Prefecture). In March of 1954, Yokozeni moved from the mainstream to the left-wing faction of the Socialist party. He then pulled the Kikkoman union out of its association with the Sōdōmei and joined it instead with the independent National Food and Beverage Workers Union which had been established one year earlier by the United Beer Workers Union. Upon executing these maneuvers— securing an independent political base within the newly founded Food and Beverage Workers Union and taking its power with him to the left wing of the Socialist party—Yokozeni ran successfully as a Socialist party candidate from Chiba for the National Assembly in 1954.

In the February general elections of 1955, however, the Kikkoman union, along with the unions of Nihon Kentetsu, Kawasaki Seitetsu, and Nihon Parupu (all in the First District of Chiba Prefecture), were implicated in a voting fraud scandal. As a result, Yokozeni, the union head, along with the assistant head and union secretary, resigned, and a new group of union officers were appointed.

Effect of Unionization Upon the Company

The emergence of an independent and active labor union within the company had two immediate and fundamental results: the formalization of rules to run the organization and a higher total wage cost to the company than would otherwise have been the case. Both of these were well foreshadowed in the *Labor Agreement* of 1950 between the union and company (The Noda Shōyu Co., Ltd., 1950: 1–50). Article 4 of this document, for example, stated that "the company in exercising these actions and responsibilities (the rights of management) will attempt to reflect as much as possible the will of the members of the union." Thus, the company was required to seek the formal approval of most employees, represented by the union, in order to exercise the rights of management.

Admittedly, some sort of tacit and informal bond already existed between the company and its regular employees and thereby limited the degree of freedom that management enjoyed in exercising its decisions. This was revealed most strikingly in the workings of the Labor Council. According to Article 16 of the Labor Agreement, a Labor Council composed of 30 persons (half from the company and half from the union) was established. Its purpose was to discuss alterations of working conditions in the company and negotiations of disputes over those alterations. Moreover, according to Article 18, fundamental matters relating to the welfare of the union members likewise fell into the domain of the Labor Council as did "any matters deemed appropriate for discussion by the Labor Council." Article 37 enjoined the company to discuss in advance any disciplinary action of an employee with the Labor Council, and, of course, any employee who objected to his/her treatment by the company would raise an objection through the offices of the union which would find its way back to the Labor Council.

In short, all areas and matters of employment within the company after 1950 became subject to specification as well as to negotiation, a far cry from the company-dominated consensus of management and labor before the war. The legalization of the labor union, the drafting of a labor agreement, the formation of a labor council within the company, and the formalization of all aspects of employment were all new initiatives as compared to the prewar period.

The other major impact of the labor union on the company was obviously to increase the total cost of labor for the company. The company was required to establish and staff committees, divert personnel, build nonproductive facilities, and generally to invest resources where it would have been otherwise unlikely to do so. More specifically, the Labor Agreement permitted company employees who were concurrently union officers to devote themselves full time to union business while on the company payroll (Article 12). Likewise, various buildings, equipment, and other tangible resources owned by the company could be used by the union without charge (Article 13). The union could object to the employment of anyone hired by the company (Article 24) and had to be consulted when anyone was to be discharged (Article 26). The company was required to re-employ most persons who had been on leave, even lengthy leaves, and could not terminate the employment of someone who accepted an appointment in the public sector (Articles 33 and 34). The company was compelled to continue the employment of persons reaching retirement age for up to an additional three years if the employee so desired (Article 42). Also, female employees over 18 years of age were forbidden to work overtime or on holidays (Article 65). In short, in these articles and in many other quarters the company was constrained in its employment practices in the postwar period in ways that were unknown in the prewar period, which added to the total cost of labor for the company.

In retrospect, the Yokozeni period of leadership of the Noda Soy Sauce Workers from 1949 to 1955 was an era of remarkable accomplishment. What had been essentially a loose association of supervisory and non-supervisory workers under the uninspired leadership of Umeda and Okada was transformed into a labor union movement of political claw and economic sinew. If the Occupation policy of democratization had meaning for workers, it was realized through labor unions which gained important wage, work, and fringe benefit concessions from companies, catapulted people into office who were more than sympathetic to the interests of labor, and provided leverage to compete with big business and big government, both of which had been long entrenched in power since before the war.

The most compelling examples of the growing power of the union, however, occurred long after the Occupation period ended. In 1959–60, the union found itself strong enough in Noda and secure enough within the newly established Chūritsurōren (Federation of Neutral Labor Unions) to resort first to work slowdowns and next to strikes to force the company to grant the concessions it wanted. During the 1960s, concessions came in three main areas: the level of compensation, retirement benefits, and the age of retirement. Although the company and union bickered over these matters, the differences were more matters of degree rather than of kind. Company and union had reached a sort of compromise where each recognized the existence and strength of the other. This tacit compromise, however, probably owed as much to a prolonged period of high annual rates of growth in per capital income and per capita national product as it did to any eagerness of company and union to get along with one another.

Company and Community After 1962
Indeed, if company and union seemed to be on the road to peaceful co-existence, company and community did not. In 1962, the Spring Labor Offensive (a fairly routine annual spring "struggle" wherein one or another of the larger labor federations demonstrates for pay increases and larger summer and year-end bonuses) coincided with the local Noda township elections. Through the efforts of the Kikkoman union, Shinmura Katsuo was elected mayor. Shinmura's victory in 1962 was the first of a half dozen or so mayoral seats to go to the Socialist party in Chiba Prefecture during the last decade. He was also the first mayor of Noda in the twentieth century who had not been a Kikkoman employee at some point in time.

The domination of city government since the early 1960s by members of the Socialist party drove a wedge into what had been a nearly inseparable association of company and community for almost half a century. Some might argue that the relationship had been one of company dominance and community dependence but no one would deny the closeness of the association.

Perhaps the best example of the schism between company and community that developed while Shinmura was mayor was the decision to build a new 1,500-seat civic auditorium and cultural center on the outskirts of Noda. The erection of this cultural palace was more symbolic than anything else, however, since an entirely adequate and well-loved cultural center, the Kofukan, already stood in the center of town —a gift from Kikkoman to the town in 1929 and still subsidized by Kikkoman through a combination of endowment funds and outright grants for over 90 percent of its operating budget. The Kofukan housed civic meetings, provided space for the town library, was used by 23 different civic and cultural groups on a regular basis, and engaged extensively in the education of the young through an in-house private foundation which provided scholarship programs, tutorials, and block grants to schools (Ishige, 1979). The Socialist government in Noda, however, thought it was bad for the town's image to be so reliant on Kikkoman or on institutions closely identified with Kikkoman. Shinmura was embarrassed that so many activities that would normally occur in town halls and institutions which were free of private attachments were, in Noda's case, taking place in buildings and programs supported by a private—and what is worse, capitalist—company. Hence the new civic and cultural center for the town, built at great expense and maintained at considerably annual deficit to the municipal budget. Fortunately (or unfortunately) for the image of Noda, use of the old but more convenient downtown cultural center has not fallen off while the new suburban center seems to be gradually establishing its own position and role in community affairs. Now, instead of being identified exclusively with soy sauce, Noda is beginning to be thought of as a town of polish and education.

Antitrust and Business Strategy

Just as the question of democratization raised concerns over the excessive concentration of corporate power in Kikkoman's relations with Noda, so too the same sorts of concerns were at issue when Kikkoman's predominant market power became a focus of antitrust inquiry in 1951 and again on several occasions in the 1960s. In 1951, price fixing among competitors was at issue, and during the 1960s Kikkoman's position as a price leader for the industry and the company's efforts to move more directly into the marketing of its products were construed as evidence of excessive market power.

In all of these actions against Kikkoman, the Japanese Fair Trade Commission (FTC) was guided by the Occupation policy of democratization. The Americans wished to create an open and competitive market with reasonable opportunity for entry into all of the product markets of a modern industrial economy. Their primary tool for doing this was to break up the concentration of ownership of the means of production which had, in their view, characterized the prewar, *zaibatsu*-centered economy of Japan. But deconcentration of ownership was in itself not a guarantee of free and open markets. Deconcentration as well as democratization of markets were both essential for the Occupation policies to succeed. Both of these legal programs found their justification in laws passed by the Japanese Diet in 1947 with the encouragement of the American Occupation government. The democratization law, if vigorously enforced, could have dismembered the large combines of Japanese enterprises. Not surprisingly, the deconcentration law was repealed in 1955, a scant three years after the American Occupation had ended in Japan.

In January 1951, the price of soy sauce, subject to government regulation by the Price Control Board, was allowed to rise to ¥56 per *shō* (1.8 liters) on the retail market. Noda Shōyu Company (Kikkoman) and three other major makers (Yamasa, Higeta, Marukin) met together in order to discuss the adequacy of this price, and finding it wanting, petitioned the Price Control Board to raise the price to ¥80 per shō. The Board was unwilling to go so far, but it did allow a price of up to ¥75 per shō to be charged for the best-quality soy sauce and an average price of ¥70 per shō for soy sauces of lesser quality. These four makers in turn informed their wholesalers and retailers of this determination and advised them to raise their prices accordingly. The Soy Sauce Manufacturers Association, following the lead of the big-four makers, established a policy outlining maximum but not minimum price levels for different quality soy sauces. They suggested a maximum price of ¥75 per shō for the best-quality soy sauce.[2]

In June 1950, the three other makers came to Noda for a meeting with Kikkoman where it was agreed that their average cost of manufacture should be ¥61 per shō and their average price to wholesalers and retailers should be ¥64 and ¥75 per shō, respectively. They maintained this agreement until October of the same year when they were told to desist by the Japanese Fair Trade Commission.

The big-four makers, including Kikkoman, did not deny that they had fixed prices among themselves but they did deny that this was done to the detriment of the consumer. Instead, they argued that their agreement was to set maximum prices for their products. Antimonopoly regulations had been developed, they argued, to protect consumers from manufacturers who overcharged for products; such manufacturers fixed minimum and not maximum prices. Thus, the soy sauce brewers, while not repudiating their collusive agreements, denied that a deleterious effect arose from them. The intent of their agreements was not to overcharge customers: indeed, it was to prevent precisely that.

The Japanese FTC parried the manufacturers' argument by asserting that the monopolistic power needed to fix maximum prices was the same power necessary to set minimum prices. Excessively concentrated economic power was undesirable in whatever form it took, and interference with the market mechanism, no matter what its nature, was unjustified. Furthermore, it was felt that the involvement of the Price Control Board in the setting of appropriate price levels with the advice of the soy sauce manufacturers did not justify their collusion on the matter of prices. The administrative guidance provided by the Price Control Board was in itself not law, not a substitute for antitrust regulation, and not a justification for makers to reach price-fixed agreements among themselves.

Although unstated during the 1950 FTC hearings, the soy sauce manufacturers harbored another, and to them more compelling, rationale for their collective behavior. The many varieties of soy sauce were a result of the widespread availability of raw materials, the ease of manufacture, and the array of local, regional, and even occupational taste preferences for soy sauce. In addition, chemically made soy sauces had proliferated after the war due to the difficulties of obtaining large quantities of good raw materials (soybeans, wheat, and salt) and to the advantages of more rapid and less expensive production of soy sauce using such chemical techniques. For these two reasons, the big-four makers of naturally brewed soy sauces felt justified in reaching their price-fixing arrangements: only by such arrangements could they and the consumer both be protected from poor imitations of their product. By guaranteeing a good-quality soy sauce of uniform taste at reasonable prices to the consumer, the makers believed that they could repel the recent advances of chemically manufactured soy sauces and of local, unstandardized brews in the marketplace. Furthermore, since so much of the cost of naturally brewed soy sauce depended on the volatility of commodity markets for cereals, especially during a period of rapid inflation for food prices in Japan, the big-four makers felt that their efforts to stabilize markets and prices were defensible.

Of course, such arguments as these were not relevant to the FTC's mandate. Manufacturing and marketing agreements among makers to share information, to fix prices, to agree on markets, and to do almost anything in concert were illegal according to Article 3 of the Anti-monopoly Act, whether or not they were conceived or executed with any fraudulent purposes in mind.

That was 1951. During the 1960s, the thrust of the FTC's investigation of Kikkoman changed. In these hearings, the company's efforts to integrate forward into marketing and distribution by encouraging associations of distributors who handled their products exclusively were held to be illegal. The hearings involved the Kikkoman-Kai, an association of distributors (*tokuyakuten*) in the Osaka area who handled Kikkoman products exclusively. They accounted for 31 percent of the sales of Kikkoman products in the Osaka metropolitan area in 1966. In September 1967, Kikkoman announced to this group that it was raising the price of its product from the factory, and in a separately called meeting asked them to raise the prices of the Kikkoman products they sold. In January 1968, Kikkoman further advised the distributors to increase the prices charged to their subsidiary jobbers for handling Kikkoman products (Kanezawa [ed.], 1977: 110).

The FTC found in this case that Kikkoman had interfered in the pricing and marketing policies of an association of distributors who were not part of the corporation itself. This was in opposition, therefore, to Article 8, Clause 1, of the antitrust laws of Japan, which clearly prohibit any manufacturer from involvement in the pricing and marketing activities of an unrelated association in the distribution sector. If Kikkoman had owned the distribution network in question in Osaka—that is, if the company owned and operated the plant and equipment associated with the exclusive distribution of its products in Osaka—this would not have constituted a violation of antitrust regulation. Since the Kikkoman-Kai was not part of the Kikkoman Corporation, however, the company's activities to set prices and policies for the resale of its products on the wholesale and retail markets were illegal. If the Kikkoman-Kai had decided itself to raise prices, that was another matter; such a decision was within its appropriate economic functions and entirely legal.

These examples of the Occupation policy of democratization as applied to antitrust regulation of monopolistic business practices seem simple enough. Kikkoman did not deny either its price-fixing activities with other manufacturers in 1951 or its pricing and marketing agreements with distributors in the 1960s. In both cases, the activities in question were not conceived or carried out covertly. Quite the contrary: Kikkoman publicly revealed its intention of gaining some measure of control over the pricing and marketing of its products.

Curiously enough, the failure of Kikkoman to guarantee retail price maintenance for its soy sauce has had more of a detrimental effect on its rivals than on itself. This was because of Kikkoman's ability as the price and market-share leader in the industry to finance simultaneously a vigorous sales and marketing campaign for its soy sauce and to inaugurate a series of new ventures in a move to diversify its product line. Other Japanese soy sauce makers were not able to attempt that then, nor are they able to do so now.

Democratization Accelerates Internationalization

Americans like to believe that the Occupation of Japan was successful. How else can one explain the prosperity and prominence of Japan in the world today—just a short generation following what must be considered one of the most totally devastating physical and psychological defeats in modern history. Thus, democratization has come to be recognized as the policy goal that guided and supported this radical transformation of the political, economic, and moral values and institutions of Japan.

Yet for all the apparent success of the Occupation of Japan and of the democratization of Kikkoman, a major question remains as to what difference these exogenous factors had on the company in the long run. Depending on which yardstick is applied, the Occupation policy of democratization can be said to have had varying degrees of effect on the company. The question to be asked, it would seem, is what would have happened to Kikkoman without the Occupation policy of democratization. The answer, I think, is that very much the same sort of transformation of the company would have occurred—

perhaps not as quickly or as completely, but nevertheless with the same overall direction and content. This belief is based not so much on conjecture as on empirical inference drawn from evidence of change already under way or likely to occur at Kikkoman. These changes appear to be part of a process of the internationalization of business practices worldwide.

In the area of family and firm, for example, there had been an obvious and growing separation of ownership and management at Kikkoman since 1925. Even before that time the trend could be discerned, but with the establishment of the Senshusha holding company in 1925, it became more clearly visible. In fact, several things were happening at once. The growing size of the company—from roughly, 1,000 employees in 1918, to 2,000 in 1925, to 3,000 in 1940, and 4,000 in 1966—resulted in a reduction in the need for managerial resources and influence drawn from the Mogi-Takanashi families. At the same time, the increasing sophistication in managerial skill and experience represented in the growing ranks of middle- and upper-level company employees signified a diminution of the need for Mogi-Takanashi family members' expertise. The appearance of new institutions other than family and lineage, such as cartel, corporation, and holding company, to carry out specialized economic functions signaled a decline in Kikkoman's dependence on the Mogi-Takanashi households. The involvement of such outside institutions as banks, investment firms, and other related companies in the management of the firm likewise resulted in a contraction of what the family was required to do. This diminution of family function was paralleled, of course, by a reduction of family size, not only among the Mogi-Takanashi households but across the country as well. This has happened as the co-resident nuclear household of a husband and wife living together on their own has become salient in all economically advanced countries during the process of their industrialization and urbanization. In short, since the early twentieth century the control and especially the management of Kikkoman has been gradually but progressively transferred from familial to nonfamilial forms of organization. In this sense, therefore, the Occupation merely speeded up a process already well under way.

Much the same sort of argument might be aimed at the issue of unions. Every advanced industrialized nation today has an industrial relations system in which unions play a large part and in which industrial relations law is based on positive rights guaranteed either to individuals or to collective bodies. While it is possible that such rights might not have been accorded individuals in Japan without the Occupation interlude, it is highly unlikely that collective bodies would have failed eventually to receive recognition of such rights. Indeed, something much like that already had occurred in prewar Japan when large companies established a system of permanent tenure for regular employees.

Regular employees of major Japanese corporations were so called because they came to enjoy a full range of employment benefits. These included the expectation of permanent employment with a firm (barring bankruptcy or some such catastrophe) and of a compensation scheme that was weighted heavily toward monetary reward calculated according to years on the job. Although these expectations never attained the status of legal rights in the prewar period, they did acquire a degree of entitlement among regular employees so that they were the equivalent of law—at least, customary law in the large corporations. In effect, these entitlements represented a kind of contract—a "compact" or "covenant," if you will—which an employer could break only with the gravest consequences (see Upham, 1981).

The Allied Occupation of Japan did little more than formalize these traditions for the regular employees of large firms. Regular workers in large corporations account for roughly 30 percent of the privately employed work force in Japan and, not surprisingly, about 30 percent of workers in Japan are unionized. Moreover, 80 percent of these belong to so-called enterprise unions wherein employees are not organized on an industry or craft basis but instead on a company basis. Such unions are private in that they are not closely affiliated with any labor group outside of the company; since they enlist both shop and office workers, they are fairly inclusive within the enterprise, but they are definitely exclusive as well, refusing membership to all but an elite corps of workers—that is, the regular workers of large firms. In short, democratization speeded along the unionization of an already privileged minority of industrial employees.

Furthermore, whether in the postwar or prewar periods, benefits such as lifetime employment, seniority-based compensation, and extensive on-the-job-training were possible only within periods of rapid economic growth for large corporations. Employment entitlements and economic advancement were irrevocably related to one another, and this correlation had little direct relationship with Occupation policy. Democratization has simply allowed the better-off workers in large firms to legalize their superior position in Japan's so-called dual economy or dual economic structure of large and small firms.

Indeed, the extension of such entitlements to regular workers and then the subsequent imperilment of them in Noda can explain a good deal of the difficulties experienced between company and community in the postwar era. At the end of the 1950s, the process of production at Kikkoman underwent a basic change from essentially a large-batch, mechanically interrelated process to an automated, continuous process technology. In this newer, more fluid process of manufacture, the basis for the special relationship of company and community was discarded: that is, the mutual interdependence of the company's jobs and the community's skilled labor was broken. In the current dry fermentation process, several tons of roasted wheat kernels and soybean grits are germinated automatically in three days' time in special, sealed culture rooms without the aid of human workers. Since 1966, one plant, Factory 7, has maintained 30 such dry fermentation process rooms. After germination, the kōji is moved automatically by conveyor and elevator to the brewing tanks for fermentation. In Factory 7, again, there are 2,100 fermentation tanks, each producing 10,000 large bottles (1.8 liters) of soy sauce every eight months or so. Using the latest hydraulic pressing machines, 90 percent of this is converted to either shōyu or shōyu oil while the remaining 10 percent is sold as fertilizer cake. As late as 1955, the conversion efficiency was 70 and not 90 percent (Tsuchiya, 1974).

Because of this change in technology, then, the company's need for manpower has declined absolutely and its need for outside skilled labor or jukurenko has dropped drastically relative to the demand of the previous three-quarters of a century. Not surprisingly, as the company's dependence on local manpower, both skilled and unskilled, has declined, relations between company and community have deteriorated, allowing for a further estrangement of the two under the series of Socialist mayors first elected in 1962.

In the area of company and community relations, therefore, the recognition of a union within the company can be seen as an extension of the entitlements gained by regular workers before the war, while the separation of company and community in a political sense since the 1960s can be understood as part of the process of technological modernization and resultant worker redundancy. Neither of these developments, in this perspective, owes much to the Occupation policy of democratization. Both of these developments, moreover, can be observed in other industrially advanced nations of the world.

Finally, the effect upon Kikkoman of democratizing the economy and preventing companies with concentrated economic power from monopolizing various product markets must be considered. It is ironic in many ways that Kikkoman, rather than numerous larger corporations, should be taken to task over this issue. The large zaibatsu escaped deconcentration of their economic power in product markets in large part because the effect of the Occupation was to dismantle holding companies, interlocking directorates, securities and personnel interlocks while leaving zaibatsu power in different product markets largely untouched. This was due to the apparent Occupation belief that little could be done about this concentration and also to the belief that most zaibatsu-shared markets as oligopolists rather than dominating them as monopolists. As a consequence, medium-sized but highly specialized firms like Kikkoman often got snared in the antitrust net that far more economically concentrated companies avoided.

Development of a New Business Strategy

After 1951, however, the company set in motion a number of new efforts which resulted eventually in a new business strategy for the firm and which owed very little to the FTC for their inception and execution. The basic problem facing Kikkoman in the 1950s and 1960s, it would appear, was less the threat of antimonopoly hearings than the threat of declining per capita consumption of soy suace in Japan. This menace to corporate fortune emerged for two reasons. First, the demand for food and food-related products is mostly inelastic—that is, as society becomes more affluent and as individuals find themselves with more disposable income, they spend less and less of it, as a proportion of the total, on foodstuffs. Moreover, because of their exotic, nutritional, or otherwise perceived value, postwar Japanese have switched increasingly from traditional to nontraditional (that is, Western), foods which do not as a rule require soy sauce as a seasoning. Thus, soon after the Occupation the executives at Kikkoman faced a deteriorating soy sauce market, a market that had accounted for 85 percent of sales in 1953 (Yamaichi Securities Co., 1955: 115).

One response to this was to try to gain an ever-larger share of a declining market and to do so by taking market share away from traditional rivals. Indeed, the price-fixing agreements with other makers that were so attractive immediately following the war were no longer so attractive, and one response to this changing market environment was the effort to establish exclusive distributors to handle Kikkoman products. These distributorships, which were initially tied closely to the company until the FTC hearings in the 1960s, have developed subsequently into an arm's-length association with the company. But Kikkoman would be a rather unimaginative company if it allowed its newly found mission to sell more at others' expense to halt there. It has continued to rely on traditional channels of distribution through *tonya* to market some of its goods, while it has created a new network of wholly owned distributors to run in tandem with the now at-arm's-length network. Most importantly, however, Kikkoman has used some of the considerable revenues that it generates as the soy sauce market-share leader to advertise its product widely and to embark on an ambitious consumer education program.

Beginning in 1955–56, Kikkoman plunged into the world of advertising and product promotion. The company began to explore in detail questions that it had neglected since its rise to dominance in the industry some three decades earlier. The amount and fluctuation of demand were studied. Research teams explored how best to advertise and expand sales. Trademark brand patterns and colors were specified and then publicized across the land. A planning and research department to coordinate these efforts was founded in 1957–58. A house-to-house education program was launched to teach consumers, especially housewives, the good points of soy sauce, how to cook with it, and how to prepare savory delicacies with it. Kikkoman provided free soy sauce to the innumerable cooking classes taken by young Japanese women preparing for marriage. Television was used heavily as a medium for advertising. The company sponsored such programs as the "International Cooking College for Housewives" in which new international dishes using shōyu were prepared. The goal of most of this was to somehow make an old product seem new, that is, to create a new image for shōyu. Overall, the aim was to advertise soy sauce and to raise the image of Kikkoman in particular in the eyes of the consumer.

The company broke out of the old distribution channels and began to sell to supermarkets and to chain and department stores. Repeating a pattern begun before the war, Kikkoman used its sales offices in smaller cities as direct distribution outlets. Beginning in 1951 with an office in Fukuoka, Kikkoman set up combined wholesale and retail offices in such cities as Nagoya, Yokohama, Hiroshima. In 1973, a subsidiary company, Kikkoman Merchandising Center, was established to coordinate sales activities around the country and to quickly respond to whatever requests were raised by sales offices and outlets within Japan. Finally, various sizes and sorts of containers for distributing shōyu were test marketed. The most popular of these, such as the Mann-Pack which combined a number of different Kikkoman products, were sold nationwide (Kinugasa, 1974: 12). Kikkoman was immensely successful in this sales and marketing campaign, raising its market share in Japan from 14 percent in 1952 to double that—28 percent—in 1965, and to triple that in 1980.

Fortunately for Kikkoman, this blitzkreig into sales and distribution was undertaken at just the right time not only to shore up the company's position in the declining market for soy sauce in Japan, but also to permit the company to sell all of its increasing production from the newly automated and highly efficient factories. In fact, by the end of the 1950s the challenge was no longer whether enough soy sauce could be made, but whether or not it could be sold. Finally, this increased production was related to increasing expenditures on research and development and increasing numbers of patent applications, as the following figures reveal.

TABLE 1

R&D Expenditures		Patent Applications			
domestic only		domestic	international		total
1961	100 index number	1961	100 index number		100
1963	201	1968	500	+ 62	562
1967	250	1969	512	+ 363	875
1970	397	1970	412	+ 263	675

(Kinugasa, 1974: 11)

Internationalization

Given the volume of production achieved by the company (4.5 million gallons annually by the end of the 1950s), it was natural that the company would eagerly begin to look overseas for markets. Moreover, once the forecasting, sales, and marketing tools that were developed for the home market were perfected, it was logical to apply them outside of Japan. So what had begun as a defensive measure to prop up soy sauce sales in a declining home market became in time an offensive maneuver to internationalize the outlook and operations of the Kikkoman Corporation.

The company already had acquired some international experience before the war, when in the late 1930s one-tenth of its production was exported. But half of that went to countries in the yen currency bloc (largely Manchuria and North China, excluding Korea and Taiwan), and most of the remainder went to Hawaii with its considerable Japanese and Japanese-American population. The postwar internationalization, by contrast, has been far different, as Kikkoman has attempted to serve a North American and Western European market of primarily non-Japanese descent. Fortunately, a good deal of what Kikkoman learned in its consumer education and television promotion efforts at home in 1955 was applicable overseas in the 1960s and 1970s.

Kikkoman's assault on the international market can be conveniently, if somewhat artificially, dated from the American presidential elections of 1956 when Kikkoman bought air time in the midst of the election coverage in America to advertise its products to the wholly non-Japanese audience tuning in to the broadcast. Shortly thereafter, certain Safeway stores in the United States began to carry Kikkoman soy sauce, and the company can be said to have begun its assault on the North American marketplace. In June 1957, Kikkoman International Incorporated was established and was soon rooted in San Francisco. Ten years later, after a decade of 20 to 30 percent rates of increase in annual sales, Kikkoman contracted on a commission basis with Leslie Food Company, a subsidiary of Leslie Salt Company in Oakland, California, to bottle Kikkoman Soy Sauce and Barbecue Marinade shipped from Japan. This relationship continued for four years, from 1968 to 1972, when Kikkoman began producing soy sauce at its own plant in Walworth, Wisconsin (which had a 2.5 million gallon capacity in the initial year of operation). Transportation costs from Japan to the United

States of brewed soy sauce were roughly one-fourth of production costs while transportation and other expenses of carrying raw materials to Japan were between 5 and 20 percent of preproduction costs (Noda Shōyu Kabushiki Kaisha, 1950). Both of these were substantially reduced by the opening of Kikkoman's Wisconsin plant. The timeliness of the decision to open the North American factory was reinforced by the United States' embargo on the sale of soybeans to Japan in 1973, a year after the Walworth factory opened. In the balance of that decade, sales in North America continued to climb at a 10 to 15 percent annual rate of increase—a rate that was not as rapid as it had been earlier but one that was calculated in terms of an expanded market and a larger market share. A good deal of this accomplishment must be credited to Kikkoman's North American marketing strategy which was and is to sell soy sauce as an all-purpose, international seasoning rather than one limited to Oriental cuisine.

Diversification

The success of Kikkoman in multiplying sales and market share both in Japan and abroad represents only half of the story of the company's response to the declining per capital market for soy sauce in Japan. The other part of the company's plan to cope with this disheartening development was to diversify its product line so as to lessen its dependency on one principal product.

In 1949 Kikkoman (Noda Shōyu Company) produced seven branded products: Kikkoman Soy Sauce, Kikkoman Sauce (a thick, gravy-like steak sauce), Manjō Sake, Manjō Tsuyu and Manjō Memmi (both soup bases for noodle dishes), Manjō Shōchū (vodkalike potato spirits), and Manjō Whiskey (Harvard Business School, 1974). Today, Kikkoman sells over three dozen branded food and food-related products (see Table 2, which identifies most of these) through a network of subsidiary companies, in addition to other investments in restaurants, recreational land development, pharmaceuticals, and food importing and exporting.

All of these new products and ventures are logical extensions of market positions and management know-how that were in Kikkoman's possession at the start of its diversification effort. Many of these products, such as the bewildering variety of sauces and juices, represent products that, although they are unsophisticated in terms of the

TABLE 2
Kikkoman's Main Products as of 1975

Kikkoman Brand Products

    soy sauce
    mild soy sauce (lower salt content)
    light color soy sauce
    teriyaki barbecue marinade and sauce
    Worcestershire sauce
    tonkatsu sauce
    memmi (soup base)
    tsuyu (soup base)
    sukiyaki sauce
    instant soy soup mix
    instant osuimono (clear broth soup mix)

Manjō Brand Products

    mirin (sweet rice wine)
    shōchū (distilled spirits)
    plum wine

Yomonoharu Brand Product

    sake

Del Monte Brand Products

    tomato ketchup
    tomato juice
    chile sauce
    mandarin orange juice

Kikko-Disney Brand Products

    fruit juice (orange, pineapple, grape)
    nectar (peach, orange)

Mann's Brand Products

    wine
    brandy
    sparkling wine

Higeta Brand Products (marketed but not made by Kikkoman)

    soy sauce
    tsuyu
    Worcestershire sauce

technology of manufacture, are nevertheless branded and packaged products that must compete with a variety of similar goods. Here, Kikkoman's already established channels of marketing for its traditional products as well as its recently enhanced advertising outlays compared to the Occupation period, give it great advantage over its rivals. This is a case, then, of driving a heavier load of goods through already well-secured marketing channels with little additional risk but with highly satisfactory returns. Kikkoman's Del Monte- and Disney-branded tomato and fruit juice products (manufactured under licensing agreements) enjoy a 30 percent market share of a very large market in Japan. Also, there are some new products which derive from the company's traditional strengths in research and development (R&D) in the areas of fermentation, brewing, and enzyme technology. The Mann's wine product line and the digestive aid preparations of Seishin Pharmaceutical Company are outstanding examples of this. Given these R&D strengths, Kikkoman can be expected to branch out into new products, such as industrial enzymes, food engineering (amino acids, yeasts, and other micro-organic matter), and perhaps genetic engineering. Finally, there are new product areas which are based on technologies related to those historically employed by the company; these include soft drink (Coca-Cola) bottling and certain aspects of restaurant operations.

Although the revenues of Kikkoman still depend heavily on the sale of soy sauce—representing 57 percent of sales in 1979 (Tōyō Keizai Shinpōsha, 1980: 124)—the company has moved away from an almost complete reliance on soy sauce in the 1950s to a point where soy sauce sales will account for no more than half of all sales by the close of the 1980s. In general, one could say that Kikkoman began its diversification program rather late compared to some of its competitors, such as Kirin, Suntory, Kagome, and Aji-no-Moto corporations, and that Kikkoman's efforts, because of their reactive rather than active character, have been somewhat half-hearted. Nevertheless, Kikkoman has diversified extensively while greatly enlarging its share of the home and international market for naturally brewed soy sauce. By any measure, Kikkoman is highly prosperous and well positioned for future growth.

In sum, since the 1950s and the realization that the market for soy sauce in Japan was not auspicious, Kikkoman has emphasized sales and marketing within Japan to great success, developed a worldwide outlook and operations, and considerably diversified its product line by relying on the marketing and technological strengths of the firm. In light of these accomplishments, which have little to do with democratization, it would seem that some other conceptual notion should be introduced to illuminate the course of postwar change at Kikkoman.

Democratization versus Internationalization
Although the Occupation policy of democratization appears to have

had undeniable impact on Kikkoman for the first decade following World War II (1945 to 1955), it would seem to have had increasingly less importance for the company since that time. By the mid- to late 1950s, the closed ownership of the company had been reversed and shares in the company were widely held and traded. Yet this development owed little to democratization. Instead, the dilution of family ownership was directly tied to Kikkoman's diversification strategy and the internationalization of its operations and activities. The need to raise capital for these new directions forced the liberalization of ownership. In short, internationalization rather than democratization has had the greater effect on reducing family control. Nevertheless, it is well to remember that the Mogi-Takanashi families in concert still retain the largest single bloc of shares in the company (about 20 percent) and friendly enterprises (Nihon Seimei Insurance Company and two Mitsubishi banks) hold another substantial share (about 20 percent). As a result, the Mogi-Takanashi families remain securely entrenched in the top management positions in the company. There has been relatively little democratization of ownership and management here even if the company has been internationalized nonetheless in outlook and effort.

The internationalization of Kikkoman's circumstances may likewise help explain the accommodation of company and community, as everyone inside as well as outside the corporation has come to realize that Noda no longer represents the nucleus of a company with worldwide assets and ambitions. Although dissatisfaction with the company is sometimes still apparent, especially as seen in local and regional elections, major antagonisms have not separated company and union or even company and community for nearly two decades. Thus, company, union, and community have accommodated one another since the Occupation period, and it is difficult to judge how much of this accommodation has been inspired by the ideal of democratization. Most of this process of adjustment, however, has come in the late 1960s and 1970s, the era of internationalization, rather than in the 1950s and early 1960s, the period when democratization was pronounced.

The FTC's imprint on Kikkoman in 1951 was to deny it a close relationship with distribution networks not owned by the company. But while this avenue of advancement was obstructed by the FTC, Kikkoman inaugurated a new sales and marketing promotion that carried the company to a greatly enhanced market share and a noticeably deepened product line. The admitted impact of democratization in the 1950s, which was to negate price and market agreements among major manufacturers, became an undisguised blessing in the 1960s when Kikkoman could employ its vastly superior financial and technological resources to crush its rivals in the marketplace in a completely legal and "democratic" manner.

These developments—the continuity of ownership and management in the firm, the formalization of company and union interdependency, the accommodation of the company and the wider community to each other, and the declining relevance of antimonopoly legislation for Kikkoman in its newer market strategy—make one chary of the efforts of government, domestic no less than foreign, to influence closely the nature of business enterprise and to control the direction of its evolution. The circumstances of enterprise growth within a particular historical and cultural context as well as the incessant need for economic accountability seem to determine the nature of business growth in Japan as well as in the Western world.

The crucial distinction between democratization and internationalization, in conclusion, was the degree of which either was voluntarily conceived and carried out. Democratization was an imposed system of Western values which often lacked resonance with established Japanese ideas and institutions. Accordingly, the effects of democratization were evident to the degree that either past practices or current beliefs of the Japanese were compatible with the goals of the Occupation. This was especially true after the 1947–48 change in Occupation policy which emphasized Japanese recovery at the expense of the institutionalization of a particular idealized vision of a postwar democratic Japan. In Kikkoman's case, democratization appeared to accelerate but not to alter various changes already underway within the company.

Internationalization, by contrast, was a voluntary process of bringing specific features of Kikkoman's business practices more in line with what was being done in large corporations in other advanced countries. The effort was more focused and less formal, and it lacked most of the eschatological character of democratization as well. Another difference between democratization and internationalization might be illustrated by the familiar function and form dichotomy. The Occupation's efforts to democratize Japan were based on a belief that function follows form. From the beginning, the conception of a democratic Japan was embodied in legal definitions and specific institutional features: the individual and not the household as the basis of society; universal suffrage for women as well as men; a more equitable distribution of farming land; a different sort of industrial relations system. From such concrete conceptions, the Occupation proceeded to design and to encourage specific institutional changes, and from such institutional changes, particular ideological and organization outcomes were expected.

Internationalization, however, is a much less precise concept than democratization, and there is little agreement in the context of a single institution, like a corporation, of what it should mean. As a result, the stress is on functionalism rather than on formalism. Functionalism, in the case of international business, is anything that will work, be effective, and be profitable. Because of the free-form character of internationalization, a variety of organizational devices and styles appear effective (see Fruin, 1981), and form most often follows function rather than vice versa. In Kikkoman's case as well, there is an evident willingness to experiment with new products, production techniques, management styles, and operational forms in the international arena. The internationalization of Kikkoman is epitomized by the openness with which the company approaches the international market today, and the range of options in products, planning, and operations that it is willing to consider. It is in this open-ended strategy of adaptation to the international business environment rather than in the closed-in character of specific institutional manipulation that the contrast between internationalization and democratization is most apparent in the history of Kikkoman after 1945.

NOTES
1. Inkyo was a kind of regency office which allowed persons who because of age, sex, or other reasons were inappropriate to assume the office of the household head to assume, in fact, that office on a temporary basis. Yōshi was a technique of adopting persons into the family for the purpose of advancing the family fortune through time.
2. Details of this antitrust case are drawn from the *Bessatsu Jurisuto,* a Japanese legal periodical devoted to summarizing and explicating legal decisions rendered in Japan (see Kanezawa [ed.], 1977: 14–15, 28–29).

REFERENCES

Editorial Committee of Kikkoman Labor Union
1977   *Kikkōman Shōyu rōdō kumiai sanjūnenshi* (A thirty-year history of the Kikkoman Shoyu Labor Union). Noda: Kikkōman Shōyu Rōdō Kumiai.

Fruin, Mark
1981   "How 'Japanese' are Japanese Manufacturing Enterprises in the United States?" *The Asia Record* (August). Palo Alto.

Hadley, Eleanor
1970   *Antitrust in Japan.* Princeton: Princeton University Press.

Harvard Business School
1974   *Kikkōman Shōyu Co., Ltd.* (No. 4–375–073). Boston: Harvard Business School, Intercollegiate Case Clearing House.

Ishige Toshiji
1979   Interview with Ishige Toshiji, director of the Kofukan (July 11).

Kanazawa Yoshio (ed.)
1977   *Bessatsu Jurisuto* (*Jurisuto* supplement), 53 (January). Tokyo: Yūhikaku.

Kawashima Takeyoshi
1957   *Ideorogī to shite no kazoku seido* (The family system as an ideology). Tokyo: Iwanami Shoten.

Kinugasa Yosuke
1974   "Takokuseiki kigyō e no senryaku—Gendai Nihon kigyō bunseki: Kikkōman Shōyu Kabushiki gaisha" (Strategy of a multinational enterprise —Analysis of modern Japanese business: Kikkoman Shoyu Co., Ltd.). *Kikkōman Shōyu Kabushiki gaisha hanbai shiryō*, 694 (August). Reprinted from *Keizai Ourai*, 4 and 5 (July–August).

The Noda Shōyu Company, Ltd.
1950   *Labor Agreement* (in Japanese). Tokyo: Yoshida Shuppansha.

Noda Shōyu Kabushiki Gaisha
1950   *Annual Report—1949* (January).

Tamaki Hajime
1956   *Kindai Nihon ni okeru kazoku kōzō* (The family structure in modern Japan). Tokyo: Shui Shoten.

Tōyō Keizai Shinpōsha
1980   *Kaisha shikihō* (Company Quarterly Report). Tokyo: Tōyō Keizai Shuppansha.

Tsuchiya Takao
1974   Unpublished interview of Mogi Saheiji in Noda (March).

Upham, Frank K.
1981   "Patterns of Violence, Litigation, and Social Change in Japan." Presented at the Midwest Regional Seminar on Japan. Evanston, Illinois (March 7). Unpublished.

Yamaichi Securities Co., Ltd.
1955   *Japanese Corporations Yearbook—1955.* Tokyo: Okamura Publishing Co.

"MANAGING HIGH TECHNOLOGY" IN AN INTERNATIONAL PERSPECTIVE: A COMPARISON BETWEEN JAPAN AND THE UNITED STATES

Koya Azumi
Frank Hull
Jerald Hage

INTRODUCTION

The characteristics of the nation-state, its people, and their culture provide the immediate environmental context within which industrial organizations operate. During the past few centuries, Western societies have undergone transformations into post-modern structures. But in Japan, this transformation has occurred with relative rapidity, especially after World War II. Today, Japan is on a technological par with the West (Moritani, 1978, 1980; Hasegawa, 1981). Yet, the question remains as to whether the Japanese have achieved technological sophistication with or without experiencing the associated characteristics of Western society.

The distinctive characteristics of the modern societies of the West include their *scale* and their *complexity*. Scale is ultimately derived from technological advances in machinery, and complexity from knowledge. The concept of scale is often suggested by applying the adjective "mass" to the systems of production, distribution, consumption, education, and communication (Chandler, 1977). These mass systems are made possible by the division of labor enabling organizations to achieve capacities far in excess of efforts by individuals. But less appreciated is the fact that this division of labor is also associated with the growth in knowledge. Knowledge bases have increased exponentially (Price, 1968). Indeed, the ultimate source of prosperity in post-modern societies is their knowledge base (Bell, 1973; Hage, 1980).

Therefore, two key characteristics are useful for comparing Japan and the West: scale and technological complexity. Both are associated with the division of labor, a key variable in the comparative analysis of societies (Marsh, 1967). Moreover, these concepts can be applied to

111

an organizational as well as a societal level of analysis. In this paper our focus is on organizations, the workhorses of society, because most frequently the Japanese challenge is seen in terms of their better organizational design (Ouchi, 1981; Cole, 1979).

Until relatively recently, the contrast between Japan and the West was stark in terms of both scale and knowledge technology. Japan produced for localized domestic markets and export goods were often craft artifacts requiring little technical expertise. Today, Japan is mass producing some goods for global markets far transcending the limits of its national borders. For example, in 1976 the United States had 87 corporations, mostly multinationals, with assets of $2.5 billion or more while Japan had only 15. If one adjusts for size and the very rapid growth, since 1976, then Japan appears to be rapidly approaching the same density in terms of corporate concentration as America. Moreover, the Japanese are entering high technology markets such as computers and silicon chips, where they are now taking out pioneering patents rather than purchase rights from Western firms.

However, the question remains as to whether the same strategies that have led to Japan's recent success will continue to work in the development of high technology products requiring the most sophisticated knowledge bases. We explore this question by comparing factories in Japan and the United States in order to explore what types of organization design seem likely to succeed both within and/or across each national context.

Our efforts to explain the success of Japanese industry relative to the West are based on comparisons using a typology of industrial organizations utilizing the concepts of scale and knowledge technology. This typology provides bench marks for estimating the extent to which organizations in similar environmental niches are structured alike regardless of national setting. To the extent that Japanese organizations do not fit into environmental niches like their Western counterparts, their form may be examined for possibly unique characteristics setting them apart from the evolutionary sequence of events observed in the West. While our theoretical framework is that of the Darwinian model of population ecology (Aldrich, 1979), we suggest that because evolution is not always an incremental process, unusual forms may emerge in times of rapid change (Hage, 1980). Using this kind of classification system we can begin to approach the question of how and to what extent the organization of Japanese industry is like and unlike that of the West. This can be answered in two ways: the distribution of forms can be different, or there can be different forms.

THEORETICAL MODEL
A Typology of Environmental Niches

In order to contrast the forms of organization in different countries, a theoretical framework is required. Our typology of forms (Hage, 1980) is derived from an open systems perspective (Katz and Kahn, 1966). Industrial organization constitutes the "throughput" part of the input-throughput-output process in which the inputs are resources that are extracted from the environment and the outputs are products (or services) that are extruded back into the environment (Azumi, 1972). We view the organizational throughput system as determined to some extent by its environmental niche in markets requiring varying degrees of scale and technological knowledge.

The environmental niches within which factories operate include at least four types: (1) small-scale, low knowledge (2) large-scale, low knowledge (3) small-scale, high knowledge (4) large-scale, high knowledge. In Figure 1, we suggest some of the characteristics of each type of market and performance.

Each of the four types of organization roughly represents a stage of chronological evolution in the United States. The traditional type of industry has existed since the classical marketplace of Adam Smith. Only in this niche do the laws of supply and demand operate at the plant level. Because the size of product demand is small or localized, there are many competitors willing to fulfill distinctive tastes in clothing, shoes, baked goods, house construction, and many services, etc. By the 1880s, many segments of the traditional marketplace were transformed by mass production techniques such as standardized manufacture of cigarettes, sewing machines, matches, business machines, elevators, etc. (Chandler, 1977). But as Chandler (1962) points out, mass production companies found it necessary to divisionalize after World War I in order to reduce the product mix for each unit organized on a product-market basis when there were customer and/or technological differences. The divisionalized form allowed for continued growth by adding on new product lines without exceeding the limits of cognition of any group of managers. More critically one saw the

FIGURE 1

	Small Scale	Large Scale
	small size	large size
	non-automated mach.	automated machines
	high uncertainty	low uncertainty
	task variability	task non-variability
	shifting, dynamic	stable, static
	uncodified knowledge	codified knowledge
	unanalyzable	analyzable
	low % engineers	high % engineers

	Small Scale	Large Scale

Low Knowledge Technology
 	
low complexity
homogeneity (few diverse functions)
low skill level
little search behav.
low % R&D
	Throughput Technology
	Craft
	Structure
	Shape: Squat
	Power distribution:
	  medium centralization
	Control by plan:
	  few rules
	  few job titles
	  short hierarchy
	Control by feedback:
	  medium A/P ratio
		Throughput Technology
		Assembly-line
		Structure
		Shape: Shaft
		Power distribution:
		  high centralization
		Control by plan:
		  medium rules
		  medium job titles
		  tall hierarchy
		Control by feedback:
		  low A/P ratio

High Knowledge Technology
 	
high complexity
heterogeneity (many diverse functions)
high skill level
much search behav.
high % R&D
	Throughput Technology
	Batch
	Structure
	Shape: Diamond
	Power distribution:
	  low centralization
	Control by plan:
	  few rules
	  few job titles
	  short medium hierarchy
	Control by feedback:
	  high A/P ratio
		Throughput Technology
		Continuous process
		Structure
		Shape: Pyramid
		Power distribution:
		  medium centralization
		Control by plan:
		  many rules
		  many job titles
		  medium-tall hierarchy
		Control by feedback:
		  medium A/P ratio

emergence of Type 4 forms, a mix of mechanical and organic structures. The chemical and electrical industries were the forerunners.

As the state of industrial art became more dependent upon advances in knowledge, small entrepreneurial companies of Type 3 were founded in the boom of the 1950s, based on what today is usually referred to as high technology. During the 1960s, many of these companies were acquired by larger companies or sometimes created as spinoffs from multi-product giants who were less interested in small markets. The tendency of companies to become multi-product conglomerates accelerated with the mergers of the mid-1960s.

One wants to keep analytically distinct the multi-organizational level, as in the divisional structure and conglomerate, from our analytical level, that is the organization. The latter has a distinctive technology and a distinctive market or customer. At the same time that the divisional multi-organizational form was being created, the mixed mechanical-organic organizational form, Type 4, emerged most especially in chemicals and electrical products. And parallel to the conglomerate at the multi-organizational level has emerged the true organic form for high technology. These parallels have not been kept distinct in the literature and are sometimes confused. Some divisional structures have only mechanical organizations as in General Motors. Some have both mechanical and mixed mechanical-organic forms as in DuPont. And some have organic divisions as well as the other kind as in General Electric. Some mechanical organizations have organic divisions as in Exxon. Likewise the range and variety of conglomerates is equally great. Our focus is on the division or organization and how it should be structured.

Examples of the Typology in the United States
The industry implied in cell 1 of Figure 1 is old; it includes crafts and such traditional enterprises as clothing, furniture, housing, restaurants, and personal services. However, optimal size tends to be small and demand is limited because taste plays such an important role. Initial investment is not high. Craftsmanship, service, or quality predominates in some cases and price in others. However, the greater the importance of price the more the mass production type of organization becomes feasible. Although there is mass production in clothing (Robert Hall), in furniture (Kroehler), in housing, and in restaurants (fast foods), it can never completely capture the market because there are so many different taste preferences. The level of task knowledge is low and what there is relies upon the training of artisans or semi-professionals. When qualitative breakthroughs occur, they usually do so in small or large companies *outside* of the industry. Thus frozen food

technology has changed the food service sector but it was adopted from another type of industry located in the small-scale, high technology niche. Structures in organizations of this type are usually simple (Mintzberg, 1979).

For the kind of industry shown in cell 2 or Figure 1, having large-scale and low-task knowledge, the initial breakthrough in mechanization occurred many years ago and the current emphasis is on process rather than product innovation (Abernathy, 1978). The many case studies of Chandler (1977) fit this quadrant. Price determines the competition in the marketplace and therefore process innovations that impact on price are critical. The basic technology is organized on a mass basis and can often utilize assembly lines. Examples include automobiles, radios, cigarettes, canvas shoes, and television. The division of the organization in this quadrant corresponds to the mechanistic model of organizational structure described by Burns and Stalker (1961) and with machine bureaucracy discussed by Mintzberg (1979).

The type of industry in cell 3 of Figure 1 (high-task complexity and low scale) is exemplified by electronics, precision instruments, airplane manufacturers, radioisotopes, robot manufacturers, hospital lab-testing companies, and the more specialized machine manufacturers and the like. Here, relative to the size of the company there is greater R&D effort. In this cell, one would expect to find the organic structures described by Burns and Stalker (1961) and adhocracy described by Mintzberg (1979).

Markets are uncertain and variable. As scientific sophistication increases, product life diminishes although not all product lives are decreasing (Mansfield, 1968). In some areas, product lives are decreasing and in other areas they are not. Thus both process and product innovations are important for industries in quadrant 3. If demand is small, essentially small-batch production, then the innovation rates must be even higher. Typically the product is desired for its unique attributes and is designed to meet customer needs. Frequently the customer is another organization who is purchasing a robot, an instrument, or highly specialized machine. Under these circumstances Research and Development (R&D) must be decentralized and almost part of the production process (Burns and Stalker, 1961). However qualitative breakthroughs are still likely.

The industries found in cell 4 of Figure 1 are diverse. Often organizations began as R&D operations (cell 3) and grew by exploiting potential product demand through further innovations until the pace of breakthroughs had to be controlled because of sunk costs in capital equipment. In those industries where R&D was essential for initial operations, *basic* research, as opposed to applied development, continues to be in the main product lines supported at a fairly high rate (e.g., chemicals, electrical equipment). However, the location of the R&D effort may be problematic. In this quadrant, quality of product is as important as price. Quality can take on a variety of different meanings, including dependability, durability, superior or extra features, convenience in use and the like.

Profits are often used for diversification by purchasing innovations from smaller, capital-poor companies (Utterback, 1971). Some of the organizations in cell 4 began as Type 2, but diversified by investing their capital in other products to hedge their bets (e.g., U.S. Steel). Market uncertainty is perhaps the major factor inhibiting large capital investments in process innovations because their ultimate payoff in terms of economies of scale is viewed as too risky. Often the firms in this quadrant attempt to control their markets rather than simply compete by cost-cutting or qualitative improvements. In the language of institutional economies, these firms often prefer a hierarchical rather than a market approach for the reduction of transactional costs (Williamson, 1975). Here high technology refers not only to devising new products, but even more to the applied sciences of marketing, purchasing, and advertising. It is organizations in this quadrant which have the most marketing, advertising, and sales personnel to merchandise a diversified array of products. There are many professionals and boundary spanners in their support staffs (e.g., Mintzberg's 1979 professional type). Although many new products are introduced, their mortality is high because of the continual threat of a competitor producing a new breakthrough. Thus drug companies and computer manufacturers have periodic upheavals. An advantage of many organizations in quadrant 4 is their power and control over their markets. Thus they can plan these changes and their innovation rate to a certain extent.

Relevance of the Typology for Japanese Industry
Although this typology seems to have a certain degree of predictive

validity so far as American firms are concerned one might expect that there would be some contrast with Japanese industry. The emergence of those types of industry heavily dependent upon so-called big science (Types 3 and 4) occurred largely after World War II in America at a time when Japanese industry was beginning to rebuild. The dominant organization model of the time was still that of Type 2, and it is into the mass production of basic goods that the major thrust of Japan's reindustrialization effort took place. However, many of the Japanese business elite decided to emphasize the quality of the product as much as the price. Normally this would mean more organizations of form 4, that is a mixed mechanical-organic structure and continuous rather than assembly-line technology.

Technological knowledge from the West was important not only in the area of production technologies but also of management and marketing practices. This borrowing from the West became a fine art. Until recently, much of the progress the Japanese have made toward competition in high technology markets has been heavily reliant upon imported knowledge. But this does not mean that the Japanese necessarily rested content with what they borrowed. They continually improved the process of production by improving both the efficiency or productivity and the quality of the product. This means an emphasis on process innovation rather than product innovation, the usual strength of R&D labs.

But the question as to how suited Japanese industries are to the development of product innovations in high technology as well as to the perfection of extant applications remains to be answered. In particular, one wonders whether there is a relative absence of Type 3 (the organic form), the one most closely associated with what we would call high technology. In this type one finds the largest rate of product innovation and basic research (Lawrence and Lorsch, 1967). The Japanese do not support R&D in basic science research as heavily as their Western competitors, their university scientists are less closely linked with industry than is the case in the United States, and the best scientists in industry are more rewarded for local applications within the company than for cosmopolitan contributions to the advancement of science. Yet, science is a disinterested, universalistic enterprise of the world community (Merton, 1968). Does the system of company-based rewards in Japanese industry hamper advances of Japanese in basic science? According to the Western notion of how science and industry advance, the Japanese may be disadvantaged in the era of high technology. On the other hand, to the extent that Japanese industry has evolved new and different organizational forms, perhaps they have an edge in the competitive struggle in high technology markets.

At the level of the multi-organization one wonders if the coalition of organizations found in Japan might not be a superior form to either the conglomerate or divisional form developed in the West. Our data do not speak to this issue but it is important to recognize that there are many aspects to the problem of comparing organizations.

Organization Structures

Our open systems approach is derived from contingency theories of organization and the population ecology model presuming in the long run that those forms of organization most adapted to their environment niche are the more likely survivors. The competitive conditions of scarce resources will increasingly affect organization forms. Having described the environmental niches, we now describe the types of organization form most appropriate for each so that we many compare Japanese and American forms.

One of the oldest lessons from biology, that form follows function, was discovered to hold in organizational analysis by Woodward (1965). However, implicit in Woodward's thinking, as well as that of Burns and Stalker (1961), is the notion that there are different kinds of function. Our typology of organization forms focuses on two kinds of functions, or performances, as being of particular concern for the survival of industrial organizations: innovation and productivity. The discovery by Burns and Stalker (1961) that the organic type was best for innovation and the mechanical type was best for productivity is the starting point for the development of our typology. For example, decentralized power structures characterizing the organic type facilitate the utilization of technical expertise in R&D. However, we go a step beyond Burns and Stalker by examining the nature of the work performed by industrial organizations as indicating the extent to which inputs of knowledge technology and large-scale resources are required from the environment. Because we base our typology on these two kinds of inputs, we suggests that there are at least four types of industrial structures. While Burns and Stalker (1961) and Lawrence and Lorsch (1967)

119

made the point that there is no one best way to organize, the result of their work has been to suggest that there are only two ways. We move beyond this by suggesting at least four best ways to organize depending upon the input resources obtained from appropriate environmental niches. Needless to say one would expect there to be more than four. Our typology can be made more complex systemically by adding another environmental characteristic.

The inputs upon which the typology is based are knowledge technology (i.e., task complexity) and scale of operations. These are basic building blocks for organization theory as indicated by the frequency with which they appear in the literature. Perrow (1967) was one of the first to call attention to the importance of knowledge technology, and the series of work by Hage and Aiken have demonstrated its effect on organizational structure (Hage, 1980). The effects of scale (often measured as size) on structure are well established in the literature (e.g., Pugh et al., 1968 and 1969; Hickson et al., 1969; and Blau, 1970 and 1972 and Blau et al., 1976). We use the term *scale* instead of *size* to indicate the volume of work being performed, regardless of the mix of men and/or machines employed. Because different kinds of outputs are being manufactured in the various factories in our sample, the scale of operations must be measured by indicators that apply to all situations. Therefore, our measure of the scale of operations in manufacturing organizations adds the standard scores for the number of employees and the automaticity of machines in order to obtain an overall estimate of plant capacity (which is closely related to shipment value of the product). This index avoids the controversy over the relative effects of size and machine technology (Scott, 1975; Kimberly, 1976) by combining producers, whether their form be human or metallic. By making a distinction between knowledge on the one hand and machines on the other, the concept of technology is divided along the lines of task complexity and scale of operations. This conceptual ordering results in two basic dimensions that we view as determining optimal types of organization structure: the knowledge required to do the work and the amount of work to be done. This conceptualization also allows one to think about organizational forms as if they were determined by the factors of production. Thus one can begin to see how economic theory and organizational theory can be combined.

The usefulness of these kinds of inputs for predicting organization structure is most apparent by reference to the types of structure described by Burns and Stalker (1961). Their mechanistic type, which corresponds with Weber's (1947) description of bureaucracy, is most suited for performing large-scale work involving relatively little knowledge technology. By contrast, their organic type, which employs relatively more professionals and technicians, is more suited for performing small-scale work where technical expertise in required. Our typology builds upon this insight by expanding the analysis to include all four of the logically possible situations (see Figure 2).

By conceptualizing scale as the number of repetitive events over time, it is possible to understand how organizational work characterized as "uncertain" (Lawrence and Lorsch, 1967), "shifting" (Thompson, 1967), "variable" (Pugh et al., 1969; Tracy and Azumi, 1976), and "many exceptions" (Perrow, 1967) has an effect on organization structure which parallels that of scale. An organization's work which can be characterized as being uncertain, shifting, variable, and having many exceptions involves few repetitive events. By contrast, events should be more repetitive if the work of the organization is certain, stable, non-variable, and has few exceptions.

Hage's (1965) definition of complexity includes two aspects: the number of diverse functions performed and the degree of trained expertise required for the organization's work. Although analytically distinct aspects, they are necessarily connected to the extent that trained intelligence is necessary to *integrate* the qualitatively diverse items. Innovative change increases complexity by increasing the number of qualitatively different entities. The number of qualitatively diverse items is a concept used in the typologies and both James Thompson (1967) and Lawrence and Lorsch (1967) although the term is labeled differently (e.g., heterogeneity). The presumption is usually made that some degree of interconnectedness exists among the diverse items. The greater the degree of this interconnectedness, the greater the relationship between the diversity aspect of complexity and the skill level of the trained experts. But in any case, both the diversity aspect of complexity and the skill aspect of complexity should have effects on organizational structure which are generally parallel.

In order to understand how the complexity of the organizational work impacts the organizational structure, it is first necessary to know what knowledge exists for dealing with the problem. Skilled employees

FIGURE 2

A Typology of Environmental Niches Based on the Inputs of Knowledge Technology and Scale

	Small Scale	Large Scale
Low Knowledge Technology (Complexity)	**Type 1: Traditional Market** Performances: Innovation in products moderate, innovation in process low. Product life moderate. Productivity low, volume fluctuates. Inputs: Knowledge base low, craftsmen and semi-professionals. R&D negligible. Machines simple and general purpose. Few employees. Market context: Many firms of varying sizes, but none dominant; essentially the classical market context. Return on Investment (ROI) usually small.	**Type 2: Low Knowledge, Mass Market** Performances: Innovation in products low, but occasional qualitative breakthroughs; process innovation moderate. Product life low. Productivity high; vol. mass & stable. Inputs: Knowledge base low, mostly unskilled workers, with some tech. experts. R&D proportionately small but with long term payoff. Machines specialized and moderately automatic in assembly lines. Many employees. Market context: Few firms of large size, oligopoly of successful firms operate in monopoly context. ROI moderate, relatively stable.
High Knowledge Technology	**Type 3: High Knowledge Specialty** Performances: Innovation in products high, process innovation moderate, relatively high likelihood of qualitative breakthroughs. Product life short. Productivity low, volume low, prototypes and small batch runs. Inputs: Knowledge base high: skills of professionals, technicians, and master craftsmen. R&D proportionately large, short term payoff. Machines general purpose with some highly technical. Few employees. Market context: Many firms in fluid competition as products constantly under development. Individuated market context. ROI extremely high for successful risks, but unstable.	**Type 4: High Knowledge, Mass Market** Performances: Innovation in products and process mode rate. Moderate likelihood of qualitative breakthroughs. Product life relatively short. Productivity moderate; volume large, efficiency hampered by product mix. Inputs: Knowledge base high: skills of maintenance workers, engineers, & professional managers. R&D moderate, both short and long term payoff. Machines are varied from general purpose to highly automatic, continuous process. Many employees. Market context: Some firms of large size and various of moderate size, shifting number of competitors, monopoly market context for major product lines, but segmentation of others. ROI moderately high, moderately stable.

are required for "search behavior" (March and Simon, 1958). But whether the knowledge structure is codified or uncodified, "analyzable" or "unanalyzable" (Perrow, 1967), paradigmatic or nonparadigmatic (Kuhn, 1962) makes a difference in how the search is optimally structured. If the knowledge for dealing with the organization's task is codified, then the work may be simplified by breaking the job down into specialized components. A high degree of expertise can still be required for dealing with specialized problems, as for example in nuclear engineering, or neurosurgery. However, the structure of the organization should be different if the knowledge base is uncodified because there is no a priori basis for subdividing the work. This in turn limits the number of generalists who can work in the same organization on the same problem, because coordination can be maintained only by feedback rather than by plan (March and Simon, 1958). Thus the nature of the trained expertise required affects organization structure.

HYPOTHESES

Inputs and Form
The characteristics of organization work related to knowledge technology (complexity) and scale of operations have predictable effects on optimal organization designs. Representative features of each of the four types depicted in Figure 2 may be stated in hypothetical form as follows:

1. Configuration
   (a) The larger the scale of input, the more the configuration is shaped like a shaft (i.e., vertical rather than horizontal differentiation along the workflow), especially if the knowledge requirement is low.
   (b) The greater the knowledge input, the more the configuration is shaped like a diamond (i.e., horizontal differentiation at the middle rather than at the workflow level), especially if the scale is small.
2. Centralization
   (a) The larger the scale of input, the more the centralization, especially if the required knowledge is low.
   (b) The greater the knowledge input, the less the centraliza-

tion, especially if the scale is small.

3. Feedback

   (a) The larger the scale of input, the less the control by feedback, especially if the work has a low knowledge requirement.

   (b) The greater the knowledge of input, the greater the control by feedback, especially if the scale is small.

4. Plan

   (a) The larger the scale of input, the greater the control by plan.

   (b) The greater the knowledge of input, the less the control by plan.

A large number of interactions are predicted. This is important because a typology based on additive or linear effects is of little value. Only as we specify some qualitative breaks can we really argue that there is more than just the familiar mechanical and organic continuum of Burns and Stalker (1961).

The first hypothesis stipulates the relationship between the nature of the work and the design of the organization, that is, structural differentiation and the division of labor. Both the degree and the shape of this differentiation depend not only on scale, but also on the kind of expertise required for the problem. If search behavior is required for small problems in areas where little codified knowledge exists, then generalists in the R&D functions are likely to be organized in a diamond-shape structure (similar to the wheel network pattern). If the problem is one which can utilize codified knowledge, then the expertise is more specialized (particularly if the organization is large-scale) and differentiation can take place at the workflow level of the organizational hierarchy. This results in more of a pyramid-shape structure. Thus organizations having equally skilled personnel (as measured by level of occupational prestige) are structured differently depending upon whether the experts are engaged in search behavior without the aid of a codified knowledge base (R&D) or in the application of codified knowledge (engineering and applied science). The key here is that as the amount of technology knowledge increases, the part codified and therefore predictable becomes less.

The rationale for hypothesis 2a is that repetitive events make it possible for informed decisions to be made at a high level because of the frequency of similar decisions (at least for those decisions pertinent to operations, but not necessarily those involving knowledge of lower level personnel). The rationale for hypothesis 2b is that skilled experts have the necessary knowledge for making decisions (Hage and Aiken, 1970). Thus the higher the percentage of skilled experts (especially if this leads to differentiation along the workflow level), then the more decentralized the level of decision making. Complexity involves judgmental or negotiated decision making instead of programmed decision making. However, negotiated decision making is not very feasible unless the organization is small, and it is generally unnecessary if the organization's work is simple.

Control by personal means or feedback is often preferable to impersonal means if the work of the organization is complex. Control by feedback can enable diverse experts to bring the greatest amount of combined knowledge to bear on a problem (e.g., committee meetings). Including the nature of control and coordination systems as a property of organizational form is desirable as several important streams of literature can be integrated by doing so. Etzioni's typology of compliance (1961) as well as Mintzberg's typology of organizations(1979) are based on the same theory.

Hickson (1966) has pointed out that most theories of organization have focused on the "specificity of role prescription" as a key dimension of organization structure, whether described by Weber's "bureaucratic type" or by March and Simon's "control by plan." However, this "structuring of activities" (Pugh et al., 1968) is made possible by the recurrence of repetitive events, which explain hypotheses 4a and 4b.

Although most of the organizational research on control by plan has focused upon bureaucratic devices, technological controls operate in a similar way as is implicit in Burns and Stalker's (1961) mechanistic type. Thus the rigidity of the throughput technology (Hickson et al., 1969) is a dimension of control by plan. Whether the mechanism of control is a machine or a bureaucratic device, the hypothesized result is similar.

Inputs and Performance
Our argument is that the input factors of knowledge and scale of operations (indicated by investment in men and machines) determine optimal organization designs for innovation and productivity respectively. By

knowledge technology (Perrow, 1967) we refer to the extent of the R&D function as indicated by employees engaged in "search" behavior (March and Simon, 1958) to find solutions to complex problems. By scale of operations we refer to the investment in men and machines that enables a large volume of input to be processed into output. Organic organizations are high in R&D allocation, mechanical organizations are large in scale.

The mechanical-organic distinction suggests that investment in the inputs of R&D and scale of operations predict innovative and productive performances respectively. The greater the R&D, the greater the innovation. The larger the scale, the higher the productivity. However, investment approaches to the problem of innovation and productivity seem to ignore the throughput processes of organization which affect the rate of return. Moreover, there are often trade-offs between alternative kinds of performance. Money spent for R&D not only detracts from funds to rationalize and enlarge current operations, it also threatens the viability of the existing production processes and product lines. By contrast, money spent for production capacity, such as machinery or manpower, directly impacts on sales (given adequate market demand). Thus management strategy must often balance relatively safe, short-run payoff in productivity gains against risky investment in R&D that may provide competitive advantages in future years. This trade-off between productivity and innovation is a general dilemma that is reduced only in high-technology markets where product lives are short.

To the extent that there is a trade-off between investment in R&D for innovation versus enlarging capacity for productivity, each of these these input factors has an opposite effect on the two performance characteristics. These contrasting effects of R&D expenditures and scale of operations on innovation rates and productivity levels may be hypothesized as follows:

5. The greater the knowledge input
   (a) the higher the innovation rate and
   (b) the less the productivity.
6. The larger the scale of operation
   (a) the lower the innovation rate and
   (b) the greater the productivity.

The rationale for hypothesis 5 is that investment in R&D is likely to pay off in terms of innovation. However, investment in R&D may not be sufficient as a cause of innovation. To the extent that characteristics of the throughput system mediate the yield of innovative output from R&D input, the structure of innovation management processes need to be taken into account.

Hypothesis 5b suggests that the greater the investment in R&D, the lower the productivity. As mentioned above, the rationale is that R&D detracts from standardizing production operations either by diverting resources and/or by innovations disrupting the fine tuning of the system.

Hypothesis 6a suggests that large-scale operations are less innovative than small ones. This hypothesis has been the subject of some controversy in the literature (Scherer, 1970). Although arguments in the tradition of Schumpeter suggest that scale is advantageous for innovation as well as productivity, evidence mounts that small organizations are more innovative relative to their size than large ones. Despite the fact that large organizations usually have more innovations than small ones (Mansfield, 1968), small organizations have more innovations per employee as demonstrated by comparative research (Scherer, 1970; Utterback, 1971; Aiken and Hage, 1971; de Kervasdoue, 1973; Daft and Becker, 1978).

Although consensus is emerging that small organizations are more innovative than large ones, the reasons for this relationship require explication. According to one line of reasoning, large-scale operations protect their capital investment in plant equipment and machinery by resisting change. Large-scale operations producing standard goods have more rigid throughput technologies and are less innovative.

According to another line of reasoning, management practices as well as economic principles are useful for explaining the negative relationship between the scale of operations and the innovation rate. Large organizations are more bureaucratically structured (Pugh et al., 1969; Blau and Schoenherr, 1971) as well as technologically rigid. Because organizations structured bureaucratically (Weber, 1947) or mechanically (Burns and Stalker, 1961) are more resistant to innovation, they have lower innovation rates (Aiken and Hage, 1971). The reason face-to-face contact facilitating innovation is difficult to achieve among a large number of employees is because the number of possible pair relationships increases exponentially with size. The bureaucratic structuring of activity necessitated by large size reduces the exchange of innovative ideas. Trust (Ouchi, 1981) is required before employees can make themselves vulnerable by proposing untested solutions to problems. Thus small size offers structural advantages for the management of the innovation process.

Hypothesis 6b suggests that large-scale operations have higher productivity. Economies of scale and reduced learning costs explain this advantage, assuming that sales volume is achieved by standardizing rather than by diversifying the product mix.

Results for the United States

Research Design
Typologies are suspect until proven guilty! So many have been created and yet none, except perhaps Weber's, has survived. The usual reaction is to ignore them. There are a number of reasons as to why previous attempts may have failed. Most were one dimensional in nature. Those that did involve more than one dimension typically took variables that correlated. One wants the opposite desideratum mainly because then one maximizes variation. Typically structure (centralization or compliance) has been emphasized. In our case we have placed an emphasis on both inputs and outputs, which in turn are related to basic characteristics of the society.

But the value of typology must be demonstrated empirically and preferably on several data sets. With this in mind, we present a secondary data analysis on two samples of organizations where data were collected for reasons *other* than the purposes of the typology, one from the United States and one from Japan. If, in fact, the data tended to support the a priori reasoning, then one would have more confidence in the typology. At the same time, given that it is a secondary data analysis, it means that one does not have all of the information one would like, that is, the most direct measures of the concepts.

The American Data
This American study is of 110 New Jersey factories that were studied by Blau's Comparative Organization Research Program in 1973 (see Blau et al., 1976; Hull, 1977). The factory sites studied here were randomly selected from among those with approximately 200 or more

employees; in fact several employed fewer than this number, the smallest being 134. New Jersey is a highly industrialized state with every kind of industry type in the two digit SIC code except tobacco, a relatively small regional industry. The sample approximately resembles the national distribution except that chemical industries are over-represented. Although the focus of the research is on industry in general, this over-representation of chemical industries (19 out of 110) is useful because this is an important industrial category with many firms requiring critical R&D effort.

Measures

The concentration of experts is the most important single indicator of the complexity dimension along the y-axis of Figure 2. This concept is crudely measured for the New Jersey factory data as the percentage of professional and technical personnel as defined by the categories of the United States census. Professional and technical personnel have relatively long training and their employment should reflect indirectly the complexity (Hage, 1965; Price, 1968) of the organization's work and relate to the degree of knowledge technology utilized.[1]

The antecedent variable which determines the rate of innovation in an organization is obviously the creative expertise of its personnel. The greater the concentration of technical experts, the greater the rate of innovation an organization should have. However, the employment of personnel with technically complex knowledge is a necessary, but not a sufficient cause of innovation. The structure of the organization is a conditional factor which intervenes between the innovative potential of employees and the implementation of innovations. Organization structure affects the extent to which experts are encouraged to utilize their creative potential, the extent to which this potential is stimulated by communications, and the extent to which innovators have the power to have their ideas implemented.

The scale dimension along the x-axis of Figure 2 is measured as the combination of labor and capital intensity. Our assumption is that it is the combination of both *men and machines* that produces the output precisely because there are trade-offs between them as economists have noted for some time. More obvious measures like the number of physical units of output are difficult to compare across different industries, a problem which also exists to a lesser extent for sales figures. By con-

TABLE 1

CORRELATES OF ORGANIZATION TYPES CATEGORIZED BY SCALE
AND KNOWLEDGE TECHNOLOGY: 1973 U.S. FACTORY DATA

	1 Tradi- tional	2 Mecha- nistic	3 Organic	4 Mixed
Organization Structure				
Configuration				
Vertical number of levels	−.25**	+.17*	−.03	+.15*
Horizontal number of sections at base divided by levels	−.04	−.15*	−.06	+.25**
Centralization				
Level of decision for marketing questions	+.05	+.34**	−.23**	−.08
Control by bureaucratic plan				
Number of kinds of written rules	−.19**	+.05	−.01	+.18**
Control by feedback				
Supervisory ratio	−.32**	−.21**	+.33**	+.18**
Input Determinants				
Knowledge technology				
% college educated	−.38**	−.28**	+.28**	+.39**
Scale (number of em- ployees plus machine automaticity)	−.40**	+.39**	−.36**	+.50**

trast, manpower and capital investment in machinery are both relatively comparable across various industrial sectors and easy to obtain.
The particular measure of scale used in this preliminary analysis is the
combination of the standardized scores of the number of employees
and the automaticity of machinery as measured by the Ambers' (1962)
scale. Hull (1977) has shown that the Amber scale is highly correlated
with capital investment, and especially if its most automatic categories
are weighted.

There is no necessary ratio between men and machines for producing the factory's output. Although size and technology have sometimes been significantly correlated in other samples (e.g., Hickson et
al., 1969), there is no linear relationship in the New Jersey data between
size and the automaticity of machinery.[2]

The two key measures of scale and task complexity described above are not correlated. This is not a trivial point! There is little advantage in using dimensions that correlate as the basis of a typology because in fact one finds that there is a single dimension. That is, of course, the problem with the Burns and Stalker's (1961) organic-mechanical continuum. While it is multidimensional, the dimensions are assumed to vary together.

Other research indicates that task complexity and personnel size are not correlated, which suggests that indeed these are important dimensions to cross-classify for the construction of a typology (Hage, 1980).

In Table 1 is the report of the characteristics of four kinds of organizational systems. To simplify the test, both the knowledge, or task complexity, dimension (as defined by the percent of professional and technical personnel) and the scale dimension (as defined by the combination of labor and capital intensity) have been dichotomized at the median value. This arbitrary cut-point makes it simple to create dummy variables to represent each of the four types. (It should be remembered that plants smaller than 200 were deliberately excluded in the sample and thus the range at the small end of the scale continuum has been attenuated in one of its two component variables).

Structure

Typologies gain additional credence if in fact their basic constituents are correlated with a number of other variables. Since both task complexity and scale have been conceived of as dimensions of input, one gains increased belief in these dimensions in particular as they predict differences in the throughput of the organization, that is, the basic structure of the workflow or production technology (Blau et al., 1976; Hickson et al., 1969; Woodward, 1965). As can be seen in Table 1, the four types do appear to have distinctive throughputs or operations technology. Factory operations which are large scale in part because of their use of automatic machinery vary not so much in the capital intensity of this equipment, but in the type of material processed, in the level of automaticity, and the production arrangement. For example, large-scale factories with assembly lines and/or machines at Amber level three (which have automatic repeat-cycles) to manipulate solid materials do not have very highly skilled personnel (see Type 2). The machine with its repeat-cycle and assembly-line arrangements reduces skill requirements drastically. However, large-scale factories with continuous process operations, which frequently involve non-solid chemicals, have relatively skilled personnel partly because so many workers have been replaced by robots or by pipes that skilled maintenance crews become a dominant segment of the labor force (see Type 4).

Scale and complexity interact in affecting the shape of the administrative configuration as indicated by the correlations of the dummy variable for each of the four types with the number of sections per hierarchical level and by the schematic diagrams shown for each. Scale increases vertical differentiation most if the organization is performing non-complex work (Type 2). Complexity increases horizontal differentiation most at the sectional level than at the divisional level if the scale is large (comparison of Types 3 and 4).

Moreover, scale and complexity also interact so that scale centralizes decision making most if the complexity is low; complexity decentralizes decision making most if the scale is low. A comparison of the correlations of the dummy variables for each of the types in Table 1 suggests this interaction effect and it is evidenced by the significantly large increase in multiple R square which is obtained in regression analysis if the product term for scale and complexity is added to the equation.

Hypothesis 3 predicts that complexity increases control by such personal means as supervisors. The correlation of scale with the supervisory ratio is $-.06$ and significantly negative if other variables are controlled in regression analysis. The correlation of complexity with the supervisory ratio is .41.

Control procedures also appear to be related to the scale and complexity of work as they have been measured. Particularly interesting is the supervisory ratio. The supervisory ratio is only a crude measure of control by feedback because the style of supervision is not taken into account. However, to the extent that a nondirective or employee centered style of supervision requires more supervisors per worker than a directive style, there should be some relationship between supervisory requirements and feedback. In any case, scale and complexity interact in affecting the supervisory ratio so that scale decreases the supervisory ratio most if the work is complex; complexity increases the supervisory ratio most if the scale is small (Rushing, 1967). These hypotheses are

FIGURE 3

INNOVATION AND PRODUCTIVITY FOR 110 AMERICAN
FACTORIES SURVEYED IN 1973

	Small Scale		Large Scale	
Low Knowledge Technology	Type 1: Traditional		Type 2: Mechanistic	
	Innovation	−.07	Innovation	−.16*
	Productivity		Productivity	
	Sales	−.29**	Sales	+.22*
	Profits	−.39**	Profits	+.45**
High Knowledge Technology	Type 3: Organic		Type 4: Mixed	
	Innovation	+.25**	Innovation	−.07
	Productivity		Productivity	
	Sales	−.04	Sales	+.15
	Profits	−.18	Profits	+.23

*p≤.10   **p≤.05

the same for such devices of decision sharing as committees.

Hypothesis 4 predicts that scale increases control by programming. Formal measures of impersonal control such as written rules are more likely to be found in large-scale organizations, especially if they are performing complex work (Type 4) rather than work which can be standardized, as is the case for the throughput in manufacturing organizations of Type 2.

Performance

The ultimate focus of this paper is upon performance measures, particularly innovation. The principal measurement of innovation used in this analysis is the logarithm of the number of patent applications over a five-year period standardized for the number of employees. The logarithm is used because the variation ranges from 0 to 3,000. The rate is standardized because it is the number of innovations per potential innovator which should be investigated rather than simply the raw number of innovations regardless of the size of the organization. Patent applications are used to indicate innovativeness because the concept is built into the measure. However, the degree of innovativeness represented by the patent applications and whether they impact on quantity (i.e., price, production, speed) or on new product quality is unknown.

The correlates of the dummy variables representing the types depicted in Figure 3 show that organizations in quadrant 3 have the highest innovation rate. This supports the notion that the organic organization is more innovative. Although the mechanistic organization is the least innovative of the four types, it is the most productive as measured by sales per employee (and also profits per employee). This contrast indirectly supports the quantity versus quality distinction, a presumption around which the typology is theoretically grounded (Hage, 1980). Moreover, it suggests that pure types, such as the mechanistic and organic, optimize contrasting advantages.

These findings are particularly surprising given the weakness of the patent measure. One would prefer to measure the number of new products and new processes over time to see how size and technology impact on innovation rates. Clearly the typology has some face validity which is enhanced by these crude data.

RESULTS FOR JAPAN

Context

Before we present comparable data from Japan it should perhaps be mentioned that a cross-national comparative study ought to include more macro-level and institutional analysis of the societies concerned. Although cross-national comparative studies are relatively new, there are already a large number of studies (Hickson and McMillan, 1981; Azumi and Hull, 1981; Lammers and Hickson, 1979). Little attention, however, has been paid to what Aldrich (1979) calls an ecological approach to organizational analysis.

In 1972 in the American manufacturing industry, 75.2% of employees were working in factories with 100 or more employees (U.S. Bureau of the Census, 1972 as reported in Aldrich, 1979: 41). By contrast, in Japan in 1978, the figure was only 41%, a figure which had remained stable for nearly 30 years. Clearly, the Japanese factory is smaller on the average than the American, and we have no clear explanation for the difference. The size of the factory has been shown to have a number of important consequences for worker attitudes and probably worker-manager relationships as well in Western Europe and United States Between 1951 and 1978 the number of Japanese factories in the manufacturing industry more than doubled and so has the number of persons working in them. There is no discernible trend in the average size of the Japanese factory except that the proportion of employees working in factories with 1000 or more workers has declined from 17% in 1951 to 13% in 1978. A representative sample of Japanese factories in Japan would clearly be far smaller in size than a representative sample of American factories. At the same time the average plant in the United States has been declining in number of employees, moving closer to the Japanese average size although still much larger.

The Japanese Data

The Japanese data to be used here is from a stratified random sample of fifty establishments in the manufacturing industry in Tochigi Prefecture in 1972. Tochigi was selected as a representative among the 47 prefectures in Japan, as it ranked about midway in terms of a number of criteria such as the percent of the labor force in agriculture, per capita income, and telephone diffusion rate. Some contrasts between the 1972 Japan and 1973 American studies are made in Appendix A.

The two samples have some quite different characteristics that raise interesting questions about the way in which the samples can be compared. Although the original Blau sample (1976) intended to exclude factories smaller than 200, in fact the range went down to 100. The range is approximately the same but the mean personnel size is quite different as is the mean parent company size. The tendency in the United States has been for the parent companies, the multi-organizations to grow larger and larger but for factory size to diminish. Part of the reason is automation but part of the reason is the building of multiple plants in a variety of locations. The Japanese have so far not followed this apparent trend towards larger parent company size and smaller plant size. In turn, this raises some interesting problems in contrasting the two nations given our concern about scale.

Although the instruments used for organizational measurement in Japan were similar to those employed by Blau in 1973 in New Jersey, they are not identical, and therefore, only limited contrasts can be made with Table 1 given earlier. Because Japanese organizations do not normally make use of distinctions such as professional and technical personnel, no such information was collected. Thus percent of college educated personnel is used as index of knowledge technology in classifying organizations in Japan.

This results in the classification given in Appendix B. Each factory is identified by the (Japanese) Industrial Classification Number, main products, number of personnel, percent of the personnel who are college educated, and a code number implying the level of automaticity of the equipment used in the plant. (Amber N = Automaticity mode + Authomaticity range).

Those plants falling into Type 1 confirm the predictions made earlier. It was predicted that the industry in Type 1 is old, and it is indeed old involving qualities of craft. Those falling into Type 2 and Type 4 also confirm the predictions although not as well as those in Type 1. One anomaly is Type 3 which is supposedly organic but contains some factories which might otherwise be found in Types 2 or 4. This anomaly may be explained by the particular circumstance of the firm at the time of data-collection. Some of the firms in this cell had lost much of their American market due to the "Nixon shock" of dollar devaluation and had to reduce their work force considerably but had kept their more educated employees, thus, greatly increasing the index of complexity.

Objective Structure

Table 2 attempts to replicate Table 1 of the New Jersey data. By and large, the Japanese data confirm the predictions and replicate the findings with the New Jersey data. We must keep in mind that since the average factory size is larger in the Japanese sample we might expect some differences to be due to size and its impact on various variables.

There are two predictions where results opposite to the American data were obtained. One is the number of levels. The prediction was that the mechanistic type would have more levels and the organic less, but the Japanese data show the opposite. This may reflect the fact that the average factory size in the Japanese sample is larger even though the parent size is smaller. As a consequence there are more levels at site. Another interpretation is that the greater number of levels may allow individuals to be promoted within the structure, especially if there is rapid growth in sales. The mixed mechanical-organic form should be the best form for competitive advantage in international trade. Centralization is another variable which does not conform precisely to the prediction. While it was predicted that the mechanistic type would be most centralized and the organic the least (as shown in the case of the New Jersey data), the Japanese data show it is the traditional that is most centralized (using here the variable "overall cen-

TABLE 2
CORRELATES OF ORGANIZATION TYPES CATEGORIZED BY SCALE
AND KNOWLEDGE TECHNOLOGY: 1972 JAPANESE FACTORY DATA

	1 Tradi- tional	2 Mecha- nistic	3 Organic	4 Mixed
Organization Structure				
Configuration				
Vertical number of levels	−.26**	−.18	+.06	+.37***
Centralization				
Level of decision on production work methods	+.14	+.15	−.24*	−.08
Level of decision on marketing	−.02	−.04	−.18	+.20*
Overall centralization	+.28**	+.01	−.09	−.20*
Control by bureaucratic plan				
Overall formalization	−.47***	+.34***	−.10	+.19*
Control by feedback				
Supervisory ratio	−.09	−.26*	+.15	+.21*
Input Determinants				
Knowledge technology				
% college educated	−.37***	−.34***	+.56***	+.20*
Scale (number of employees plus machine automaticity)	−.53***	+.39***	−.33***	+.37***

tralization" rather than its component item having to do with marketing decisions) and the mixed form the least. There is relatively little difference between the mechanistic and organic types in this respect, although the signs are all in the predicted direction. Yet it is the decentralization of power to professional experts that most characterizes scientifically and technically innovative companies in the United States. The lack of association between college education and industrial innovation in Japan provides a sharp contrast with the West (Azumi and Hull, 1981).

Perceived Structure
The 1972 Japanese data are enriched in comparison with the New

TABLE 3

Some Additional Correlates of Organization Types

	1 Tradi-tional	2 Mecha-nistic	3 Organic	4 Mixed
Context				
Parent company size	−.20*	+.16	−.15	+.16
Parent company age	−.21*	+.43***	−.19*	−.06
Size relative to parent company	+.23*	−.25**	+.15	−.11
Market share	−.36**	+.29**	−.06	+.14
Structure				
(As perceived by rank and file)				
Division of labor	+.19	+.15	−.35**	−.06
Hierarchy of authority	+.24*	−.05	−.07	−.11
System of procedures	+.04	+.01	−.35**	+.22*
System of rules	−.06	+.03	−.05	+.06
Impersonality	+.16	−.37***	+.03	+.21*
(As perceived by rank and file, foremen, and managers)				
Amount of influence of rank and file	−.12	+.32**	−.21*	−.02
Control graph slope	−.14	+.17	−.35***	+.26**
Total amount of control, or par-ticipativeness	−.13	+.29**	−.30**	+.08

*p≤.10   **p≤.05   ***p≤.01

Jersey data in that questionnaire data are available for samples of managers, foremen, and workers in 40 of the 50 factories. Perceived measures of structure include Hall's (1961) measures of bureaucracy and Tannenbaum's (1968) control graph scores. As shown in Table 3, the mechanical organizations in the sample had employees experiencing the least impersonality and perceiving themselves as having the greatest degree of participation. These results contradict the experience of employees in the mechanical type in the United States (Blauner, 1964). The mechanical organizations in this Japanese sample have reduced the negative consequences of bureaucratic, rigid workflows.

The relatively human work place experienced by Japan's employees in the niche where the most alienated workers are usually found in America requires explanation. As shown at the bottom of Table 3, the contextual niche enjoyed by factories of the mechanical type suggests that site size is small while parent company is well established and enjoys an appreciable market share. These companies are probably the ones most likely to provide their employees with lifetime employment and other benefits. The best management practices, including quality circles, are probably also found in factories in this niche. In any case, factory workers in Japan's mass production factories have higher morale than employees in other factories.

The employees in the mechanical type in this sample had significantly higher morale than employees in any of the other types (+.31, the exact opposite of the correlation for the organic type—not shown above). This contrast illustrates the great difference in the mechanical-organic distinction between the United States and Japan. In Japan, the mechanical type seems to include many of the elements of the organic type. The specialization of trained experts did not develop in Japan's labor markets as in the United States; nor did the inter-organizational division of labor between dirty mass production work and clean R&D work. Thus these results suggest that scale has effects which are more similar in the United States and Japan than is the case for knowledge. The question then becomes the extent to which Japan's utilization of technical specialists may change during the era of high technology.

Performance

Although the 1972 Japanese data do not contain information regarding innovation, Azumi's 1970 survey of 44 companies has information on patent activities. (For further information on this sample, see Tracy and Azumi, 1976; Hull 1977). A partial test of the typology (using sales and R&D as a percent of sales) provides the results that are shown in Table 4.

Figure 4 shows that innovation and productivity have a negative relationship to each other as predicted and again it is the mechanistic type that is most strongly associated with productivity. It shows further that the organic type is positively associated with innovation but unlike the New Jersey factories, its positive association is superceded by an even stronger association of the traditional type with innovation.

FIGURE 4

INNOVATION AND PRODUCTIVITY FOR SOME JAPANESE FACTORIES

	Small Scale		Large Scale	
Low Knowledge Technology	Type 1: Traditional		Type 2: Mechanistic	
	(A) Innovation	+.25*	(A) Innovation	−.24*
	Productivity	−.18	Productivity	+.63***
	(B) Productivity	−.19	(B) Productivity	+.11*
High Knowledge Technology	Type 3: Organic		Type 4: Mixed	
	(A) Innovation	+.24*	(A) Innovation	−.39**
	Productivity	−.29**	Productivity	−.08
	(B) Productivity	−.04	(B) Productivity	+.09

(A) 44 Japanese factories surveyed in 1970   * $p \leq .10$
(B) 50 Japanese factories surveyed in 1972   ** $p \leq .05$
     (innovation data not collected for B)   *** $p \leq .01$

Moreover, the mechanical type is best associated with productivity in the 1972 data.

The fact that some of Japan's most innovative companies achieve high rates of innovation without spending R&D dollars suggests that technology has been borrowed or is embedded in the practices of the firm. Indeed, the responsibilities of Japanese workers, unlike their American counterparts, often include finding better ways of performing. However, these data do confirm the advantages of scale for productivity and the advantages of small size for innovation, the elements upon which the typology is based. But in the case of the 1972 data on Japan, it is companies in the organic niche that do not conform very well to prediction.

DISCUSSION

What does our analysis of the American and Japanese factories suggest in the context of our discussion of overall "internationalization" or increasing complexity of the world environment?

When we speak of the emergence of new types of organizations and link the emergence with that of a new type of environment, we do not, of course, suggest that the environment changes in an incremental or revolutionary fashion. Change is evolutionary and more or less gradual and the Type 1 environment persists even when Type 4 emerges. Thus, currently all four types of environments exist; therefore, the corresponding four types of organizations coexist. What is claimed is that along with increasing knowledge complexity the organic and mixed mechanistic-organic types will become relatively more numerous. Inasmuch as innovation and productivity generally are negatively correlated in the short run, and for survival the organization needs to maintain a delicate balance of both, we should point out that the best strategy for either innovation or productivity or both is a function of the location of the organization in the typology. A further analysis of quadrant 4 suggests that the organization in this cell *needs* both organic and mechanistic features to be innovative and productive. To emphasize either results in failure. Another empirical study of Japanese companies also suggests that for a firm to be adaptive, it needs both organic and bureaucratic elements (Sakakibara et al., 1980).

But as our theoretical model suggests in Figure 1, organizations competing in high technology, mass markets are usually less innovative than the smaller "organic" organizations found in the specialty niche (Type 3) and less productive than the "mechanistic" organizations competing in mass markets (Type 2). Although more complex forms of differentiation may emerge within this type, our analysis suggests that the limitations of organizations of this type may help explain the contrast between Japan and America in terms of productivity and innovation.

In sum, we suggest that Japanese have enjoyed a unique niche in the world marketplace. Innovation rates have until recently been supported by borrowing. Their huge marketing conglomerates have enabled relatively small firms to compete in world markets while remaining specialized (thus maximizing economies of scale). Their small size has also been conducive to innovation.

In the long run, it appears that Japanese organizations must become more like their Western counterparts in the generation and dissemination of scientific knowledge and that the insularity in the competing world markets mediated by trading companies provides only a temporary barrier. But we do not want to suggest that Japan will merely become like the West. The West has many lessons to learn from Japan (e.g., Ouchi, 1981; Pascale and Athos, 1981) and the current strong interest in Japanese practices shown in the United States may result in greater convergence between the two countries.

NOTES

1. This measure of the skill aspect of the complexity dimension is significantly correlated (.30) with the other aspect: the number of 21 diverse functions performed at the site as measured by an expanded version of Bakke's (1959) list.

2. Scale measured as the combination of men and machines is more highly correlated with plant sales (.51 for the 42 factories supplying this information) than either size or automaticity separately. The same is true for the correlation with capital investment (.77 for the 40 factories supplying this information).

The combination measure of men and machines is related to some other key concepts. For example, the combination scale measure is correlated .17 with the percentage of factory sales produced by standardized production, which corresponds with such concepts as stability and non-variability. The combination measure of scale is also correlated .28 with a measure of the kind of expertise, the ratio of personnel in engineering functions (uncodified knowledge).

APPENDIX A

COMPARISONS OF 1973 U.S. STUDY BY PETER BLAU
WITH 1972 JAPAN STUDY BY KOYA AZUMI

	1973 U.S.	1972 Japan
Research site	State of New Jersey	Tochigi Prefecture
Sample size	110	50
Mean personnel size of factory	497	947
(Standard deviation)	(553)	(986)
Median personnel size	360	550
Range of personnel size	100–4000	100–4500
Parent company mean personnel size	38480	6748
Mean % production workers	57	67
Mean number of subunits directly under chief executive officer	5	3.4
Mean number of vertical levels	5	8
Mean executive span of control	7	5.6
Mean span of control of first line supervisor	21	15.8
Functional specialization (Aston)	12.4	9.1

APPENDIX B

CLASSIFICATION OF 50 JAPANESE FACTORIES SURVEYED IN 1972

	ICN Products	Knowledge Technology % Coll. grad	Scale Size	Amber N
	Type 1: Traditional			
211	Quilts, carpets	2.1	288	4
222	Lumber	0.7	160	4
231	Kitchen furniture	0.0	105	2
289	Prophylactics	2.0	452	4
211	Apparel	1.5	270	3
221	Wooden barrels	1.5	282	4
352	Boilers, tanks	1.5	337	4
181	Ham, sausage	3.9	182	6
375	Lenses	0.1	1009	4
203	Yarn	2.2	363	5
282	Rubber shoes	1.0	548	2
294	Leather shoes	2.0	1073	4
	Type 2: Mechanistic			
309	Lime	2.0	427	7
339	Metal springs	2.6	450	7
348	Machine parts	3.3	550	6
361	Auto parts	2.7	290	6
375	Cameras	0.9	1200	8
241	Pulp	2.1	528	5
304	Tiles	2.8	401	6
354	TV tubes	0.6	1200	5
377	Clocks	3.0	705	5
281	Tires	1.2	1445	6
354	TV sets	1.5	1630	4
354	Tape recorders	3.0	946	5
354	Communication equipment	2.0	4500	6
354	TV sets	3.2	1855	6
	Type 3: Organic			
242	Pulp, paper	12.0	112	4
251	Newspaper	36.0	161	4
266	Insecticide	10.0	110	5
316	Steel rollers	12.0	350	5
202	Yarn	3.0	378	4
333	Oil stoves, tape recorders	6.7	712	4
369	Forklifts	19.6	600	3
323	Aluminum products	4.4	1122	3
354	Tape recorders	13.0	489	4

ICN Products		Knowledge Technology % Coll. grad	Size	Scale Amber N
Type 4: Mixed				
206	Synthetic yarn	5.4	360	6
342	Agricultural machinery	3.5	475	6
203	Treated yarn	11.6	413	6
323	Aluminum products	7.6	831	5
348	Sewing machines	7.6	936	5
351	Transformers	10.0	727	4
361	Auto parts	8.0	768	7
181	Ice cream	15.5	1225	4
321	Aluminum products	3.8	2586	5
323	Copper	6.5	1672	5
343	Engines	12.0	1782	8
352	Refrigerators, air conditioners	4.2	4500	6
362	Trains, planes	6.1	3300	3
396	Vinyl products	6.5	1930	4
302	Cement	4.0	598	5

REFERENCES

Abernathy, William
  1978 *The Productivity Dilemma: Roadblock to Innovation in the Automobile Industry.* Baltimore: Johns Hopkins University Press.
Aiken, Michael, and Jerald Hage
  1971 "The Organic Organization and Innovation." *Sociology*, 5: 63–82.
Aldrich, Howard
  1979 *Organizations and Environments.* Englewood Cliffs, N. J.: Prentice-Hall.
Amber, George S., and Paul S. Amber
  1962 *Anatomy of Automation.* Englewood Cliffs, N. J.: Prentice-Hall.
Azumi, Koya, and Jerald Hage
  1972 *Organizational Systems.* Lexington, Mass.: D. C. Heath.
Azumi, Koya, and Frank Hull
  1981 "Comparative Organizations." *International Journal of Comparative Sociology.*
Bakke, E. W.
  1959 "Concept of the Social Organization." In M. Haire (ed.), *Modern Organization Theory.* New York: Wiley.
Bell, Daniel
  1972 *Post-Industrial Society.* New York: Free Press.
  1973 *The Coming of Post-Industrial Society: A Venture in Social Forecasting.* New York: Basic Books.

Blau, Peter M.
 1968 "The Hierarchy of Authority in Organization." *American Journal of Sociology,* 73 (January): 453–67.
 1970 "A Formal Theory of Differentiation in Organizations." *American Sociological Review.* 35: 208–218.
 1972 "Interdependence and Hierarchy in Organizations." *Social Science Research,* 1: 1–24.
Blau, Peter M., and Richard Schoenherr
 1971 *The Structure of Organizations.* New York: Basic Books.
Blau, Peter M., et al.
 1976 "Technology and Organization in Manufacturing." *Administrative Science Quarterly,* 21 (March): 20–40.
Blauner, Robert
 1964 *Alienation and Freedom: The Factory Worker and His Industry.* Chicago: University of Chicago Press.
Burns, Thomas, and G. M. Stalker
 1961 *The Management of Innovation.* London: Travistock.
Chandler, Alfred D.
 1962 *Strategy and Structure: Chapters in the History of Industrial Enterprise.* Cambridge, Mass.: MIT Press.
 1977 *The Visible Hand.* Cambridge, Mass.: Harvard University Press.
Cole, Robert E.
 1979 *Work, Mobility, and Participation.* Berkeley: University of California Press.
Daft, Richard, and Selwyn Becker
 1978 *Innovation in Organizations: Innovation Adoption in School Organization.* New York: Elsevier.
de Kervasdoue, Jean
 1973 "Efficiency and Adoption of Innovation in Formal Organizations." Unpublished Ph.D. dissertation, Cornell University.
Etzioni, Amitai
 1961 *A Comparative Analysis of Complex Organizations.* New York: Free Press.
Hage, Jerald
 1965 "An Axiomatic Theory of Organizations." *Administrative Science Quarterly,* 10 (December): 289–320.
 1980 *Theories of Organizations.* New York: Wiley.
Hage, Jerald, and Michael Aiken
 1970 *Social Change in Complex Organizations.* New York: Random House.
Hall, Richard H.
 1961 "An Empirical Study of Bureaucratic Dimensions and Their Relations to Other Organizational Characteristics." Ph.D. dissertation, Ohio State University.
Hasegawa Keitaro
 1981 *Ekonomikku sūpā pawā no himitsu* (Secrets of an economic superpower). Tokyo: Asahi Evening News.
Hickson, David J.
 1966 "Convergence in Organizational Theory." *Administrative Science Quarterly,* 11 (September): 224–37.

Hickson, David, and Charles McMillan (eds.)
 1981 *Organization and Nation: The Aston Programme IV*. Westmead, Hampshire: Gower.
Hickson, David J., D. S. Pugh, and D. C. Pheysey
 1969 "Operations Technology and Organization Structure: An Empirical Reappraisal." *Administrative Science Quarterly*, 14 (September): 378–97.
Hull, Frank
 1977 "Task Uniformity, Technology, and Organizations: A Comparative Analysis of Factories in the United States and Japan and a Case Study of an American Marketing Corporation." Unpublished Ph.D. dissertation, Columbia University.
 1979a "Scale, Task Complexity, Task Variability, Technology and Structural Differentiation as Determinants of the Supervisory Ratio." Presented at the Eastern Sociological Society meeting.
 1979b "Robots, Energy Slaves, and Other Technological Determinants of the Supervisory Ratio." Presented at the Southern Sociological Society annual meeting.
Katz, Daniel, and Robert L. Kahn
 1966 *The Social Psychology of Organizations*. New York: Wiley.
Kimberly, John
 1976 "Organizational Size and the Structuralist Perspective: A Review, Critique, and Proposal." *Administrative Science Quarterly*, 21 (December): 571–97.
Kuhn, Thomas S.
 1962 *The Structure of Scientific Revolution*. Chicago: University of Chicago Press.
Lammers, Cornelis, and David Hickson (eds.)
 1979 *Organizations Alike and Unlike: International and Inter-institutional Studies in the Sociology of Organizations*. London: Routledge and Kegan Paul.
Lawrence, Paul R., and Jay W. Lorsch
 1967 *Organization and Environment: Managing Differentiation and Integration*. Boston: Harvard Graduate School of Business Administration.
Mansfield, Edwin
 1968 *The Economics of Technological Change*. New York: Norton.
March, James G., and Herbert A. Simon
 1958 *Organizations*. New York: Wiley.
Marsh, Robert M.
 1967 *Comparative Sociology*. New York: Harcourt, Brace and World.
Merton, Robert K.
 1968 *Social Theory and Social Structure*. New York: Fress Press.
Mintzberg, Henry
 1979 *The Structuring of Organizations*. Englewood Cliffs, N. J.: Prentice-Hall.
Moritani Masanori
 1978 *Gendai Nippon sangyō-gijutsu ron* (Industrial technology of modern Japan). Tokyo: Tōyō Keizai Shinpōsha.
 1980 *Kokusai hikaku Nippon no gijutsu-ryoku* (International comparison: Japan's technological power). Tokyo: Shōden-sha.
Ouchi, William G.
 1981 *Theory Z: How American Business Can Meet the Japanese Challenge*. Reading,

Mass.: Addison-Wesley.

Pascale, Richard Tanner, and Anthony G. Athos
1981 *The Art of Japanese Management: Applications for American Executives.* New York: Simon and Schuster.

Perrow, Charles
1967 "A Framework for the Comparative Analysis of Organizations." *American Sociological Review,* 32 (April): 194–209.

Price, James L.
1968 *Organizational Effectiveness: An Inventory of Propositions.* Homewood, Ind.: Irwin.

Pugh, D. S., et al.
1968 "Dimensions of Organization Structure." *Administrative Science Quarterly,* 13 (June): 65–105.
1969 "The Context of Organization Structure." *Administrative Science Quarterly,* 14 (March): 91–114.

Rushing, William
1967 "The Effects of Industry Size and Division of Labor on Administration." *Administrative Science Quarterly,* 12 (September): 273–95.

Sakakibara K., Okumura A., and Nonaka I.
1980 "Nihon Kigyō ni okeru Soshiki no Kankyō Tekiō" (Adaptation to Environment by Japanese Enterprises). *Keiei Ronshū,* 21: 28–52.

Scherer, Frederick
1970 *Industrial Market Structure and Economic Performance.* Chicago: Rand McNally.

Scott, W. Richard
1975 "Organizational Structure." In A. Inkeles, J. Coleman, and N. Smelser (eds.), *Annual Review of Sociology,* 1: 1–20. Palo Alto, Calif.

Tannenbaum, Arnold
1968 *Control in Organizations.* New York: McGraw-Hill.

Thompson, James D.
1967 *Organizations in Action.* New York: McGraw-Hill.

Tracy, Phelps K., and Koya Azumi
1976 "Determinants of Administrative Control: A Test of a Theory with Japanese Factories." *American Sociological Review,* 41 (February): 80–94.

Utterback, James
1971 "The Process of Technological Innovation Within the Firm." *Academy of Management Journal,* 14: 75–88.

Weber, Max
1947 *The Theory of Social and Economic Organization.* New York: Oxford University Press.

Williamson, Oliver E.
1975 *Markets and Hierarchies: Analysis and Antitrust Implications.* New York: Free Press.

Woodward, Joan
1965 *Industrial Organizations: Theory and Practice.* Oxford: Oxford University Press.

JAPANESE WORK-RELATED VALUES IN A GLOBAL PERSPECTIVE

Geert Hofstede

> *Perhaps the time is ripe for*
> *us to consider the world as a*
> *single social system and each*
> *nation but one of its units.*
> *(Koya Azumi, 1974: 535.)*

Are There National Value Systems?

Difference and similarity are like *yang* and *yin*. Any pair of things is different and similar at the same time; it depends on the context into which we put them, whether they will look different or similar. The same holds for people. Two American professors who look very different to their students will look very similar to a bus driver in Tokyo.

Identifying "Japanese values" versus "American values", "French values," etc., presumes that in a global context, the values of one Japanese will look similar to the values of another Japanese and different from the values of any American or any French person. This smells of unjustified generalization and stereotyping. In fact, if we are able to in some way measure values, we rarely find that on a given value a Japanese will score similar to any other Japanese and different from any American. Differences found in measurements of a value are usually of a statistical nature. The distribution of a certain value in a sample of Japanese respondents differs from its distribution in a sample of, say, American respondents, but the two distributions usually overlap to a considerable extent, as pictured in Figure 1. To illustrate Figure 1, let me assume that we have been measuring "the desirability of order at work." In this case, the distribution in Japan is likely to be more like country *b*, and in the United States more like country *a* (Hofstede, 1980: chapter 4). On the average, Japanese attach a stronger desirability to order at work, but it is easy to find a Japanese with a lower need for order than most Americans, and vice versa.

It makes sense to speak of national values in cases in which there is a significant shift between the distributions from one country to another, that is, for which the distance *a-b* in Figure 1 is large compared to the differences found within each country (the width of the *a* and *b* curves in Figure 1).

Identifying national values also presumes agreement on what we mean by a "value." In my research, I have defined a value as "a broad tendency to prefer certain states of affairs over others" (Hofstede, 1980: 19). Those values for which we do find differences between nations (according to Figure 1) are rarely isolated phenomena; they are part of value systems which can in turn be seen as "Patterns of Culture" (Benedict, 1934) rooted deeply in the history of a nation, transferred in institutions like families and schools, and reinforced by the rewards and penalties of daily life. We can sometimes recognize them in a country's legislation, literature, religion and any other manifestation of "culture" in the broad, anthropological sense. They change over time, but slowly; because once they are "programmed into" the minds of a generation, it is difficult to de-program that generation; and each generation tends to transfer them to the next.

National value systems that differ from one country to another provide an explanation of differences in collective behavior between nations. Why do some countries have a history of periodic revolutions, while others change their governments in less dramatic ways? Why do some populations at some periods in history support bellicose leaders, while others do not? Why do some perform economic miracles, while others under similar economic conditions do not? (Kassem, 1974). National value systems also help to explain the stereotypes that people in one country tend to hold about people in another, and they contribute to the actual relationships that develop between countries.

A Values Study Within a Multinational Corporation

My book *Culture's Consequences* (Hofstede, 1980) describes a study of national work-related value systems which started in a large multinational corporation, headquartered in the United States. This corpora-

FIGURE 1
The Distribution of a Value for Two Country Samples

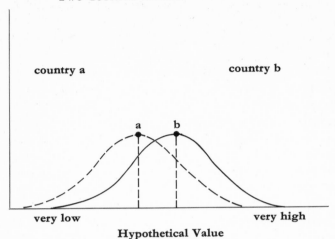

Relative Frequency of Value

country a   country b

a   b

very low   very high

Hypothetical Value

tion which I am calling "Hermes" conducted a series of paper-and-pencil surveys between 1967 and 1973 of the work satisfactions, attitudes and values of its employees around the world. In my study, I have used the existing body of survey data from the Hermes corporation to look at differences in answers about *values* only, (not attitudes and satisfactions) between employees in similar jobs but different countries. Altogether, I used data from 40 countries, collected in 20 different languages, on over 100,000 questionnaires. Most parts of the corporation were surveyed twice with the same questions, around 1968 and around 1972, so that it is possible to see value shifts over this time period.

To some people it seems bold to draw conclusions about national value systems from data collected within one multinational corporation, however large. There is no doubt that employees in, say, Japan, who take employment in a foreign multinational, are not a representative sample of the Japanese population. However, the essential point is that the research compares Japanese Hermes employee values with the values of Hermes employees in 39 other countries—Thai Hermes employees, French Hermes employees, etc.—people in the same types

150

of jobs and working for the same corporation, but of a different nationality. Nationality is the only variable on which these Hermes employees differ systematically—it is the only variable that can provide an explanation of the systematic differences found in the values data gathered.

The nationality of the Hermes employees is related to the language in which they took the surveys: Japanese in Japan, French in France, etc. It would therefore be possible that differences in scores would be due to the translation of the questions. This hypothesis, however, could be disproved; it appeared that groups of nationals of different countries who answered the same questions *in English*, nevertheless showed similar national differences as found in the Hermes data (Hofstede, 1980: 68). Also, a statistical study of Hermes data collected in Japanese, French and English showed that the patterns of correlations between answers on the same questions in these three different languages were reasonably similar (Hofstede, 1980: 61).

Paradoxically, the analysis of Hermes employee survey data did not provide any information on the corporation itself. This is because it only compared national groups *within* Hermes, and did not compare Hermes with something else. This is similar to the problem of Archimedes: without a "fixed spot on which to stand" (outside Hermes) I cannot "move the earth"—in this case, know Hermes.

The analysis of the Hermes data did allow, however, the classification of national work-related value system differences among the 40 countries involved. These were differences among the *mean* values of national groups; what I measured where distances like *a-b* in Figure 1. The unit of analysis was the *country*, not the individual employee. I call this an "ecological" data analysis as opposed to an individual data analysis. Ecological data are data referring to an entire social system, in this case a country.

Four Dimensions of National Culture

The Hermes data for the ecological analysis consisted of mean scores on about 50 questions for 40 countries (a matrix of $50 \times 40 = 2000$ numbers). Using statistical techniques (correlation and factor analysis), I could search for underlying value systems that would explain the differences in mean values between the countries in the most parsimonious way. I found four such underlying value systems, which can also be called "dimensions of national culture." The names I chose for them are Power Distance, Uncertainty Avoidance, Individualism versus Collectivism, and Masculinity versus Femininity. They will be described below. These four dimensions represent basic value choices that apply *globally,* that is, they are relevant to all 40 countries. Together they explain about 50 percent of the value differences between countries as found in the Hermes data. They therefore leave another 50 percent of the differences unexplained; this is the part that cannot be understood by global factors, but is due to specific local factors, as well as to measurement error.

The concept of dimensions of national culture is known from comparative anthropology. Various anthropologists have argued that there must be a framework to which cultural differences can be related, because all societies share a number of basic questions. To each of these questions, a range of answers is possible and different answer choices characterize different societies. In a review article about "National Character," Inkeles and Levinson (1969: 447) have suggested the basic questions which they believe are common to all societies.

1. Relation to authority.
2. Conception of self, including the individual's concept of masculinity and femininity.
3. Primary dilemmas or conflicts, and ways of dealing with them, including the control of aggression and the expression versus inhibition of affect.

The four dimensions which I identified in the Hermes data cover Inkeles and Levinson's basic questions remarkably well, as we shall see below.

The outcome of my analysis of the Hermes data has been a numerical score for each of the 40 countries on each of the four dimensions. This set of scores has allowed me to test the validity of the Hermes findings against data from other sources. For example, I derived scores for the Power Distance of nations from the answers of Hermes employees to certain value questions. Other researchers, however, have also studied national values very similar to Power Distance but using different questions on different respondent groups, for example, on university students. To the extent that these other studies covered the same countries as I did, their scores should be statistically significantly correlated with my Power Distance scores for these countries.

A search of the literature of the various social sciences showed significant correlations between one or more of my four dimensions and values scores from 14 other multi-country studies. These studies were carried out between 1963 and 1978 and covered between 5 and 19 countries from the 40 in the Hermes sample. Five of the studies were done on representative samples of national populations, through public opinion research firms; the other 9 are samples of managers or students (Hofstede, 1980: 326–27). However, the literature also revealed non-survey data about countries that could be conceptually related to one or more of the Hermes dimensions. For example, Power Distance relates to inequality in society, and one measure of this is the inequality of income distributions. Income inequality represents an "ecological" characteristic, a measure of a society as a whole. I found significant correlations between one or more of the Hermes dimensions and 19 different ecological characteristics, collected in 24 studies, covering between 5 and 39 countries from the Hermes sample (Hofstede, 1980: 328–29).

Finally, in a search for the origins of the national value differences found, I have correlated the Hermes scores with some fundamental economic and geographic characteristics of the 40 countries: their wealth (per capita income), economic growth, geographic latitude, population size, population growth rate, population density and finally the size of the Hermes subsidiary in that country. This part of the analysis showed several significant correlations, some of which I shall refer to below (Hofstede, 1980: 330–31).

Apart from these quantitative, statistical relations between national value scores from the Hermes study and other data, qualitative insight could be gained from descriptive studies of societies that scored particularly low or high on a dimension. In this respect it was revealing to look not only at what is average for a given society, but also at what is extreme. Every country has its "lunatic fringe" of people holding national values to an extreme degree. The lunatic fringes manifest themselves in collective activities which are typical for that country, even if they are only supported by a small minority of its population. These activities can be innocent, like hobby clubs, or not so innocent, like militant political or religious splinter parties or terrorist gangs. Every country has its own brand of extremists; and studying the values of the extremists helps to understand the dominant value systems of the country as a whole. The extremists represent the tail ends of the distributions pictured in Figure 1.

Description of the Four Dimensions

Power Distance represents the answer of a society to the fundamental problem of inequality between people. There is inequality in all societies; but some try to minimize it (small Power Distance) while others have institutionalized hierarchical systems in which high and low have their place (large Power Distance). The Power Distance dimension is obviously similar to Inkeles and Levinson's basic question of "relationship to authority" (see above).

The Hermes data reveal that a country's Power Distance norm is reflected not only in the values of the leaders, but also in the values of the followers. In large Power Distance countries most of the powerless people actually *prefer* to be led by powerful (autocratic or paternalistic) leaders, much more so than in small Power Distance countries; a minority rejects being led at all. In small Power Distance countries people like a mutual dependence between leaders and followers. Systems of government in countries reflect the national Power Distance norm. Large Power Distance countries tend to have autocratic regimes which cannot be reversed by popular vote, only by revolutions; but such revolutions are likely to exchange one autocratic regime for another. Small Power Distance countries tend to have pluralistic regimes with power checks and balances, in which changes in government can take place by popular vote. In work organizations, countries with large Power Distances show centralization, many levels of management and privileges for managers. Countries with smaller Power Distances tend to have work organizations with decentralization, flatter organization pyramids, and forms of worker consulation of representation.

Uncertainty Avoidance represents the answer by a society to the fundamental problem of the one-way arrow of time. Human life proceeds from birth to death in an inescapable sequence of past, present and future; and at any time in any society, the future represents the unknown; the only certainty about it is that it contains death. Some societies live easily with the uncertainty of the future (weak Uncertainty Avoidance). In such societies, any type of uncertainty is taken more lightly; people do not feel a strong need for formal rules, they want as few rules as possible. Deviant opinions and behaviors of others are easily tolerated, morals are flexible, and opportunism is a virtue. People are relaxed and not supposed to get upset easily, and there is social disapproval of the public expression of emotions, anger or aggression. Children in such societies learn to contain their emotions.

Other societies constantly feel the uncertainty of the future as a threat against which they have to defend themselves (strong Uncertainty Avoidance). In these societies, people feel a strong need for formal rules to go by. There is little tolerance of deviant ideas and behaviors; what is different is considered dangerous. Nothing should be unexpected and such societies strive for a known world. They believe in absolute principles and Truth with a capital T. However, in spite of the control of uncertainties which such societies try to exercise, life is experienced as threatening; there is more tension and a higher anxiety level. In these societies, people cope with their anxieties by hard work: their need for working hard comes from the inside, they can't be stopped. But also, these societies generally allow their members to cope with tension and anxiety by expressing emotions and behaving aggressively, at least on certain socially approved occasions. The Uncertainty Avoidance dimension is related to Inkeles and Levinson's basic question number 3: "Primary dilemmas or conflicts, and ways of dealing with them, including the control of aggression and the expression versus inhibition of affect."

Individualism, with its opposite pole Collectivism, represents the answer by a society to the basic problem of the relationship of one individual to another. In some societies which I call "Collectivist," this relationship is tight. People are born as members of in-groups of which they are supposed to remain an integrated member all their lives; their individual fate is to a large extent determined by the interest of their in-group. They sacrifice individual interests in exchange for protection by the in-group. In such societies, people think in terms of "we" rather than "I." They are not supposed to have private opinions different from the opinion of their group. Their loyalty to their in-group may carry over to other social systems. It starts in the family but may also manifest itself in the work organization. In the Collectivist society, people expect their private life to be invaded by the groups to which they belong. The penalty for not maintaining the proper relationship with the group is a feeling of shame, and loss of face. Because a Collectivist society is based on in-groups, people let their attitude to others depend on whether the other belongs to their in-group or to an apparent out-group (this is called "Particularism"). For effective work and business relationships in such a society, it is necessary to establish a relationship first, through which the out-group member can become "adopted" as an in-group-member.

Other societies, which I call "Individualist," maintain loose relationships between people. Individuals are supposed to take care of themselves and their immediate family only. They learn early in life to distinguish their "I" from any "we." In such societies it is considered a sign of strength of personality to have a private opinion, different from others. People's relationships with work organizations tend to be calculative and they will change work organizations easily if they expect a better deal elsewhere. They expect their work organizations to respect their private lives. The penalty for misbehavior in such societies is a feeling of guilt (rather than shame), and loss of self-respect (rather than loss of face). In an Individualist society, there is a feeling that all others should be treated in the same way ("Universalism" rather than "Particularism"; see Parsons and Shils, 1951). The Collectivism-Individualism dimension is related to one aspect of Inkeles and Levinson's basic question number 2: the "conception of self."

Masculinity, with its opposite pole Femininity, represents the answer of a society to the basic problem of the existence of two sexes. Biologically, the only absolute difference between the sexes is their role in procreation: men cannot have babies. All other differences between the sexes are statistical rather than absolute (more or less like Figure 1): Men are on the average taller and stronger, women have on the average more endurance and finger dexterity. However, these statistical biological differences do not dictate the *social* roles that a society should choose for its men and its women. In this respect, a range of answers is possible. Nevertheless, all known societies do reserve for their men primarily the achieving role outside the house, and for their women the nurturing, caring role inside the house. Where societies differ is on the degree to which this social role division is made absolute. In some societies which I call "Feminine," men are supposed to care for children, for others, and for the weak almost as much as women are. Men are supposed to care for the quality of life and for a comfortable, beautiful environment as much as women are. Men are not supposed to be as-

156

sertive or aggressive toward others any more than women are. It is a virtue for men to be modest and yielding; demonstrative manliness is socially frowned upon. Relationships at work are at least as important as work performance and results. There is a general sympathy for that which is small, slow, and weak, and a distrust of whoever tries to excel beyond others. Women in these societies do not in large numbers try to take men's roles because they also reject assertive or aggressive behavior; but when they want to take a traditionally male job, they meet little resistance.

Other societies, which I call "Masculine," maintain a strict role separation between men and women. Men are supposed to achieve, to perform, and to behave assertively and, at times, aggressively. At work, relationships are maintained because of their contribution to performance and results. There is a general sympathy—even among the women—for that which is big, fast, and strong. There is a belief in and admiration for supermen. Children are stimulated to excel in their studies. Women are supposed to look after the house, the quality of life, and the beauty of the environment. Women are supposed to serve men. Where women step into men's roles, they will only be successful if they exhibit at least as much assertiveness, competence and aggressiveness as most men do. However, the unique (because non-shared) role of women in a masculine society gives them a unique power as well: women often dominate in the home. The Femininity-Masculinity dimension is obviously related to Inkeles and Levinson's basic question number 2: the "conception of self, including the individual's concept of masculinity and femininity."

Table 1 gives a summary of the meaning of the four dimensions. It should be stressed again that the elements belonging to each dimension were not chosen arbitrarily. They are the outcome of an empirical, statistical study: first, of 40 countries using the Hermes value differences, and subsequently of data from other studies correlated with the Hermes data.

Japan's Position of the Four Dimensions

From the Hermes survey data, I have composed for each country its position on the four dimensions. For this purpose, I used the mean scores in the countries on those value questions which in the statistical analysis were most representative for each dimension (for the details

TABLE 1

A SUMMARY OF THE FOUR DIMENSIONS

Small Power Distance	Large Power Distance
Trend in society to minimize inequalities.	Institutionalized hierarchies in which low and high have their place.
People like mutual dependence between leaders and followers.	Most of powerless people prefer a strong leader; a few reject any leader.
Pluralistic regimes with power checks and balances.	Autocratic regimes, changed by revolutions.
Decentralization preferred.	Centralization preferred.
Flatter organization pyramids.	Many levels of management.
Worker representation or consultation.	Privileges for managers.

Weak Uncertainty Avoidance	Strong Uncertainty Avoidance
Ease and equanimity in the face of uncertainty.	Nothing should be unexpected; desire for a known world.
As few rules as possible.	Strong need for formal rules to go by.
Deviant opinions and behavior easily tolerated.	Intolerance of deviance; what is different is dangerous.
Morals are flexible.	Belief in absolute principles.
Opportunism is a virtue.	Belief in Truth.
People not easily upset.	High tension and anxiety.
Hard work only when necessary.	Inner urge to work hard.
Emotions should be contained.	Emotions and aggression may be shown at times.

Collectivist	Individualist
People are born into in-groups of which they remain an integrated member.	People develop into un-integrated individuals.
Individual interests should be sacrificed to the group in exchange for protection.	People are supposed to take care of their immediate families only.
"We" thinking.	"I" thinking.
No private but group opinions.	Private opinions expected.
Loyalty to work organization.	Calculative relation to work organization.
Private life may be invaded by group and work organization.	Work organization should respect private life.
Penalty: shame, loss of face.	Penalty: guilt, loss of self-respect.
In-group members treated differently from out-group members: particularism.	All others should be treated the same: universalism.

TABLE 1 (continued)

Feminine	Masculine
Overlapping roles of men and women.	Strict role separation between sexes.
Men should care for children, others, the weak, the quality of life and the environment.	Men should achieve and perform, women should care and be concerned with the quality of life.
Men should be modest and yielding and not more assertive than women.	Men should be assertive and aggressive; women should serve.
Demonstrations of manliness frowned upon.	Admiration for supermen.
General sympathy for the small, the slow, the weak.	General sympathy for the big, the fast, the strong.
Distrust of whoever tries to excel.	Children stimulated to excel.
Little resistance to women in men's jobs if they want them—but they often don't.	Women not accepted in men's jobs or only if they are more assertive than men.

of the computation see Hofstede, 1980: chapters 3–6). By a linear mathematical transformation, I made all index values fit a scale between 0 and 100 (120 for Uncertainty Avoidance), in which a country which is low on a dimension scores close to 0 and one which is high, close to 100. The resulting index values are listed in Table 2.

In Table 3, I have further simplified Table 2 by comparing Japan with only six other countries: France, Germany, Hong Kong, Sweden, Taiwan, and the United States. Table 3 shows the relative rank of these countries on the four dimensions, in which the lowest scoring country is 1 and the highest scoring, 40. Unfortunately, I have no data for the People's Republic of China. The data for Hong Kong and Taiwan, however, can at least show how countries with a Chinese cultural heritage compare to Japan. Data for South Korea are available in the Hermes data bank but they were left aside in the first analysis because of their relatively small sample size. They will, however, still be analyzed, together with data from about ten other countries; I expect the results to be available in late 1981.

Table 3 reveals that Japan, in comparison to the 39 other countries in the Hermes sample, scores about in the middle on Power Distance and Individualism, and near or at the top of the list on Uncertainty

TABLE 2
Index Values for the Forty Countries
on the Four Dimensions

Country	Abbre-viation	Power Distance	Uncertainty Avoidance	Individ-ualism	Masculinity
Argentina	ARG	49	86	46	56
Australia	AUL	36	51	90	61
Austria	AUT	11	70	55	79
Belgium	BEL	65	94	75	54
Brazil	BRA	69	76	38	49
Canada	CAN	39	48	80	52
Chile	CHL	63	86	23	28
Colombia	COL	67	80	13	64
Denmark	DEN	18	23	74	16
Finland	FIN	33	59	63	26
France	FRA	68	86	71	43
Great Britain	GBR	35	35	89	66
Germany (F.R.)	GER	35	65	67	66
Greece	GRE	60	112	35	57
Hong Kong	HOK	68	29	25	57
India	IND	77	40	48	56
Iran	IRA	58	59	41	43
Ireland	IRE	28	35	70	68
Israel	ISR	13	81	54	47
Italy	ITA	50	75	76	70
Japan	JAP	54	92	46	95
Mexico	MEX	81	82	30	69
Netherlands	NET	38	53	80	14
Norway	NOR	31	50	69	8
New Zealand	NZL	22	49	79	58
Pakistan	PAK	55	70	14	50
Peru	PER	64	87	16	42
Philippines	PHI	94	44	32	64
Portugal	POR	63	104	27	31
South Africa	SAF	49	49	65	63
Singapore	SIN	74	8	20	48
Spain	SPA	57	86	51	42
Sweden	SWE	31	29	71	5
Switzerland	SWI	34	58	68	70
Taiwan	TAI	58	69	17	45
Thailand	THA	64	64	20	34
Turkey	TUR	66	85	37	45
USA	USA	40	46	91	62
Venezuela	VEN	81	76	12	73
Yugoslavia	YUG	76	88	27	21
Mean		52	64	50	50
Standard Deviation		20	24	25	20

(Hofstede, 1980: 315)

TABLE 3

Relative Rank of Japan and Six Other Countries on the Four Dimensions

Country	Power Distance	Uncertainty Avoidance	Individualism	Masculinity
France	32–33	31–34	30–31	12–13
Germany (Federal Republic)	11	20	26	32–33
Hong Kong	32–33	3–4	9	24–25
Japan	19	37	19	40
Sweden	6–7	3–4	30–31	1
Taiwan	22	21	5	14–15
U.S.A.	15	9	40	28

(1 = lowest, 40 = highest)

Avoidance and Masculinity. Japan's middle position on Power Distance suggests that inequality is more accepted in Japan than in the United States (but only marginally so), Germany and Sweden. However, Taiwan, Hong Kong and France accept inequality more easily than Japan does. On a global scale, Japan has a moderate need for hierarchy.

It is remarkable that while many Americans consider their country the world's model of democracy, the United States scores not as low on Power Distance as 14 other (Western) countries. In American work organizations, for example, the belief that there should be "managerial prerogatives" is strong, and forms of worker representation or consultation find relatively little sympathy. American style "participative management" means that the initiative for the employees' participation is generally with the manager, not with the employees.

Japan's extreme position (37 out of 40) on Uncertainty Avoidance suggest that there are only few countries (Greece, Portugal and Belgium) for which the need for order and predictability in society is as pronounced as in Japan. It suggests a high level of pressure for social conformity, and a strong inner urge to work hard. In this case, Japan finds itself close to France. Germany and Taiwan score in the middle, while the United States, Hong Kong and Sweden score towards the low end.

FIGURE 2
Country Clusters Based on All Four
Dimensions Taken Together

COUNTRY
(see Table 2)

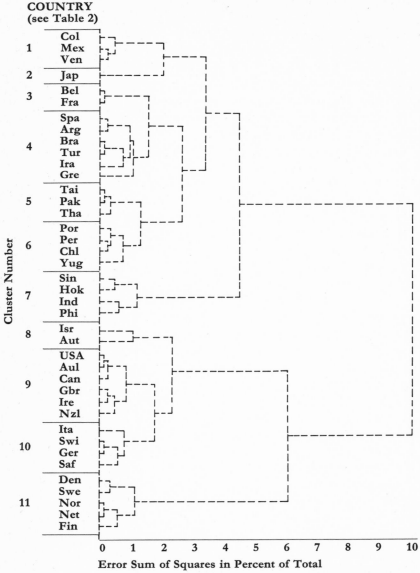

Error Sum of Squares in Percent of Total

Program YHAK(H. Forst, Cologne and F. Vogel, Kiel) Dendrogram, Wards Method. Variables: PDI, UAI, IDV, MAS
(Hofstede, 1980: 334)

162

Japan's middle position on Individualism characterizes it as "Collectivist" in comparison to other wealthy countries (Germany, France, Sweden, the United States) but as "Individualist" in comparison to other Asian and Third World countries (Taiwan, Hong Kong). The Individualism score is strongly related to national wealth (per capita income). The correlation coefficient between the Hermes Individualism Index and the 1979 per capita Gross National Product of the 40 countries is .82. For two sets of data coming from such completely different sources, this level of correlation is amazingly high. In Table 2, we found that countries with an Individualism score below Japan's are without exception poor countries, and those above Japan's without exception relatively rich countries.

Japan's extreme position (40 out of 40) on Masculinity identifies it as a unique case in this respect. It suggests that in no other country in the Hermes sample the sex role separation is as strict as in Japan, which is a defendable proposition even without the Hermes data. It also suggests a very strong performance orientation of Japanese men, in comparison to men from other countries. Japan in this case finds itself relatively close to Germany and the United States, two other "masculine" countries. Japan's opposite pole on this dimension is Sweden (which shows that Femininity is not incompatible with economic success); France and Taiwan score moderately Feminine.

Some students of Japan have argued that Japan is a unique case, that there is no country like it. The scores for Japan on the four dimensions demonstrate that only on one dimension, Masculinity, does Japan score "unique," that is, beyond all the other 39 countries in the sample. In other respects, Japan is no more "unique" than any other country on the list. The data in Table 3 also show that there is not such a thing as a "Western" value system to which the value system of Japan or of Asia can be opposed: France, Germany, Sweden and the United States are all very different from each other in some respects. America is not too different from Japan on Power Distance; France is similar on Uncertainty Avoidance, Germany on Individualism and Masculinity; only Sweden opposes itself to Japan on all four dimensions. Nevertheless, what is unique about Japan in the data of Table 2 is that no other country is similar to it on all four dimensions.

In Figure 2, I show a computer-produced "dendrogram" which groups the 40 countries according to the similarity of their scores on all four dimensions taken together. The horizontal axis indicates the percent of error which we have to tolerate to be able to consider 2 countries as scoring exactly alike. Thus, Belgium and France, Brazil and Turkey, Switzerland and Germany score very much alike without error tolerance. If we accept 10 percent error, the United States, Australia, Canada, Great Britain, Ireland and New Zealand all form one cluster. However, in the "dendrogram" of Figure 2, Japan is the country that stays alone longer than any other country. We need to accept 20 percent error before we can group the data from Japan with those of Colombia, Mexico and Venezuela.

Origins of Japan's Position on the Four Dimensions

The quantitative picture as presented by Japan's scores on the four dimensions is in reasonable harmony with comparative qualitative pictures of Japanese society and work organizations drawn by students of Japan, both foreign and Japanese, such as Benedict (1946), Whitehill and Takezawa (1968), Kawasaki (1969), Dore (1973), Azumi (1974), Yoshimori (1976) and Murayama (1977).

The origins of the value position of Japanese in a global perspective should obviously be sought in Japan's history. We find evidence of extreme masculinity in the role of the *samurai* with its stress on masculine assertiveness and honor and its absolute sex role separation. High Uncertainty Avoidance fits with the history of an insular society, which deliberately kept itself isolated from the rest of the world for centuries. In both cases, the contrast between Japan and the Chinese culture countries of Hong Kong and Taiwan is striking, and this has been confirmed by many authors.

Japan's average position on the Individualism scale must be seen in temporal perspective. There is evidence (Hofstede, 1980: chapter 8) that Individualism increases when wealth increases. There is little doubt that Japan today is more Individualist than in 1945, and that the increased wealth of the Japanese has contributed to this. But the history of Japanese society over the past centuries shows elements reflecting Collectivism (as compared to Western countries) as well as Individualism (as compared to, for example, China). Japanese capitalism was fostered by the state and did not arise from individual initiative and competition like in Great Britain or the United States. On the industrial scene, Japanese companies strike their Western competitors by their ability to cooperate (Americans speak of "Japan, Inc."). Japanese employees show a relatively stronger loyalty to their firm than employees in, for example, the United States (Marsh and Mannari, 1977). On the other hand, Japanese society is built on lineal families (one couple of each generation), not extended families like in China. Younger sons have to leave the parental home and are forced into other activities, which makes Japanese society considerably more dynamic than Asiatic societies based on expandable extended families.

Japan's average position on the Power Distance scale reflects the coexistence, puzzling to some Westerners, of a strong sense of hierarchy with the consultation of subordinates and consensus decision making. (Sasaki, 1973; Yoshimori, 1976). The power of the superior is not absolute. Azumi (1974: 522) stresses that loyalty in Japanese history was directed towards a position, rather than towards that position's occupant. This points to institutional power rather than personal power which fits with high Uncertainty Avoidance but moderate Power Distance. We find a similar situation in the German-speaking countries, in which Uncertainty Avoidance is moderate and Power Distance low.

Some Consequences for Japan's Further Development and Internationalization

Any type of prediction, of course, is speculative but I shall try anyway. In the period 1950–75, Japan showed a rate of economic growth unparalleled by any other nation. I have studied the relationships between economic growth for 1960–70 (the period preceding the Hermes surveys) and the Hermes value dimensions. It appears that, if we take all 40 countries together, there is no relationship. However, if we take only the 19 wealthier countries (which include Japan) it is the countries with lower Individualism, stronger Uncertainty Avoidance and larger Power Distances (among these wealthier countries) that have shown the faster growth (Hofstede, 1980: 330). In comparison to other wealthy countries Japan meets all three criteria. However, this is only true for the post–World War II period. If we take the 1925–50 period, we find, for example, that it is the wealthy *weaker* Uncertainty Avoidance countries that grew more in this period (Hofstede, 1980: 205); this is because it includes World War II, in which the countries with stronger Uncertainty Avoidance (and stronger Masculinity: Germany,

Italy, Japan) played a more aggressive role at first, and suffered greater losses later on.

Now we are clearly entering another historical period (say 1975–2000) and it remains to be seen whether the particular value configuration of Japan is functional or dysfunctional for further economic development in this new period. Of course we should also ask ourselves whether the values themselves will remain unchanged. The Hermes data indicate for the 1968–72 period a sizable worldwide shift toward greater Individualism, a weaker shift in a majority of countries toward increased Masculinity and smaller Power Distances, and some indication of increased Uncertainty Avoidance. However, these shifts do not substantially affect the order in which the countries appear on the dimensions, and there is no sign of convergence between countries (scores are not becoming more similar); rather there is evidence of divergence (value differences between countries are becoming larger). I therefore assume that Japan will retain its relative value position as we saw it in Table 3 for the foreseeable future as well.

The combination of strong Uncertainty Avoidance and moderate Collectivism has placed Japan in an excellent position for the production of quality goods, and it will probably continue such production. Quality production presupposes a strong sense of order, avoiding the unexpected; moderate Collectivism allows mutual help in achieving quality objectives, as we find in the Japanese quality control cycles which have acquired worldwide fame. Other countries—like the United States—try to copy them, but I doubt whether managers in these other countries realize the role which national value systems play in making the quality control cycles possible.

Some of the new global problems which make the 1975–2000 period different from the previous one, are, besides the maintenance of world peace, the shortage of essential materials and energy, and the maintenance of an unpolluted environment. Conservation of energy is not just a technical or economical problem; it has all kinds of societal and value implications. There is a triangular relationship between a society's wealth, its Individualism, and its per capita energy consumption. Japanese values are shifting towards greater Individualism, but the energy shortage may be a factor that effectively curbs this process, for example by reducing the use of private cars. On the other hand, the more Japan is able to maintain its relatively Collectivist value system, the easier it will be for people to share resources, thus saving energy. The generation and use of energy in a nation, however, also has a symbolic meaning. A statistical analysis (Hofstede, 1980: 315) shows for example that across 14 Western European countries, maximum allowed driving speeds on highways correlate significantly with Uncertainty Avoidance and Masculinity. More Uncertainty Avoiding countries sanction the expression of aggressiveness through pressing the accelerator. More Masculine countries sanction faster driving as a symbolic expression of Masculinity. "Energy" itself is a Masculine symbol, and the search for small and slow, energy-saving solutions of industrial problems may not be politically popular in strong Uncertainty Avoidance, high Masculinity Japan. For the protection of the environment, a Masculine value system is not an asset either. My analysis (Hofstede, 1980: 297) suggests that in more masculine countries so far priorities have been given to economic growth, even at the cost of sacrificing the environment, while only the more Feminine countries have at times reduced economic growth in the interest of conservation. Tsurumi (1977) has pointed to the different ways in which (Masculine) Japan and (less Masculine) China attack their pollution problems. Pollution will continue to present Japan with huge problems and may force it to measures which conflict with its Masculine values.

As far as Japan's internationalization goes, a strong Uncertainty Avoidance value system does not help make the average Japanese flexible abroad, nor does it facilitate understanding among the Japanese public for other countries' values. Benedict (1946: 225) has already remarked that the Japanese seemed to adapt less easily in the United States than Chinese or Thai. On the other hand, Japan's industrial success at home has led Japanese enterprises to a considerable expansion abroad, for which an understanding of the different thinking prevalent in other nations is essential, and they are learning by experience. It is likely that the success of Japanese enterprises abroad depends at least partly on the match between pre-existing local value systems and the value systems in the Japanese home company. Being more collectivist than most American and European managers, Japanese may have a relative advantage in countries or parts of countries in which collectivist values still prevail.

A crucial factor in the success of Japanese business abroad is the selection of managers for overseas assignments. As stated above, the strong Uncertainty Avoider is not the best foreign representative. However, within a country, values differ between individuals, as is pictured in Figure 1, so it is possible to select those with a relatively high tolerance for uncertainty (weak Uncertainty Avoidance) for working abroad. These very people may have a problem communicating with their home base, however. A strongly Uncertainty Avoiding society does not treat with kindness its sons or daughters who return with foreign ideas, as Kawasaki (1969) experienced. However, this problem is not unique to Japan. Minear (1980) shows that among Americans who studied Japan in the 1940s, those best able to understand Japan were those least appreciated by their American leadership. To a large extent, of course, Japan's international problems in the future are the world's problems. Japan is not so different, and other countries are not so different. Let us hope that we will succeed in resolving our problems together.

REFERENCES
Azumi, Koya
    1974   "Japanese Society: A Sociological View." In A. E. Tiedemann (ed.), *An Introduction to Japanese Civilization*. New York: Columbia University Press.
Benedict, Ruth
    1934   *Patterns of Culture*. Boston: Houghton Mifflin. 1959 ed.
    1946   *The Chrysanthemum and the Sword: Patterns of Japanese Culture*. New York: New American Library. 1974 ed.
Dore, Ronald P.
    1973   *British Factory—Japanese Factory: The Origins of National Diversity in Industrial Relations*. Berkeley, Calif: University of California Press.
Hofstede, Geert
    1980   *Culture's Consequences: International Differences in Work-Related Values*. Beverly Hills, Calif.: Sage.
Inkeles, Alex, and Daniel J. Levinson
    1969   "National Character: The Study of Modal Personality and Sociocultural Systems." In G. Lindzey and E. Aronson (eds.), *The Handbook of Social Psychology*. 2d ed. Vol. 4.
Kassem, M. Sami
    1974   "A Tale of Two Countries: Japan and Britain." *Columbia Journal of World Business,* 9 (2): 35–48.
Kawasaki Ichiro
    1969   *Japan Unmasked*. Rutland, Vt.: Charles E. Tuttle.
Marsh, Robert M., and Mannari Hiroshi
    1977   "Organizational Commitment and Turnover: A Prediction Study." *Administrative Science Quarterly,* 22: 57–75.

Minear, Richard H.
    1980   "Cross-cultural Perception and World War II: American Japanists of the 1940s and Their Images of Japan." *International Studies Quarterly*, 24 (4): 555–80.
Murayama Motofusa
    1977   "The Oriental Paradigm in Business Value Systems." In Y. H. Poortinga (ed.), *Basic Problems on Cross-Cultural Psychology*. Amsterdam: Swets and Zeitlinger.
Parsons, Talcott, and Edward A. Shils
    1951   *Toward a General Theory of Action*. Cambridge, Mass.: Harvard University Press. 1967 ed.
Sasaki Naoto
    1973   "A Comparative Study of the Decision-Making Process: Japan and the West." *Sophia Economical Review*, 19 (2–3): 37–46.
Tsurumi Kazuko
    1977   "Some Potential Contributions of Latecomers to Technological and Scientific Revolution—A Comparison Between Japan and China." In R. Dahrendorf et al., *Scientific-Technological Revolution: Social Aspects*. Beverly Hills, Calif.: Sage.
Whitehill, Arthur M., and Shin-Ichi Takezawa
    1968   *The Other Worker: A Comparative Study of Industrial Relations in the United States and Japan*. Honolulu: East-West Center Press.
Yoshimori Masaru
    1976   *Japanese Management: A Comparison with Western Management Style*. Fontainebleau: INSEAD.

POLITICAL PRINCIPLES
AND JAPANESE SOCIETY

Kamishima Jirō

Introduction

Ever since the Age of Discovery, the molding of the world has been dominated by the expansion of the West. Along with this expansion, the cognitive framework that originated and developed in the West has come to acquire universality. Despite the fact that the center of the Western world itself shifted after World War I from Western Europe to the United States, and that this European-American world has undergone significant changes in the very process of subjugating the non-Western world, particularly after World War II, the Western frame of reference has largely remained intact. That is, the European-American world has by now not only successfully permeated the four corners of the world geographically; it has also generated a situation in which the peoples of the world, especially intellectuals, have adapted themselves to westernization and come to consider that the proper cognition of the world is possible only by making Western cognitive tools their own. Japanese intellectuals have by no means been exceptions.

But problems inevitably arise when we try to understand Japanese situations within the Western cognitive framework. These difficulties have heretofore been explained away by Japanese intellectuals as manifestations of Japanese "backwardness" or of the "distortion of modernity." Some have even reduced the whole range of problems to the "uni-ethnicity" of the Japanese nation—a virtual intellectual fraud. On the contrary, the real problem lies in the framework itself.

In order to overcome this pitfall, it is necessary for the Japanese to extract their own cognitive framework (which could be developed into a universal one) from within the very situations in which they find themselves, just as Europeans and Americans have done. This paper, albeit no more than programmatic and confined to the field of political science, is a step in this direction. In order to tackle this job, I will tap the Japanese heritage in the following ways. First, I will go back to the rich reservoir of the Japanese language, hoping that it might possibly shed light on some aspects of reality that the Indo-European languages have not been able to grapple with.

Secondly, I will take advantage of the peculiar history of Japan which for a long time has enthusiastically imported, accepted and accumulated the advanced cultures of China, India, the Orient, Western Europe and the United States. This tradition is helpful in extracting a new cognitive framework, through the comparison of different frameworks which are already blended together in our own culture. The new framework generated in this way could perhaps enable us to decipher the massive changes that are taking place in today's world and the realities of the emergent international society.

My book *Kindai Nihon no seishin kōzō* (The Mental Structure of Modern Japan), published in 1961, analyzed the mental structure of modern Japanese by tracing it back to early modern times when its prototype was established. In doing so, I constructed a theory of middle range, the *mura* model, based on existing political theories inherited from the West. The mura model seemed legitimate with respect to Japanese society up to the time of publication. Later, the steep economic growth of the 1960s almost totally obliterated the basic structure of the mura itself. Consequently, the model seemingly lost its utility in analyzing contemporary Japan. At the same time, however, the fragments of the mura archetype still exist in various situations. If this is the case, I consider it worth identifying these remnants in order to understand Japanese society. If we can reconstruct the fragmented mura and, through this process, abstract proper cognitive tools, then we might be able to discern clearly the rationality in what has hitherto been construed as irrational.

Two Types of Society: JUNKA (Familiarization) and IKA (Strangerization)

Since the end of the war, discussions on Japanese society and culture have been one of the most popular topics among Japanese intellectuals. The basic question seems to be, what kind of society is Japan? It is, therefore, of great importance to understand the fundamental characteristics of Japanese society. But how are we to grasp these characteristics?

Yanagita Kunio, who made a gigantic contribution to the establishment of folklore studies in Japan from the end of the Meiji era to the postwar period, once remarked that the natural environment of the Japanese islands was unique, and that the situation in which the Japanese found themselves was quite remarkable (Yanagita, 1954: 163). His ideas on this subject can be summarized as follows: First of all, Japan is an insular country, and according to Yanagita, this was decisive in the formation of its society. Secondly, he pointed out that "group mindedness" has existed ever since, or even before, people came to inhabit the islands of Japan.

Arguments proposed by various authors can be regarded as so many attempts to understand the kind of society that Yanagita described. Among these arguments, there can be distinguished two different sorts, one of which can be termed "the theory of unitary society," another "the theory of cultural pluralism." The former emphasizes the homogeneous nature of Japanese society, maintaining that it is composed of a unitary race, that its language is a unitary language, and that, accordingly, its culture is of a unitary nature. The latter theory of "cultural pluralism," on the other hand, emphasizes the heterogeneity of Japanese society. According to this theory, Japanese society is held to be composed of several races and cultures. This theory was first formulated by Oka Masao, who studied under Yanagita and assisted him in editing *Minzoku*, a journal of ethnology, under his leadership. He later took leave of Yanagita when this journal was discontinued, and went to Vienna to study ethnology. According to his doctoral thesis *Cultural Layers of Archaic Japan* (*Kultur-Schichten in Alt-Japan*, 1933), Japan was made up of five different cultures. This marked the launching of the theory of cultural pluralism in Japan. Thus, after the war, several versions of "cultural pluralism" were proposed, the most important of which was the one presented by Katō Shūichi in the book *Hybrid Culture* (1956). In this well-known work, Katō made a distinction between thoroughbred culture and hybrid culture, describing the Japanese culture as the latter type. According to him, all cultures alike take in and assimilate heterogeneous elements from other ethnic groups. However, the hybrid culture takes the exogenous elements into its very core.

On the basis of this theory of hybrid culture, let us now examine in detail how elements of Japanese culture are put together. The work worthy to note for our present concern is *The Chrysanthemum and the Sword* by Ruth Benedict, which has played an important role in the arguments on Japanese culture since the end of the war. Published in 1946, this work has attracted the attention of so many intellectuals that one could not discuss Japanese culture without reference to it.

In the opening remarks of the book, Benedict makes an interesting observation that the expression "but also" frequently appears in the literature on Japan, i.e., Japan is such and such a country, *but* the opposite is *also* true. The reader repeatedly finds this kind of puzzling account in the description of Japan; similar phrasing also appears in discussions among Japanese. For example, when a Japanese tries to criticize the opinions of somebody else, he often begins his statement in the following way: "I do not mean to say anything against you, but I would like to make several remarks." Despite such phrasing, his opinion often is just the opposite of the other person.

In comparison with this, the way Westerners state their opinions in debates is quite different. They begin their statements by such expressions as "my opinion is different from yours," or "I do not agree with you." In spite of such expressions, what follows afterward often does not differ much from what the other person stated. Such a difference in the manner of speech, I think, is of more significance than it might appear. When a Japanese says, "I have nothing against you," what he really means is not that he has the same opinion as the other person but rather that he will act together with other people as a member of the community. After making this explicit, he goes on to state his own (or group) opinion. In contrast to this, by stating "my opinion is different," a Westerner means not that his opinion is substantially different from the other person's but that he wishes to state his own opinion as distinct from that of the other person. Despite the difference in the process of the discussion, similar results are obtained, provided that the discussion is presided over by a skillful chairman, since co-ordinating different opinions is an ideal in both societies.

Thus we can distinguish between two different types of society. Let us consider again our organic model. Human beings have relationships with the human environment as well as with the material environment. These two relationships provide the basic conditions for human life. Man has to establish a relationship of material metabolism with the environment. On the other hand, he also has relationships with other human beings and exchanges symbols with them. We can call the latter relationship mental metabolism. Eating food, for example, can be regarded as a behavior of physical metabolism. By taking food into one's body, one fills the stomach. In order for his stomach to become full, however, he himself, not any other person, must eat. Therefore, this physical metabolism provides the condition for the uniqueness of man. However, when a mother feeds her child, even if she herself is physically hungry, she feels satisfied. Thus, human relationships play a very important role even in such a simple behavior as eating. We can see from this example that the human individual is characterized by mutuality as well as uniqueness. Both of these elements are indispensable components of human beings.

These two aspects of life are fulfilled by the corresponding functions of *ika* and *junka*, which could be translated as strangerization and familiarization. The former signifies the tendency to estrange oneself from others, the latter to adapt to them. In any society, which is by definition composed of plural selves, both ika and junka functions are at work simultaneously. However, it seems that one or the other of the two is operating more forcefully in concrete historical situations. If this is indeed the case, we can classify societies into two types: one in which ika prevails (strangerizing society), and the other in which junka does (familiarizing society). The former tendency ultimately results in a class society, and the latter in a "diffuse" society where heterogeneous elements coexist without clear demarcations among them.

As an interesting manifestation of the estrangement tendency, a Japanese would feel difficulty in being the first to speak in discussions or conferences. When he does speak he would almost never fail to preface his speech with, "I am of the same opinion, but. . ." In contrast, the Westerner's preface would rather be, "I am of a different opinion." For the Japanese, a straightforward disagreement is expressed either among intimate friends or by a person in a clearly superior position. The former is acceptable because one knows that his disagreement would not hurt the intimate relationship; the latter because the expression is legitimated by authority. Similarly, in a class society, disagreement is openly expressed because the definition of the situation is fairly simple: one is talking either with his peers, i.e., those who belong to the same class, or with those who belong to other classes, in which case one can rely on the spiritual and physical support of his own class.

The phenomena of strangerization which emerge in the interaction process among human beings is based on the uniqueness of the human individual. On the other hand, the mutuality between individuals provides the basis from which the phenomena of familiarization derive. Both strangerization and familiarization are necessary for social life to be maintained, but the extent to which these two modes of social interaction are conspicuous is not always the same either at the individual level or at the social level; in some cases strangerization becomes predominant, in other cases familiarization, and a given society will have its own way of balancing the two. In cases where familiarization predominates over strangerization in a given society, I would like to use the expression "society of familiarization"; when the opposite is true I would like to call it a "society of strangerization."

In the relatively classless society of familiarization, various heterogeneous elements coexist side by side, so that a hybrid culture is likely to arise. In the other type of society, homogeneous elements gather together to form distinct classes exclusive of each other. Put differently, collectivities are easily developed which assert an individual existence of their own. Such a situation, needless to say, contributes to the development of individualism.

When comparing the differences between Western and Japanese societies, it is often said that Japanese society lacks recognition of the individual personality while in Western societies a condition favorable for the growth of the individual personality was formed early in history. This comparison, however, is not very adequate. It should be noted that in class societies, collectivities first assert their unique, individual existence, and from this situation individualism gradually develops. Just as a class makes its individuality distinct by forming a consistent standard of membership of its own, the individual becomes independent as a subject by taking himself as a measure of everything. This is how the individual personality is maintained in Western societies.

What we find in Japanese society is a different kind of individual personality. Here an individual shows his personality by taking other people as his measure. This is sometimes taken as evidence of the lack of individual personality, but this is not the case. Let me cite an example to illustrate my point. When you fly an airplane there are two ways to go about it. The pilot can control his plane by taking as a reference either the body of the plane or the environment outside the plane, that is, the horizon in this case. The former way of piloting is called "inside out," and the latter "outside in." In either of these cases, the pilot cannot control his plane without sober personal judgement (Hamaguchi, 1977: 252–54).

These considerations lead us to the following conclusion: that individual personality can remain intact not only in a society of strangerization (in the form of individualism) but also in a society of familiarization in a different form. Now that the basic framework has become clear, I wish to analyze the characteristics of these two types of society in more detail.

Society in an Insular Situation
Western societies fall into the category of "societies of strangerization" while Japanese society falls into the "societies of familiarization" category. In a society of familiarization a mixture both of ethnic groups and of cultures takes place. One might wonder whether America is not classified as a familiarization society together with Japan, since different races and cultures do coexist there. However, in the case of America, familiarization proceeds only within certain limits. Different ethnic groups are assimilated only to the extent that they all get the same American citizenship, and that is just about the extent of it. Note also that immigrants in America often live in ethnic residence districts distinct from surrounding areas. This obviously prevents the mixture of races.

In contrast to this, the process of mixing goes on to a far greater extent, even at the level of the family in Japan. This definitely distinguishes Japanese society from, say, American society, and makes Japan a typical example of the familiarizing society. The most important single factor that gave Japanese society its peculiar character was its geographical situation, as Yanagita recognized. Although Japan is sometimes compared to England, this comparison is not very adequate, for England is separated from the European continent by only about 20 miles, which is far closer than the distance between Japan and the Asian continent. Also note that the coastline of the Japan Sea is rather smooth, while the coastline of the Pacific is much more intricate. Thus its geographical features give us an impression that it is somewhat closed to the continent and open toward the Pacific Ocean.

Japan is surrounded by the sea on all sides, with several ocean currents flowing alongside. The largest of these currents is the Japan Current (Kuroshio), which runs northward from the coast of Formosa along the Pacific coast up to the west of Okinawa, where it divides and moves north as the Tsushima Current. These currents run into the Tsugaru Strait as well as the Soya Strait. From the north, on the other hand, the Kurile Current runs southward down to the northern coast of the mainland. We also find the Riman Current running southward along the coast of the Japan Sea. Thus Japan is situated where these various currents run against each other. The pattern of these currents suggests the probability that people and things came floating to Japan from the continent as well as from southern islands. Therefore, people and things of various sorts must have continued to come to Japan, and with them information about the outside world. But the opposite situation was unlikely to happen. As we can see from the way ocean currents run around the islands, it is more difficult for people to go out from these islands than to come in. This is an important point for us to bear in mind when we try to understand the nature of Japanese society, for it was on account of this geographical condition that Japan formed a kind of insular microcosm separated from the rest of the world.

The same remark stands true for the communities which were formed within Japanese society as a whole. The intricate geography full of mountains, valleys, and rivers hampered communication among these communities. Just as Japan as a whole was a microcosm insulated from the continent, each of the communities was a microcosm separated from the others by the natural environment. And as if enclosed by magic mirrors, those who were inside these communities could see what was going on outside them, but it was difficult for those on the outside to know what was going on within these communities.

Because of the ocean currents a journey to the Asian continent required the development of navigation. Even after sailing vessels began to be made, they had to wait for the seasonal monsoon winds to send the vessels to the continent. Shipwrecks were not infrequent, as the examples of Abe no Nakamaro and Ganjin show. Cultural exchange was obviously accompanied by great costs and risks, which only the central government could bear. Only the court could be directly in touch with the culture of the continent. Sophisticated cultures usually came to the capital first, and then gradually spread to the rest of the country. The pattern by which culture was propagated was thus established, and corresponding standards of cultural evaluation were gradually formed. As Yanagita Kunio pointed out, these standards took the capital to be culturally sophisticated and the countryside vulgar.

Another important factor which greatly influenced the development of Japanese society was its population density. There were many densely populated communities already in the Edo period. For example, in as early as the middle of the eighteenth century, the population of Edo was 500,000, that of Kyoto 500,000, and Osaka 400,000. These figures surpass those of most other cities in the world developed in the eighteenth century.

Kishimoto Minoru, in *Population Accumulation in Japan* (Nihon no jinkō shūseki), estimates the distribution of population in the Edo period and makes an interesting point. According to his estimate, among the areas that contained more than 3 percent of the entire Japanese population in 1750 were the areas around Osaka and Hyōgo, Aichi, and Niigata. The distribution changed in 1885. Though Osaka still held more than 3 percent of the total population, the proportion in Niigata decreased, and Hiroshima and Fukuoka increased instead. Although Tokyo does not appear as a densely populated area in the figure, this is due to the method of the estimation, for Kishimoto, while taking as the basis of his estimation the countries (*shu*) of those days, allocated the population according to today's administrative division. Since the Musashi district, in which Edo was situated, spreads over Tokyo, Kanagawa, and Saitama prefectures, this unduly reduced the population size of Edo (Kishimoto, 1968: 46–47).

What is to be noted in these figures is that Niigata held a remarkably great proportion of the entire population. This is accounted for by the fact that Niigata was a rich rice-producing district. We should also note that merchant shipping had developed to a great extent on the coasts of the Japan Sea during the Edo period. Japanese society, of course, depended on rice as its primary source of nutrition. Compared to barley, unpolished rice is very rich in nutrition. This is one of the reasons that Japanese communities could grow so dense. Historians estimate that communities based on rice farming were established in Japan in the Yayoi period. Rice farming was the legacy of the Yayoi culture. There are also aspects of the culture of the Jōmon period which facilitated the growth of the population. In the Jōmon period primitive farming based on taro cultivation had been practiced. Since Japan consists of a number of small islands and is surrounded by the sea on all sides, this primitive farming is believed to have been accompanied by fishing. In primitive fishing the catch was distributed to all— "A piece for those who took part, a piece for those who couldn't." This custom, practiced until very recently on Gaja Island, seems to be an expansion of the spirit of primitive fishery. This tradition of equal distribution was handed over to the farming society established in the Yayoi period, and its spirit lingered even after people left the mountains and started farming on the plains. While taking over the custom of equal distribution on the one hand, they produced rice with rich nutritive value on the other. The conditions were thus favorable for population growth.

As the population increased, intimate communication relationships developed within these communities. This tradition of close communication was also transmitted to later periods, and even after the modern industrialization process began, Japan remained a country with a strong urge for close mutual communication.

Japanese Politics

We have considered Japan's unique geographic and cultural heritage, and thus, can account for various heterogeneous elements found mixed with each other in Japanese society and culture. In some cases, exogenous elements remained intact and unmixed, just as if they had been put in a capsule or, to use an actual example, a storehouse such as the Shōsōin Temple treasure house. Customs and ideas, as well as things, often retain elements of the past. It was for this reason that Katō Shūichi characterized Japanese culture as "hybrid culture."

The Japanese language is a very good example of the hybrid nature of Japanese society, for its development seems to be different from that of many other languages. Indo-European languages, of which Germanic and Celtic languages are the derivatives, stemmed from the ancient Indo-Hittite language. These languages developed by repeated differentiation. The same holds true for the languages of Uralian descent. Japanese, however, did not follow such processes of development. It was, as I see it, compounded of varieties of language introduced into Japanese society by different ethnic groups coming from divergent areas of the world. In this respect, Japanese is, as it were, a language of assimilation, made from a concoction of various sorts of languages, and should be regarded as distinct from languages of dissimulation which develop through differentiation and purification. Not only the language but also the Japanese race and the culture in general must have been formed through a similar process.

As I have already made clear, it was above all the geographical situation that played a decisive role in determining these fundamental characteristics of Japanese society. Faced with this situation, the newcomers to the islands were forced to live in harmony with those already there. Put differently, Japan was a society with a strong assimilating coercion, where heterogeneous elements had to live together with each other. Those who lived in this society, therefore, must have had some kind of familiarizing obsession. Such a situation, no doubt, was typical of a familiarizing society. The strangerizing society presents a sharp contrast to this. It is typically organized as a class society, where coercion works as the regulative mechanism. People living in this type of society tend to develop a strangerizing obsession.

In the familiarizing society, mutuality rather than individuality becomes the dominant social principle, and on the basis of this principle people tend to develop a compulsive idea that they have to act in accordance with others. As a result, in Japan different lineages, cultures, and languages mixed, and a new culture and language were created. Since Japanese society thus made it imperative for people to get along with each other, political integration tended to assume a "soft" and "gentle" form. It rarely, if ever, assumed a violent form of administration based on the military power.

Political integration based on military power (i.e., ruling by conquest) presupposes the division of a society into two different categories: the conqueror on the one hand, and the conquered on the other. On the basis of this division, political integration is attained by the exercise of military power; that is to say, the conquered are either killed or enslaved. The ruling class and the ruled are, therefore, in constant opposition. Various conflicts which could occur between these classes also tend to be settled by violence. Consequently, the ruling class and those ruled are likely to develop heterogeneous cultures exclusive of each other.

Since there is always the chance of rebellion, it is necessary for the rulers to take measures to cope with rebellion and prepare for a possible defeat. For this reason, the ruling class is often required to secure for themselves some safe place where they can take flight in case of danger. The geography of Japan, however, made it extremely difficult for the ruling class to take such measures, and this partly explains why conquest by violence and the subsequent political administration based on the sword was difficult to attain. Political integration took on a completely different aspect, and the state was established on a totally different basis in this country.

When outsiders happen to come drifting into Japan, they are in a state of powerlessness in most cases. It is extremely unlikely that these powerless people could conquer and dominate those who had already gained power. However, if they happened to have a sophisticated culture from which the natives could benefit, these people might be trusted and respected. It is possible in this case that the native people voluntarily submitted to the newcomers and made them their political leaders. In fact, this seems to have been the dominant style of political rule in Japanese society. For those at the top to remain in power, it was necessary to maintain their superior level of culture. It was for this reason that Japanese rulers have made continuous efforts to incorporate the fruits of the advanced civilization developed on the continent.

Thus, it seems proper to characterize continental societies as basically strangerizing and oceanic ones as familiarizing. In political terms, the former tends to develop "hard" politics based on military force, and the latter to develop "soft" politics based on sentiments. With the preceding considerations as precepts, let us now turn to the field of political science as more narrowly defined.

For this, it is necessary to relativize existing political theories. The key concepts in these theories have been Conflict, Domination, and Autonomy, but they are not without their own limitations. This leads me to hypothesize some new ones around which to organize new theories. Physics has broken matter into molecules, atoms, electrons, protons, nuclei, etc., and, at the same time systematically reorganized them, for example, in the form of the periodic table of elements. I am suggesting that political science, too, can break down the logic of the world of politics into elements and locate them in its own orderly "periodic table." In this spirit, I will, in the rest of this paper, take up the challenge of formulating a basic framework for a new kind of political perception.

Political Principles

To the political principles of Conflict, Domination, and Autonomy, I have added "Kikyō" (involution or involvement), "Karma," and "Assimilation" (see Table 1).

No political community functions on the basis of a single principle alone, but rather on multiple, interwoven principles. These principles are related both to economic production and to social interaction. Concerning the former, three modes of economic labor can be distinguished: collecting, rearing, and fabricating. On the other hand, there are also three modes of social interaction: empathy, representation, and alienation. By combining these modes, therefore, we get a diagram with nine cells (Table 2). The political principles enumerated above can fill in six of these cells, which leaves three other cells empty, as is shown in the table. Other political principles have yet to be discovered to fill in these cells, and so the scheme I propose in this paper is of a provisional nature. Now let me briefly explain each of the principles starting with the more familiar ones.

Conflict and domination. What I term conflict is the principle by which political integration is achieved in a situation of radical opposition. It has been widely held that the *ultima ratio* of conflict is violence or force of arms, which I think is mistaken. Rather, it could be reduced to personal commitment for which one makes a furious dash for a cause, without thought for one's life. A Japanese book on the art of war, *Tosenkyo,* written as early as the eleventh or twelfth century, already pointed this out in the concept of *shin'ei*. This volume integrated the military tactics of the Minamoto family and the Ōe family, and it formed the basis of traditional Japanese military tactics, presenting a sharp contrast to the Chinese military tactics advocated by Suntze (Kamishima, 1972: 192–96). (Incidentally, the military tactics of Suntze were later introduced to Europe, and provided the basis of

TABLE 1

POLITICAL PRINCIPLES

Components	Conflict	Domination	Autonomy	Assimilation	Karma	Kikyō Involution or involvement
Ultima Ratio	mana (morale)	violence	self-determination	civilization (potlatch)	karma	jinshin (volonté générale)
Group Structure	friend-enemy	dominance-submission	consociation	center-periphery	pratitya or samutpāda (reciprocity)	matsurō-shirasu (pietas-nonviolent reign)
Organization	order	command	persuasion	indoctrination	dharma	yosashi (devolution)
Activities	disorder	resistance	protest	zào, fǎn	yoga	mono no aware (sensitization)
Social Change	rise & fall	violent revolution	reform	cultural revolution	saṃsāra (panta rhei)	naru (Werden)
Value	life	justice	self-sufficiency	affluence	śānti	serenity
Social Base	reifying constraints	strangetizing constraints	anarchic constraints	apolitical constraints	de-imaging constraints	familiarizing constraints

TABLE 2
FORM OF INTERACTION

Economic Production	Empathy	Representation	Alienation
Collecting	karma		conflict
Rearing	kikyō (involution)	assimilation	
Fabricating		autonomy	domination

modern military tactics used by Napoleon. He is said to have carried a translation of Suntze in his pocket.) Suntze's teaching runs somewhat as follows: If you have a military force 10 times as strong as that of the enemy, besiege the enemy and wait until he surrenders; if your force is 5 times as strong, make an active attack on the enemy; if you have a force of the same strength as the enemy, fight to the best of your ability; and if you have a force weaker than the enemy, take to flight, for it is sheer folly to stock to a battle which you are certain to lose.

The principles laid down in *Tosenkyo* are radically opposed to this. The book denounces the tactics of Suntze as based on fraud. Emphasizing the importance of spirit and morale, the authors of the volume regard fixed determination as more valuable than anything else. According to the authors, to go forward and fight to the end is the only way to win the battle regardless of the numerical strength of the military force. As compared with the volume by Suntze which exhorts one to become a fox when necessary, *Tosenkyo* extolls remaining a lion under any circumstances.

The spirit shown in *Tosenkyo* was handed down to later generations in Japan. For example, this spirit can be found almost in pure form in *Hagakure,* an old document which recorded the teachings of Yamamoto Tsunetomo. Yamamoto was a samurai in the Nabeshima *han* (clan) who survived the Warring Countries period, and the ethics in his teaching makes him the legitimate successor to the spirit of *Tosenkyo*. Just like the authors of *Tosenkyo,* Yamamoto acknowledges only going forward, without retreating even for a minute, as the legitimate way of the samurai. "The way of the samurai is nothing else than to die"— this well-known opening phrase shows in what spirit this book was written. He idealizes the Nabeshima clan to the level of an absolute value which is unrivalled even by the shōgun or by the *tennō* (emperor), and for which one can sacrifice everything, even one's life. For this reason, his doctrine was deemed dangerous by the authorities of the shogunate government, and *Hagakure* remained a banned book until the middle of the Meiji period.

To cite a more recent example, we could see the same tradition of conflict at work in the Second World War. As is well known, the Japanese leaders at that time emphasized the importance of spiritual power. According to their understanding, they were fighting a battle between the white races with material power and the colored races with spiritual power. While Americans were trying to build material strength to prepare for battle, the Japanese were trying to reinforce their spiritual power. And while Americans were making attempts to develop new and better kinds of radar, the Japanese were training to see in the dark. The final measure that the Japanese resorted to in the last phase of the battle was the well-known fanatic suicide tactics. This obviously reminds us of the teachings of *Tosenkyo* and *Hagakure,* and, indeed, could not have taken place without this tradition.

Despite the fact that Japanese society was formed as a familiarizing society in which conflicts seem unlikely, the principle of conflict took a severe form in this country. The strangerizing element, smoldering in a latent form, engendered severe conflicts within some small circles of the society. Thus losers of a battle were often pursued tenaciously by the ruler, and if caught they were usually not allowed to live.

Through these severe conflicts, the ultima ratio of the conflict principle took clear shape. The concept of "the original spirit" which appears in the *Kojiki* and *Nihonshoki* explicates this ultima ratio. According to these volumes, this original spirit was what started history and gave life to man. This concept closely resembles the concept of *mana* in the Melanesian and Polynesian islands.

The custom of *harakiri* is directly related to the tradition of conflict. This tradition is so deeply rooted in Japanese culture that the custom of harakiri remained even after the Meiji Revolution. Compared to Japan where the principle of conflict took a clear form relatively early in history, it developed only gradually in Europe. True, theoretical studies about conflict were made by various authors such as Thomas Hobbes, Herbert Spencer, Karl Marx, Friedrich Nietzsche, Georg Simmel, Carl Schmitt, Harold Lasswell, and Ralf Dahrendorf.

It is extremely doubtful, however, whether the essence of conflict has been made clear enough.

For example, an eminent political theorist of Nazi Germany, Carl Schmitt, made efforts to lay bare the concept of politics and believed that the recognition of different groups of people as friends and enemies was the starting point of all politics. On the assumption that the political engenders violence and force as its necessary outcome, he tries to understand politics by taking as his reference point war, rebellions, and violent revolutions. He could thus make clear the hidden structure of the conflict principle. Nevertheless, his thinking bears resemblance to that of Suntze in some respects, for both approve the assumption that the outcome of a battle depends on the numerical strength of the military force. In assuming thus, one is forced to introduce machinations into one's political thinking to cope with the case in which the military power of the enemy surpasses that of one's own in strength. In consequence, his political thinking led to the elucidation of the principle of domination rather than that of conflict. The ultima ratio of the conflict principle itself remains unclarified in his theory.

The same remark can be applied to Machiavelli, who laid the foundation of modern political science. It is well known that he advocated above all else violence and fraud (which he called the "tactics of beasts") as effective measures of political domination. We can cite many other authors in Europe who developed the logic of domination based on violence and fraud. They are all related to the tradition of Suntze and can be contrasted to the Japanese tradition in this respect.

The reason the principle of domination has attracted so many European authors should be clear enough. European societies provided the stage on which bloody scenes of domination by conquest unfolded again and again. Domination is attained through violence, by which the conquered become the ruled class. Since the class societies subsequently formed are characterized by a constant class opposition, the ruling class takes violence as the ultima ratio. On the other hand, violent revolution easily comes to be justified as a legitimate right on the part of the ruled class.

Let us summarize these remarks on conflict. As Table 1 shows, the ultima ratio of the conflict principle is mana or morale. The latent structure based on this conflict principle is "friend-enemy." One might note here that it was Carl Schmitt who abstracted this aspect as a political theory. The organizational principle that results from conflict is "order" (*chi*) which is a condition where the victor-loser relationship is frozen. The typical activities under this condition tend to aim at liquidating the frozen relationship, and we designate it as "disorder" (*ran*). What we call "rise and fall" (*kobo*) in the political arena is the result of such activities. The kind of value pursued is "life" (*seimei*) in both the physical and spiritual senses of the word. The underlying social base is "reifying constraints" (*bukka kyōsei*).

The second principle is "domination" (*shihai*). Machiavelli said that the monarch needs to be both a lion and a fox, and he is echoed in Suntze. Inasmuch as "violence" (*bōryoku*) is the ultima ratio, artifice is indispensable. The prevalent structure here is "dominance-submission" (*shihai-fukujū*); and the activities tend to be "resistance" (*teikō*) against command. The value pursued is "justice" (*seigi*), which goes, needless to say, counter to its ultima ratio. Such a society is based on "strangerizing constraints" (*ika-kyōsei*).

Autonomy and assimilation. In European societies, political power gradually was concentrated in the monarch under the absolute state that emerged after the end of the Middle Ages. It was through this process of concentration of political power that the concept of sovereignty took shape. This, however, is but one side of the story, for accompanying this process were such historical events as the riots of the peasantry and the rebellions of the bourgeoisie. These rebellions brought forth the concept of sovereign rights of the people.

Therefore, two antagonistic movements have characterized the political history of modern Europe. The theory of the divine right of kings on the one hand and the theory of "representation" on the other are the direct outcomes of these movements. Thus, the logic of domination and the logic of autonomy were formulated and developed out of this situation. The relationship between these two logics was by no means simple. The latter logic was often caught in the former, and doctrines of domination were stated and legitimated by the terminology of autonomy. This is how such terms as self-government and self-control came to be used. It is interesting to note that the terms which originally were applied to the determination of one's fate by others were transformed to mean a situation where one has authority over one's own fate.

The logic of domination took the shape of *raison d'état* in the process of the development of colonial markets by European countries. This actually justified robbery and massacre by the state, for according to the concept of raison d'état, the state had a reality of its own and a law of motion independent of the individuals. It was only after World War II that this concept was radically challenged.

So as to prevent the power of the state from growing too large and corrupt, various political devices have been contrived. The theories of the separation of powers were formulated by John Locke and Montesquieu; a pluralistic theory of the state elaborated by Harold Laski, and the theory of poliarchy developed recently by Robert Dahl are other examples of the attempts to guarantee an institutional basis and to secure opportunities for political participation. The logic which has served as the guiding principle for such movements was, needless to say, the logic of autonomy. In order to examine this principle, it is necessary to study Rousseau, who eagerly talked of the ideal of democracy in his *Social Contract* (1762).

Rousseau's assumption is quite different from, indeed, the opposite of Machiavelli's, for he develops his theory on the assumption that man is honest and faithful in the state of nature. On the basis of this assumption he formulates the principle of autonomy which provides the foundation of the theory of democracy. The kind of democracy which he described was "democracy under the oak tree," that is to say, direct democracy where everyone can participate directly in the determination of things.

Since it is extremely difficult to apply the principle of direct democracy to large scale modern societies, direct democracy is naturally replaced by representative democracy. To be sure, at the outset when this system began, it was relatively clear that delegates were to act in accordance with the intention of the electorate. Representative democracy, however, makes it almost a necessity that delegates use their own discretion at least to a certain extent. It was for this reason that the concept of the "collective will" of the people was worked out. Delegates were not conceived to be representing the individual voters any more but the collective will in general. By this concept, therefore, delegates come to be authorized to force their intention upon the electorate. Ideas similar to this are already expressed in the work of Hobbes; the theory of national representation or the national political party developed by Edmund Burke can be cited as other examples.

Representative democracy, institutionalized in this way, obviously degenerates into something different from the original ideal. Domination is substituted for autonomy before one is aware. The element of domination is intermingled surreptitiously with that of autonomy in the institution of democracy, and in fact this institution has switched autonomy into a form of domination. The principle of autonomy, developed in theoretical forms in Europe, has always been followed by the principle of domination.

Max Weber, for example, elaborating the sociological theory of domination in *Wirtschaft und Gesellschaft* (1922), distinguished three types of domination on the basis of legitimacy: traditional, charismatic, and legal. Interpreting his description according to the framework I set forth in this paper, his interest lay in the mechanism by which the autonomy principle was transformed to the domination principle and the way in which the latter was indoctrinated by the terminology of the former. The autonomy principle was, therefore, conceived by Weber as inseparable from domination principle.

To be sure, there are attempts to separate these two and extract the autonomy principle in its purity. An American political scientist Charles Meriam tried to base his political theory on the concept of coordination; Robert Plunger also set power politics clearly against autonomy of the citizens and tried to develop the theory of political participation. At any rate, the core concept of the autonomy principle is self-determination, and in the case where self-determination is made an inalienable right, it easily leads to anarchism. W. Godwin, P.J. Proudhon, Max Stirner, etc., all deemed self-determination of great importance and maintained that social determination should be complete codetermination. For this reason social solidarity cannot but take the form of a loose alliance in their thought.

In Japan, Kōtoku Shūsui, Ōsugi Sakae, Ishikawa Sanshirō, and Tsuji Jun were influenced by these European theories. But of more importance are the theories elaborated apart from these European versions of the autonomy theory. Andō Shōeki, a unique philosopher who advanced materialism in the Edo period, Tanaka Shōzō (a thinker in the Meiji period who has recently come to be reevaluated as a democrat as well as a forerunner of the anti-pollution movement), and Gondō Seikyō, who is said to have had a great influence on the young military officers involved in the coup d'état of May 5, 1932, were all theorists of autonomy in Japan. Gondō Seikyō developed a unique theory of "*shashoku* autonomy." *Sha* and *shoku* in this Japanese word mean respectively the deity of earth and the deity of crops, so that "shashoku autonomy" might be translated as "earth-crop autonomy." What he meant by this was the ideal state in which the political affairs of the nation are run by autonomous local communities. He considered this form of political integration to have existed in the tradition of Oriental societies and contrasted his doctrine with the political doctrine introduced from Europe after the Meiji Revolution. According to him, the latter leads to government by authorities, while the former leads to government by people themselves.

One of the distinctive features of the Japanese version of autonomy theory is that violence is denied as a means for achieving the ideal. In European versions, on the contrary, violence is usually conceived as indispensable to realize self-determination.

Summarized briefly, the ultima ratio of the autonomy principle is self-determination. The latent pattern of grouping is "consociation." The method of organization here is "persuasion" (*settoku*), and the corresponding activities "protestation" (*igi*). Change takes the form of a "dualistic evolution" (*gubun-shinka*), that is, evolution on both sides of merits and demerits (Zhāng Bing Lin, 1906). The value pursued is "self-sufficiency" (*jisoku*). Operating at the social base is "anarchic constraints" (*museifu-kyōsei*).

Let us now turn to the principle of assimilation. In order to make this principle clear, I will begin by introducing an interesting custom practiced in various primitive societies. This custom, which is called "potlatch" in a Canadian Indian tribe and is known as such in cultural anthropology, is described by several authors. In these societies, a person who wishes to become the leader of his tribe treats neighbors in an extravagant way and thereby raises his social status. This custom is by no means limited to these primitive societies. Leadership based on a similar custom is also found in Japan. For example, those of high social status were implicitly constrained to give alms. The higher the social status, the greater amount he had to give. If he acted against the custom, he was ridiculed as stingy.

The custom of potlatch is widely distributed over the areas around the Pacific Ocean and is found in China as well. The tributary commerce ancient China developed with surrounding countries is a good illustration. The expression "tributary commerce" is a bit misleading in this case, for by paying tribute to the Chinese rulers, other countries could expect even greater returns from China. Chinese rulers considered themselves to be world leaders under *noblesse oblige* to benefit the surrounding backward nations with the fruits of their sophisticated civilization.

In fact, a similar principle is advanced in a form of political theory by Confucian philosophers. Rejecting the politics of power, the Confucianists recommend the politics of virtue as the ideal way for the political rulers to follow. According to their teaching, therefore, the Chinese rulers have to extend the benefits of their civilization gradually to the surrounding barbarian areas and make the barbarians follow them.

Thus there has been a form of political integration similar to potlatch, which I term the assimilation principle. It goes without saying that political integration on the basis of this principle alone could not have continued, especially in great empires such as China. For these empires to subsist, it was necessary to plunder as well as to give. The assimilation principle was therefore inseparably related to the domination principle. Even today, the traditional principle of assimilation, handed down from Confucianism, seems to remain active in the political thinking of the Chinese people. This, perhaps, was the cultural background which enabled China to denounce in bitter tones Soviet socialism as socialist imperialism.

While the assimilation principle has existed in the nations located in the Pacific sphere including Japan and China, and in various hunting tribes, attempts to theorize about it in clear terms are also found in today's Western countries. Kenneth Boulding, for example, in his work *Economy of Love and Fear* (1973), which called into question economic theories based on the concepts of exchange and exploitation, introduced the concept of "gifting" into his economic theory. His thinking can be understood as an attempt to adjust economic theory to the contemporary political situation where autonomy and assimilation are gaining in importance as principles of politics.

The fourth principle, then, is "assimilation," whose ultima ratio is benevolence of "civilization" (*bunmei*), material as well as spiritual. The potlatch of the North American Indians, tributary trade of China, and alms-giving in Japan are concrete expressions of this principle. The type of structure prevalent in this case is a center-periphery (civilized-uncivilized) relationship (*Naigaikai*); organization is achieved through indoctrination (*kyoka*); and political activities take the form of *zào, fǎn*, a Chinese expression which originally meant childish temper tantrums, but was refined as a political concept by Mao Tse-tung. In trying to achieve the value of "affluence" (*hō-jō*), activities in such a society are essentially cultural revolutions. Contemporary Chinese have a term (*hōsoku*) which actually combines this value of affluence with self-sufficiency. At the social base of the assimilation principle are "apolitical (non-action) constraints" (*mui-kyōsei*).

Karma and kikyō (involution). The movement of non-violent resistance founded by Gandhi is a case in point to illustrate the principle of karma. His thought, indeed, is very difficult to understand without assuming the karma principle. Especially noteworthy in Gandhi's thought is that he made a distinction between the law of the beast and the law of humanity. This naturally reminds us of the distinction between the two laws of politics traditionally recognized in India: *artha* (which is the law of material interests) and *dharma* (the sacred law).

The *Arthasastra* provides us with the idea of artha. The author, Kautilya, was a head advisor to the king Chandragupta of the Mauryan dynasty from the late fourth to the early third century B.C., and the book, which develops a very realistic theory of politics, is comparable to *The Prince* by Machiavelli. In this book, the author sets forth three component elements as the basis of the state: bureaucracy, armed force (i.e., a standing army of about 500,000), and a secret service for the supervision of the bureaucrats. He preached that the state be administered on the basis of these institutions.

Thus a systematic theory of artha had been established by as early as the beginning of the fourth century B.C. in India. The political theory based on dharma was formulated and put into practice as its antithesis in the third century B.C. under King Ashoka. The theory later was crystallized in the *Bhagavad Gita*, a poem thought to have been written in the first century A.D., which extolled the law of non-violence and emphasized the greatness of the power brought forth by truth, love, and non-violence. Gandhi was greatly influenced by the *Bhagavad Gita*. Thus political ideas based on the concept of dharma which have existed in Indian society ever since ancient times were transmitted to

Gandhi through this poem. It was out of this tradition that his philosophy of non-violence was born.

The ideas formulated in the Hindu society were transmitted to China through Buddhism, and then to Japan by way of China. For example, Taoism in China is very similar to Hinduism in its theoretical posture. Therefore, when Buddhism was transmitted from China to our country, Hindu elements in Taoism were also brought in and disseminated to the public at large. Beliefs and rituals of Shintoism were amalgamated with these exogenous elements and the logic of karma permeated Japanese society. Under the influence of these elements a very unique political theory was elaborated in Japan by Andō Shōeki, a philosopher who advanced a preeminent materialist philosophy as early as the eighteenth century. His ideas were excavated by Kanō Kōkichi and were studied by Herbert Norman. Although Andō criticizes Confucianism, Taoism, and Buddhism in his works (*Shizen shin'eidō,* and *Tōdōshinden*), he by no means altogether rejects the ideas in these philosophies. In fact, notions similar to the karma principle can be found in his own work.

As an example of Andō's interpretation of karma, imagine the misery and total exhaustion present during a famine. Under such circumstances, eating cooked vegetables and grains would keep one alive and enable one to call forth his powers of action. Andō concludes that it is not the man himself but the food he eats that causes his action (Andō, 1981: 46). Andō's idea sounds very much like karma, according to which all human actions are thought to be connected with each other, no action arising without a causal action preceding it, so that these actions form an infinite chain of causes and effects. Just the doctrine of karma, Andō's thinking seems to be based on the assumption that chains of action and reaction exist in nature. From this standpoint he deems it of great importance for man to plough for himself, and proposes to reform the "state of selfish laws" where those not engaged in ploughing can have everything their own way and those ploughing for themselves are envious of them. "The state of nature" based on everyone's ploughing will not be realized without reversing this status quo. "Ploughing for oneself" (*chokkō*) is regarded as the primary agent or the ultimate cause of all other actions.

To be sure, Andō's ideas about social reform are often criticized by modern political scientists as unrealistic. In fact, his theory of social reforms might appear inadequate in the eyes of those who conceive of reform in terms of the domination principle and who consider violent revolution to be the only possible measure of social reform. However, this criticism is not to the point, since Andō's theoretical framework itself is based on a different principle. He obviously denied struggles by force, relying instead on *saṃsāra*, and hoped that a "righteous leader" would appear to realize his ideal of social reformation. The latent political structure in such a society would be *pratitya* or *samut-pāda* (*engi*), where everything is linked to everything else. It follows then that the organization of this society is ruled by dharma (*riho*) and activities by *yoga* (*zendatsu*). The value pursued is *śānti* (*heian*). At the social base lies "de-imaging constraints" (*muka-kyosei*). Finally, Andō's political theory is characterized not only by the karma principle but also the principle of involution to which I will now turn.

Basic to the principle of kikyō is an understanding of the term *jinshin*. Since the Meiji era jinshin (people's heart) has come to be widely used. Although the word itself existed before the Meiji era, its meaning was different. In the Edo period, jinshin had almost the same meaning as *jinyoku* (man's desires), but it gradually came to signify the collective feeling in people's hearts during the closing days of the shogunate. This change in meaning seems to have been influenced by the idea of public opinion introduced from Western countries. In other words, jinshin contains two different concepts: the traditional concept of the heart on the one hand, and the Western concept of public opinion on the other.

Therefore, the Japanese words *jinshin* and *yoron* (meaning public opinion) have subtle differences in nuance, and accordingly these two terms have been used in different contexts. What has worked as the ultima ratio in the political tradition of our country, as I see it, is jinshin and not public opinion in the strict sense of the term, and I will label the political principle based on jinshin as the kikyō principle.

This last principle of kikyō (involution or involvement) has as its ultima ratio jinshin which is similar to Rousseau's *volonté générale* in the Western political vocabulary. But, while the latter is a static concept, the former is more dynamic. Politics in such a society follows the jinshin, but it can only be inferred since there is no specific institution or agent to evaluate it. The prevalent structure here is *matsurō* ("pie-tas")-*shirasu* ("non-violent reign"). Shirasu has been understood as government in post-Meiji Japan; but government for Inoue Kowashi, who drafted the Meiji constitution, meant to manipulate and administer men who are treated as things. In contrast, he rightly understood shirasu as a means to reflect social conditions as a mirror does, and thus to attend to popular demands (Inoue, 1969: 644). On this concept of shirasu he drafted the first article of the Meiji constitution. In his original draft the article reads: "The Empire of Japan is to be reigned (*shirasu*) by the *tennō* of the single lineage that has continued ever since this country began." However, when the official text was written, this expression was changed, and the term *tōchi* ("govern") replaced shirasu. The Japanese political leaders obviously tried to found their regime on the domination principle. But politics could be founded on the kikyō principle, as Inoue was clearly aware.

Matsurō, on the other hand, means to do things voluntarily. It is clear, then, that matsurō-shirasu is completely different from dominance-submission. The method of organization is *yosashi* ("devolution"), which could also be designated as *go-inin* ("mandate"). For a person to be qualified for the mandated authority, he must have a certain humane capacity which in Japanese is called *kiryō* and *utsuwa*. (By way of caveat, it should be pointed out that these words can also refer to capability which is different from capacity.) The corresponding activity is *mono no aware* ("sensitization"), which refers to a sensitive response to what happens in one's surroundings. Change is achieved by *naru*, which could be approximated to the German concept of *Werden*; Andō Shōeki's *shizen* is also related. The value of *seimei* ("cleanness" or *sérénité*) is pursued; and at the social base lies "familiarizing constraints" (*junka kyōsei*).

I have thus far explained the six principles which I consider to be most basic for understanding political phenomena. However, it should be pointed out that there is no society where only one political principle operates. Rather, what we observe in any society is a combination of two or more principles with different emphasis placed on each. That is, politics not only in Japan but in other societies could be understood more properly by looking at it as a combination of several principles. For instance, the combination of kikyō and domination would serve as a cognitive framework to understand particular political phenomena, such as the rise of fascism in the period between World War I and World War II, or dictatorship in the Third World after World War II.

FIGURE 1

Kikyō (involution)

Assimilation   Domination

Conflict   Autonomy

Karma

Development of a Combination of Political Principles in Japan

I will now examine how these six political principles developed in Japanese society. Using a hexagon, the political principles are placed at the vertices and we can show how they are related to each other (Figure 1). I will use this chart to show the pattern of political development in Japanese society.

However, first it is necessary to note once again that the political system of Japan's insular society is different from that of the continent. The most important point is that while exogenous groups can come in and dominate society by force on the continent, such a situation is unlikely to happen in the insular society, which is based on the kikyō principle. Conflict, however, is implicit in both societies. In the insular society scarcity of resources, for example, can cause severe conflict. The combinations of principles which provide the starting points of development for continental and insular societies are shown in Figure 2.

How, then, were the six principles combined in the political development of our country? I propose a pattern of eight stages of develop-

FIGURE 2

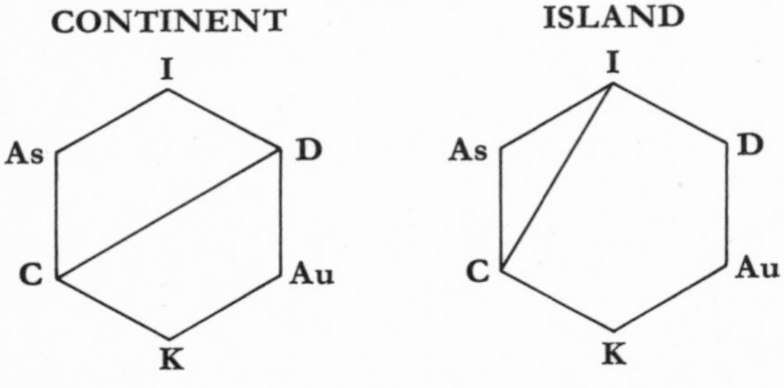

CONTINENT

I

As   D

C   Au

K

ISLAND

I

As   D

C   Au

K

FIGURE 3

I. Murakimi System

II. Okimi System

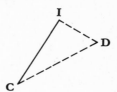

III. Sumera mikoto System

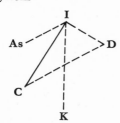

IV. Ritsuryo System

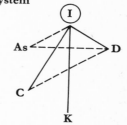

V. Kamakura Shogunate

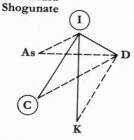

VI. Tokugawa Shogunate

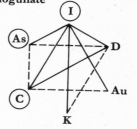

VII. Meiji Constitution

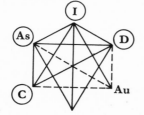

VIII. Showa Constitution

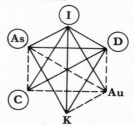

ment (Figure 3), each with a particular combination of political principles. The first two steps are the *murakimi* (rulers of small scale communities) system and *okimi* (rulers of greater scale communities) system. The murakimi system belongs to the period when small mobile groups, separated from each other, were scattered over the country. At this stage the conflict principle was included in the involution principle. As these groups began settling down, small communities arose, and the necessity of mutual negotiation among these communities brought forth a political system of a higher level, which I call the okimi system. At this stage conflicts among the communities became manifest. The conflict and the domination principles thus took shape.

What comes next is the *sumeramikoto* system. At this stage, when Confucianism, Taoism, and Buddhism were introduced into Japan, the assimilation principle together with the domination and karma principles, appeared in the Japanese political system.

The *ritsuryō* system corresponds to the fourth stage, which began in about the middle of the seventh century A.D. The principles of kikyō, assimilation, karma, conflict, and domination came to be interrelated at this stage.

The fifth stage began in the eleventh century with the establishment of the Kamakura shogunate. At this stage when the shogunate tried to achieve political integration of the country by force, the principles of kikyō and domination assumed central importance as political principles.

The sixth stage is the Tokugawa shogunate. At this time a council system developed under which ministers of the shogunate made decisions by consultation. The political system under the Meiji constitution becomes the seventh stage. Political institutions of Europe, mainly based on the principles of domination and autonomy, were introduced into Japan at this point. And finally, the system under the Showa constitution which was established after the war heralds the last stage. The autonomy principle now found a firm basis.

It can be seen from the outline above that the Japanese political system has been influenced by various political institutions developed in other parts of the world.

To turn to the present, we are witnessing increasing deviation from the domination principle; that is, the world seems to be moving toward the other five principles. Let me point out, then, that the more we resort to a framework in which the domination principle is the most powerful explanatory variable, the less visible our contemporary political phenomena will appear. A new political scientific framework is called for, although, to be sure, I am not denying the utility of social psychological explanations.

In concluding this paper, let me emphasize a point which is indispensable for a full appreciation of what I have discussed above. As some have already pointed out, the major concerns of postwar Japan—"democratization," "modernization," and "internationalization"—have shared a common denominator, namely, the question of international understanding. Stated differently, Japan has not been very successful in achieving international understanding—not only under occupation, but also in the tumult over U.S.-Japan partnership and in the more recent economic friction over trade imbalances. The waves of interest in Japanese people, culture, and society can be seen as parallels. Despite its surface appearance, international understanding has not been enhanced. Rather, ever new suspicions and distrusts are generated, and they arise in similar patterns.

As I see it, the problem lies precisely with those who are usually referred to as "internationalists"; namely, the groups of people composed both of Japanese and non-Japanese who are, in a sense, intermediaries between Japan and the rest of the world. Once discrepancies and conflicts occur in negotiations between any two or more countries, it is not only the nature of issues that has to be scrutinized, but also the framework within which the issues are perceived. In the case of Japan, unfortunately, the same groups of people with the same cognitive framework have functioned as the vehicles for solving international negotiations. Naturally, specific responses have varied according to specific issues. But it appears that the framework itself, the format with which to approach the issues, has remained intact. And this in fact accounts for the never-ending series of international misunderstandings. In order to overcome this difficulty, the best shortcut to take might be to replace the conventional groups of "internationalists" with new ones. But this is a virtual impossibility, partly because there would arise problems concerning vested interests, and partly because it would lead to lack of continuity in international negotiations. Perhaps it is more plausible for us to try to change as much as possible the cognitive framework of the already established "internationalists," and to keep the membership of the groups as mobile and open as possible.

REFERENCES
Andō Shōeki
    1981   *Kōhon shizen shin'eidō* (Nature's guidance). Annotated by Yasunaga To-shinobu. Tokyo: Heibonsha.
Hamaguchi Eshun
    1977   *Nihonrashisa no saihakken* (Rediscovery of Japaneseness). Tokyo: Nihon Keizai Shimbunsha.
Inoue Kowashi
    1969   "Goin sonkō (Collected works of Inoue Kowashi)" (1895). In *Inoue Kowashi* (document), vol. 3. The Library of Kokugakuin University.
Kamishima Jirō
    1972   "Jōmin no seiji gaku" (Politics of the Common Man). Dentō to Gendaisha.
Kishimoto Minoru
    1968   *Nihon no jinkō shūseki* (Population Accumulation in Japan). Kokon Shoin.
Yanagita Kunio (ed.)
    1954   *The Japanese*. Tokyo: Mainichi Shimbunsha.
Zhāng Bing Lin
    1906   "Jufēnjinhuā." *Minbāo*, no. 7, Zālū 2.

RELIGION IN JAPAN:
NATIONAL AND INTERNATIONAL DIMENSIONS

Robert N. Bellah

Religion and Modernization

For a long time Japan has been singled out among the non-Western nations as an example of successful modernization. In the early twentieth century, many Asian nations looked to Japan as an example and many Europeans urged them to do so. Again after 1945, Japan became a singular example of successful modernization in the non-Western world. But quite recently, for the last five or ten years or so, Japan has been offered as an example not just to the non-Western world but to the Western world as well. As Ezra Vogel has been pointing out, Japan has in many respects replaced the United States as the chief example of a successfully modern nation.

I am not sure how useful it is to argue who is really Number One. Perhaps both the United States and Japan are too obsessed with that idea. But it is nevertheless true that our two nations are clearly among a very small handful of the most modern and the most successful nations in the world today.

Before we discuss what religion might have to do with the success of American and Japanese modernization, let us consider a bit more closely just what we mean by a modern society. Certainly, whatever else a modern society means, it is an economically dynamic society. Indeed one major synonym for modernization is economic development. Economic development involves many things: science, technology, the complex organization of factories and corporations. But it also involves a certain kind of motivation. It involves making a profit. Even in a socialist economy, profit is important. An economy that did not produce a profit at all would be in deep trouble. More than a few economies in the world today are in that kind of trouble, whether they are socialist or capitalist. But the profit-motive, or the pursuit of self-interest, is not only an inevitable accompaniment of a developed economy; an emphasis on the maximization of profit, on individual and/or collective self-interest, is a characteristic feature of the world's most successful economies and most modern societies. Both Japan and the United States excel in a highly competitive spirit that is concerned with the advancement of self-interest.

Yet we know that the unrestrained pursuit of self-interest has been condemned by all the great traditional religions and philosophies of the world as morally evil and socially destructive. Consider, for instance, the beginning of the Book of Mencius. King Hui of Liang remarks that since Mencius has come such a long way he must have something to profit (*rieki*) the kingdom. But Mencius takes offense. He asks why we should even mention the word "profit" when all that matters is benevolence and righteousness (*jingi*). If one talks of profit then "those above and those below will be trying to profit at the expense of one another and the state will be imperiled." In Christianity and Buddhism avarice or greed are among the very worst sins. Islam and Christianity traditionally forbade the taking of interest on loans as a sinful form of profit. Merchants were viewed with suspicion in traditional societies, both Western and Asian, precisely because of their concern for profit and the pursuit of self-interest. Aristocrats and farmers in such societies were held in higher regard because they were felt to be less directly concerned with money and profit. And in general such suspicion in traditional societies was well-founded. Excessive concern for self-interest rapidly led to corruption that undermined the patterns of traditional social life. Corruption led to inefficiencies in government, excessive pressure of taxation on the peasants, weakening of state power, military and bureaucratic, and often widespread rebellions and a change of regime. The Chinese dynastic cycle is only the most vivid of many such examples in the annals of traditional society.

Viewed in this perspective modern society would seem to be the great exception to traditional wisdom. Here is a kind of society that inflames self-interest and the profit-motive and yet rather than destroying itself as Mencius predicted, succeeds in marvelous ways entirely unknown to traditional society. Whether in the long run Mencius is right or wrong I will consider later. We must first consider how it is possible for successful modernizing societies to arise that both depend on the energy of self-interest and yet avoid the fate that Mencius predicted.

It is here that we will want to consider the role of religion, at least certain forms of religion. In the case of America, de Tocqueville argued that religion was one of the keys to our success. Unlike traditional religion, according to de Tocqueville, American religion is fundamentally democratic. It encourages people to organize themselves in churches and congregations and to take responsibility for their own group life. While leaving the individual free to participate actively in social life, including economic life, indeed strongly encouraging such participation, religion nonetheless reminds the individual that he is not alone and that his self-interest is only a part of the larger interest of society. Thus, religion encouraged the pursuit of self-interest and yet controlled it at the same time. It produced what de Tocqueville called "self-interest rightly understood." In this way, religion helped to provide the energy for economic growth while restraining those destructive features that traditional societies had feared. Max Weber later developed this argument when he linked the Protestant Ethic to the spirit of capitalism. Through this kind of religion, the pursuit of self-interest, which in traditional society is always seen as ethically destructive, could itself become ethical. What was required was what de Tocqueville called a certain kind of "mores" (*dōtoku*); that is, ethical practices embedded in daily social life—what could be called a "moral ecology" —that allowed for a strong and cohesive society with a vigorous spirit and high morale, while at the same time rapidly developing economically.

When we turn to Japan, what is interesting is that we find certain similarities. Here, too, even before 1868, there was a certain vigor in economic life. And here too, this economic activity went hand in hand with ethical practice rather than being mutually destructive. In *Tokugawa Religion*, which I published over 20 years ago, I tried to examine those religious tendencies in pre-modern Japan that provided an ethical context for economic activity. I used the figure of Ishida Baigan (1685–1744) as a particularly vivid illustration of those tendencies. Baigan had taken the ethico-religious teachings of his day and molded them into a way of life for the merchant class that justified their economic activities, including their legitimate concern to make a profit, at the same time that it provided a context of ethical obligation. Baigan strongly disapproves of an unethical pursuit of self-interest. He insists on honesty (*shōjiki*) which means avoiding trickery, sharp-dealing, and not paying one's debts. But making an honest profit is perfectly in accord with the Way of the Sages. Baigan argues that when merchants engage in ethical economic activity they are as honorable in their own way as samurai or farmers. They too are making a contribution to the good of society. In this way Baigan helped to undermine the low opinion of merchants and of economic activity common in feudal society. He did this not just by arguing for economic freedom but by arguing for the possibility of a genuinely ethical economic life.

Ninomiya Sontoku (1787–1856), coming nearer to the end of the Edo period, exemplifies even more clearly the tendencies I wish to emphasize. Sontoku had a strong commitment to increasing production. He spent his life in what we would call today "rural development," helping backward and impoverished villages reclaim their wasteland and greatly improve their output. But Sontoku, like Baigan, placed his concern for economic activity in religious and ethical context. He even claimed that it was his first ambition to improve men's souls. He said, "My cherished desire is to reclaim the wilderness of men's spiritual fields (*kokoro no ta*), sow good seeds received from heaven—benevolence, righteousness, propriety and wisdom—harvest the good seeds and sow them again and again, so that the good seeds are spread throughout the nation." Actually Sontoku made no great distinction between work in the physical fields and work in the spiritual fields, for he believed that productive labor for the good of family, village, and nation was the best spiritual discipline.

Sontoku, like Baigan, made a distinct contribution to the notion that the economic activities of ordinary people are worthy of honor and respect if carried out in an ethical way. Baigan had said that every man is a small heaven and earth. Sontoku argued that all of us are, like Shakamuni, entitled to regard ourselves as worthy of respect equal to anyone. But it is important to note that though Baigan and Sontoku implicitly criticized the feudal class hierarchy and argued for the spiritual dignity of the common man, they did not support a radical economic individualism freed of ethical and social constraints.

Whereas economic modernization in many parts of the world has destroyed traditional structures and led to breakdown or stagnation, in Japan and the United States economic development and the older texture of social and ethical relationships seem to have reinforced each other. For a long time after 1868, the older ethico-religious ideology survived to give spirit and meaning to new forms. A strong sense of family solidarity on the one hand and a vigorous sense of duty in the occupational and political spheres on the other kept commitment and morale high in Japanese society. Even after the formal ideology collapsed at the end of World War II, social practices in family and work place retained their vitality. It is not that there has not been conflict in Japanese society nor that the central values of social solidarity have not been criticized, but in spite of all the conflict and criticism the effective vitality of Japanese society has continued and provided the basis for stunningly sustained economic growth.

Modernity is supposed to lead inevitably to secularization. Many have predicted the total dissolution of religion or at least its grave weakening. Scholars have argued about to what degree these predictions have come true. Certainly among intellectuals in both Japan and America, religion is not a very strong force. But often intellectuals have not been able to see that they are in the minority and that their own views keep them from seeing how alive religion is in the larger society and among the common people. In Japan today it is estimated that there are 180,000 religious bodies actually incorporated with the government as religious juridical persons, and perhaps a total of as many as 230,000 such bodies exist altogether. In the very midst of Japan's postwar boom the new religions grew so rapidly that they have been recognized all over the world.

Religion in Japan and America has played the role of keeping the individual from being completely isolated, has checked an unprincipled pursuit of self-interest, and has reinforced a whole pattern of ethical practices which have made for a viable and effective society. In these ways religion has counteracted the materialistic and radically individualistic implications of our modern economy. Religion has indeed helped keep alive the impetus toward economic growth by helping to prevent the economy from destroying its own social base.

Religion and the Crisis of Modernity

During the 1950s and early 1960s, so-called modernization theory was very popular. This theory took it for granted that economic growth and technological development were good, and that all societies would seek them were they not prevented by certain unfortunate barriers created by their "traditional" culture and society. Certain societies were put forward as models of modernity and other societies were urged to "catch up" with them by becoming as similar to them as possible. America and Western Europe were the prime examples but increasingly Japan also was put forward as a model of modernity.

By the late 1960s and early 1970s modernization theory was in retreat for a number of reasons. Among other criticisms, the question was raised as to whether modernity was a viable pattern at all. The process of modernization seemed to create political instabilities that threatened a constant breakdown, with the ultimate threat of nuclear holocaust always lurking in the background. As the 1970s advanced it became clear that there were serious problems with the world economy and that the great boom of 1945 to 1970 was not going to continue. As if these troubles were not enough, more and more people began asking whether the pattern of life of modern societies, even when they are successful and prosperous, is really deeply satisfying for human beings.

Modernization intrinsically seems to cause a variety of problems including atomization, alienation, rootlessness, and meaninglessness. It undermines older patterns of belief but it puts nothing in their place. In all these respects it would seem legitimate to defend older patterns that made life more meaningful and more moral. And yet when that defense becomes strident and dogmatic, uncritically rejects everything that is foreign or different, and finally leads to the exaltation of the nation so that it threatens others militarily, this whole process seems to justify the worst fears of the enlightenment rationalists. Are not religion and all patterns of particular solidarity irrational and destructive? Do they not stand in the way of a world community which can only be built on reason and science? Is there any way out of this impasse?

Some Japanese have been critical of modernization almost from the beginning, not infrequently from a religious point of view. Japan has already undergone one great crisis with respect to modernity in its modern history, the effort to overcome the modern (*kindai o chōkoku suru*), that affected the masses as well as the intellectuals. Among the first stirrings of a religious critique of modernity were to be found certain Christians who rose above the temptation to see their religion as merely an effective instrument for modernization. Uchimura Kanzō (1861–1930) was perhaps the greatest example. His deep Christian convictions led him to clash with the demands of modernity at a number of points, perhaps most dramatically in his anti-war activities. But in later life his stress on the second coming of Christ was clearly an expression of a deep religious dissatisfaction with the course of modern Japanese history.

Similar tendencies were found in Buddhism. When Japanese Buddhism began to disentangle itself from the system of state control that had dominated it in the Edo period, there were many who apprehended a religious truth in considerable tension with any existing society. Among Pure Land Buddhists Kiyozawa Manshi (1863–1903) had particularly broad influence. His teaching was to "simply enslave yourself to Buddha." From that standpoint of religious truth one could critically view one's society and make judgements about it. From the Zen point of view Suzuki Daisetsu developed a comparable position. Indeed Suzuki offerred Zen not only to Japanese intellectuals but to Western intellectuals as well as a point of clear vision in the midst of the confusion of the modern world. Among those Japanese who picked up Suzuki's teachings was the greatest of modern Japanese philosophers Nishida Kitarō (1870–1945). Nishida's philosophy has been called conservative and certainly he was no radical social critic. Yet a position that asserts absolute nothingness (*zettaiteki mu*) as the deepest religious truth must implicitly at least call into question the whole modern quest for power and wealth. Nothing, finally, could be more illusory from the point of such a religious understanding than the whole process of pursuit of material gain whether through military or economic means.

During the ultra-nationalist period, such intellectuals as Watsuji Tetsurō and Miki Kiyoshi, attempted both to criticize modern society and to envision a way of "overcoming" it. They drew from Japanese tradition and from a wide range of partially conflicting Western sources, including both Marxism and Romanticism. The alternative offered, since it was in effect an apology for the new military regime, was really no solution, but only caused a deepening of the anguish. Yet much of their criticism of modernity remains unanswered to this day. The shallow optimism of much postwar official ideology, even though ostensibly liberal and democratic, does not compare in depth with the earlier analysis.

By the late 1960s Japan was clearly shifting from a period of admiring the foreign to being proud of what is specifically Japanese. But what has occurred is a deepening disparity between the Japanese view and that of the rest of the world. For the world today does not see Japan as unique, special, and particular, set off from all the world by a history unlike any other, as many Japanese see themselves. Rather the world views Japan today as quintessentially modern: rational, scientific, efficient, the very face of the future if that is the way the world is going. It is possible that Japan has become the most successful modern nation just when much of the world is beginning to have profound doubts about the whole idea of modernity. But will Japan itself contribute to the search for alternatives to modernity? There are some reasons why this is not too likely at the moment. For one thing it is easier to criticize modernity when it is failing than when it is succeeding, and Japan continues to be strikingly successful.

Ever since the end of World War II there has been something of a spiritual vacuum in Japan. No moral consensus has replaced the one that collapsed with the lost war. In 1960 Prime Minister Ikeda proposed as a national goal doubling the national GNP. That goal did provide a certain momentum and by now has been much more than met, but many Japanese were not happy with it. Somehow merely endlessly increasing GNP did not seem a very noble or a very profound value. As Katō Shūichi said, we are interested in life, not a standard of living. Throughout its modern history Japan has tried desperately to catch up, following whomever seemed to be most successful at any given time. Now Japan has caught up and surpassed everyone else. For the first time Japan has no one to look to but herself.

Civil Religion: The National and International Identity of Japan
One way to understand the response of the Japanese people to the challenge of modernity is to examine that important cluster of symbols and sentiments which, following Rousseau, I have called "civil religion." This term, which unfortunately is not very clear in English, has caused a great deal of discussion. Originally, of course, civil religion simply referred to the religion of the city. Historically, that meant the ancient cities of the Western world, Athens, Rome, i.e., the pre-Christian classical world in which the only religion was "civil religion." Civil religion can be thought of as a "common religion" or a "culture

religion," to use the term of Professor Ikado Fujio. It is a form of religion which, as a kind of "atmosphere," pervades an entire society. While conceptually distinct from institutional religions (into which one is born) and associational religions (which one joins voluntarily), civil religions nevertheless have both institutional and associational aspects. In America, for example, the associational dimension of civil religion is prominent. After all, American civil religion was the product of a nation formed by a conscious, voluntary act. Indeed, the first statement of American civil religion is contained in the Declaration of Independence which calls upon nature and nature's God to legitimate the new nation. There are also associational aspects to the Japanese civil religion. Modern Japanese history begins with a deliberate, conscious act in the Meiji Restoration. In recent history, the effort to symbolize Japanese national identity with events like the Tokyo Olympics or the Osaka World's Fair also bring out a more actively conscious kind of symbolism. But in the main, the Japanese case seems to be more closely related to the institutional side of civil religion. It is linked to a ruling family and an imperial lineage that goes back "for ages eternal"; that is, it has no conscious beginning and is rooted in a particular relation to the land and in relation to kinship in the mythical sense. According to this view, all Japanese are one family of which the Imperial House is simply the main branch.

Today, however, among the more viable aspects of Japan's civil religion I might mention the peace movement and the movement to protect and preserve the natural environment. The peace movement began rather early in modern Japanese history, mainly within the Christian community. In the postwar period, Fujii Nichidatsu, a leader of a small branch of Nichiren Buddhism, has devoted his life to the peace movement. He spent many years in India hoping to share his Lotus Sutra piety with spiritually receptive Indians. In recent years he has developed a close relation to some of the leaders of the American Indian Movement who have seen in his teachings some similarities to their own traditional beliefs. Fujii is not trying to establish an international organization of his own but to open channels of communication of the spirit. The terrible experience of being the only society to be attacked with nuclear weapons may have meaning in itself, provided that this experience is taken as a call to clarify to the world the horror of atomic war and the fact that it must not happen again.

The problem of the destruction of the natural environment, pollution, and the illnesses and suffering that come from lack of regard for the human consequences of industrialization have been the focal points of another side of Japan's civil religion. Again, I think this has a religious dimension in Japan perhaps more than in other parts of the world because of the very deep Japanese tradition of love for and respect for nature. Nature itself has been seen as a kind of religious "revelation."

In short, one of the most important aspects of self-identity in an "internationalizing" Japan must be sought for in the transformation of a civil religious tradition reaching back to antiquity. I believe that symbol systems of this sort are inevitable. Knowing that they can be used for evil ends, as they have been both in Japan and in the United States, we might wish we could simply get rid of them. For example, there are some people in Japan who wish that Yasukuni Shrine would simply go away. But this is not going to happen. We are not going to eliminate symbols of national identity. If we try to do so, we will only make ourselves irrelevant and without influence.

Japan is in many respects the polar opposite of the United States. Japan is as racially, culturally, and linguistically homogeneous as the United States is pluralistic. There is indeed religious pluralism in Japan but the religious division of labor has worked well for a long time and there are not many tensions to be worked out, except, perhaps, in connection with some of the new religions. But if Japan is culturally homogeneous in a way rare among modern nations, that does not mean Japan can simply relax into a comfortable particularity. For Japan is a part of a pluralist world and even more dependent on that world than most nations. Japan's great economic success has placed her in the center of the world's gaze. As was once said of America, "The eyes of all peoples are upon you." The narrow island country (*semai shimaguni*) is now an economic superpower and a model of modernity for all nations. Thus Japan too has special responsibilities. Japan for a long time has been extraordinarily open to the culture of the rest of the world and yet in a way invisible herself. Everything of importance gets translated into Japanese but almost nothing, except perhaps novels, gets translated out of Japanese into foreign languages. The language barrier will not quickly disappear, but Japan's invisibility is surely over. What kind of society Japan has been able to build, how respect for tradition has or has not been combined with modernity, these are things from which the world expects to learn. What happens in Tokyo or Osaka has a meaning in America or Europe, or even Africa, that it never had before. Thus how Japan attains universality in the midst of its homogeneity and particularity will be closely watched abroad from now on. Japan has a role to play as a citizen of the world not only economically but also culturally.

The Zen teaching that the deepest religious meaning is apprehended in the midst of daily life is to be remembered. It is the development of viable patterns of moral life for individuals and groups that will let the light of transcendence shine through. The abstract meaninglessness of so much of modern life can be countered only by the concrete practice of human decency in daily life, which also means political life. It is only a religion that comes alive in practice that will speak to our condition and make the modern world habitable for human beings.

THE HOLLOW ONION:
THE SECULARIZATION
OF JAPANESE CIVIL RELIGION

Winston Davis

Since the 1960s, the Japanese press has been glutted with books and articles searching for a national identity. Known rather grandly as Japan Theory (*Nihonron*), this literature includes ruminations on culture, society and national character. Needless to say, each of these subdivisions is also a "Theory". The Theory of Japanese Culture is a study of the uniqueness of Japanese consciousness as expressed in literature, language, religion and the arts. The "soft-shelled" side of the Theory, these studies cover roughly what a Marxist calls ideology. The Theory of Japanese Society attempts to simplify the confusing details of local history, changing family and political structures, and other historical and sociological complexities, reducing them to a set of easily grasped, intuitively convincing patterns. At best, the Theory of Japanese Society helps one see basic, shifting trends in the development of the country (see Yasuda, 1980: 3–14); at worst, it degenerates to a confluence of modernization theory and collective narcissism. Finally, the Theory of the Japanese People deals with who the Japanese themselves are, their national character and personality. Some of these Theories entertainingly dwell on the characteristics of the Japanese rather than on their character. Many seek to delineate an idealized, unimodal personality at the expense of the rich variety of personality types. Although bibliographies have been compiled of these Theories (see Nomura Sōgō Kenkyūjo, 1978), both their diversity (ranging from the banal to the academic, categories that are not always distinguishable) and their sheer volume make describing the parameters of the movement a difficult task.

While the names of the authors of the Theory may not be recognized by many Western readers, one could describe the phenomenon ostensively by listing some of the principal Theorists, people such as Nakane Chie, Isaiah Ben-Dasan, Doi Takeo, Kawai Hayao, Okonogi Keigo, Hamaguchi Eshun, Yoneyama Toshinao, Sera Masatoshi, Sakuda Keiichi, Aida Yūji, Mita Munesuke and many others. Since national self-images, like identity itself, are socially constructed through a process of interaction with "significant others," what foreign scholars have written about the Japanese also figures in the creation of Japan Theory. Names like Ruth Benedict, Edwin Reischauer, Robert Bellah and Ezra Vogel come to mind. All of these writers have tried, in one way or another, to spell out the essence of Japanese culture or the unique significance of Japan and her people in the modern world.

Before describing the Theory of Japanese Culture as a publishing event, I should point out an important shift, one might even say transformation of the self-image of the Japanese people during the past ten years. This change has been noted by many scholars and has been charted statistically by the opinion surveys conducted by the Japanese government every five years called *The Survey of the National Character* (Hayashi et al., 1975). What is especially significant in the findings of this survey is the steady growth of national self-esteem in recent years. As the memory of the lost war recedes and as economic recovery turns into a worldwide conquest of unprecedented scale, the Japanese have taken greater pride in their country and in being Japanese.

Two recent events stick in my mind as especially symbolic of this transformation of the national consciousness. The first was the pronouncement by the late Prime Minister Ōhira that America is no longer a superpower. While greatly exaggerated, this statement by America's foremost Asian ally seems to reflect a new Japanese perspective on international relations, a new readiness for independence and, perhaps, a new sense of vulnerability.

The second event which symbolized the emergence of a new Japan was a short television series aired in Japan late in 1979. At that time, Suntory Whiskey Company sponsored a series of seminars called "Japan Speaks" (or more accurately translated, Japan Insists). The seminar was graced by the presence of Claude Lévi-Strauss, Robert Jay Lifton and Daniel Bell, Western scholars of worldwide reputation who took their places with lesser luminaries from Japan. Ezra Vogel, whose book *Japan as Number One* is, itself, symbolic of the new Japan,

213

introduced the series addressing his Japanese audience in fluent Japanese, standing on the White House lawn. Since Harvard, where Prof. Vogel teaches, is nowhere near Washington, I presume that either Suntory flew him to Washington to tape the interview, or else that the White House scene was dubbed in behind him. In either case, what was striking was the symbolism: a Harvard professor standing in front of the White House talking about (as I recall) *Japan* as Number One. Since the Japanese had long believed that America was Number One, symbols of American legitimacy—a Harvard professor and the White House itself—had to be trotted out to make the message credible. (One can easily imagine how ridiculous the Japanese would have found all of this had the same prologue been delivered, say, by an assistant professor at the University of Florida from the beaches of the Sunshine State). The commercials from the sponsor were also revealing. One showed New York's Statue of Liberty holding a bottle of Suntory whiskey in her uplifted hand. Another featured I Musici ensemble playing Bach melodies. In English, beneath the picture, were the words "I Musici plays J. S. Bach for Suntory." Here, in short, was a magnificent array of potent, legitimating symbols—Harvard, the White House, the Statue of Liberty, and Bach—symbols of the educational, political and artistic excellence of the West. All were now pointing eastward, to Japan—or at least to Japanese whiskey. And all were pointing to a Japan which now could "speak" and even "insist."

The consciousness of the new Japan is being distilled today not just by the Suntory Foundation, but by the various authors of Japan Theory. The general drift of this literature can be summarized under the following five points:[1]

I. The first and most important characteristic of the Japan Theory movement is that it is not comparative research. This may sound contradictory because these books are filled with comparisons of Japan and other countries. The reason why I maintain that it is not comparative research is that the authors generally take the uniqueness of Japan as their starting point or fundamental presupposition. Truly comparative research is interested in contrasts, degrees of difference, and the continua of human experience which makes the study of foreign cultures so interesting. But Japan Theory will have none of this. It assumes the uniqueness of Japan and sets out to prove it by a random

214

selection of data. A related point is this: the so-called comparisons which one does find in Japan Theory almost always compare Japan with America and Western Europe, i.e., with Japan's so-called trade partners. I have yet to read a Japan Theorist who tried to compare Japanese customs in an unbiased way with, say, those of an African tribe. I mention this because in my own research on Japanese religions comparisons with African or Indian customs have often seemed both helpful and revealing. This unwillingness to engage in comparative studies which are truly comparative is, I think, indicative of the sub-liminal ethnocentric tendency of much of the Theory. Japan Theory is interested primarily in the contrasts between Japan and her industrial competitors, contrasts which confirm the uniqueness of Japan. That a list, however long, of ad hoc, bilateral differences does not constitute uniqueness seems to be a lesson waiting for learning.

II. The positions taken by the various Theorists are complementary or supplementary ones. That is, the images they develop of Japan are not clear-cut alternatives to anything in particular. Instead, they tend to generate lists of typically Japanese characteristics—i.e., the Japanese are hard working; they understand each other by a mysterious form of nonverbal communication; their society is based on groups and not on individuals; they indulge (*amayakasu*) and accept indulgent relations (*amaeru*); they make clear distinctions between in-groups and out-groups; they have a vertical social structure; and they are inept in foreign languages. To make sure that analytical levels are thoroughly confused, the fact that they live in a small, island country is generally thrown in, somewhat gratuitously. (Actually, how gratuitous the last point is can be questioned. G. K. Chesterton, for example, once pointed out that ". . . the patriot never under any circumstances boasts of the largeness of his country, but always, and of necessity, boasts of the smallness of it" [Chesterton, 1904: 134].) After giving this pinwheel of national characteristics a good spin, an author brings it to a halt on the one he feels is most propitious for unlocking the mystery of the whole society. Often, this leading characteristic will be given a catchy name that will appeal to the mass media. It is important to bear in mind that the Theorists are competing nowadays in a literary marketplace filled with readers whose appetite for new self-images is already satiated, if not quite jaded. For this reason, Theorists in search of the national essence (and a publisher) are forced to concoct a steady stream of new appellations for Japan. Like the name of God in theology, the names of Japan never exhaust their divine subject: the society of Protean Man, the society of Moratorium Man, the vertical society, the miniaturizing society, the society of the eternal child, the maternal society, and—my favorite—the hollow onion. Each one of these characteristics becomes a prism or a lens through which the whole society can be viewed.

III.   Closely related to my previous point is the third aspect of the Theory: Japan Theory is vague. Because the images it generates are ambiguous, there is no way to select or judge between them. The Theory gives us no way to select the most adequate or accurate characterizations of the Japanese people. For this reason, the Japan Theory cannot be said to be a theoretical problem at all. Nor has it given rise to truly academic (i.e., "dialectical") discussions (*ronsō*). The prose of many of the Theorists is so nebulous that one does not know whether they are celebrating the status quo or whether they would like to reform the country and its national character in some way. When Theorists argue, it seems that they themselves do not really know what their colleagues have been trying to say. Although it is difficult to decode the political persuasions of Theorists, I suspect that in most cases it is well to the right of center.

Although Theorists assume a descriptive posture, their writings have clear normative overtones. By telling the reader who the Japanese are, they are, indirectly, telling the Japanese who they *ought* to be and how they *ought* to behave. One cannot dismiss such literature lightly simply because it tends to be platitudinous. Platitudes, when they describe the life of a people, tend to become norms. As such, Japan Theory may someday—perhaps even today—play an important role in social control. In this connection, the favor which the Japanese government has bestowed upon the Theory of Nakane Chie seems to be of singular importance. According to Mouer and Sugimoto, "The Foreign Ministry had Nakane's *Japanese Society* rewritten for its 'official' presentation on Japanese society. Entitled *Human Relations in Japan,* it was first published in 1971 and serves as the volume in the ministry's public information series on Japan for distribution overseas at its embassies and consulates" (Mouer and Sugimoto, 1979: 12). Obviously the government finds something very gratifying about the image of Japan which she creates—that of a unified, consensual, classless society in which all work and cooperate (under benign "vertical" supervision) for the good of all.[2]

IV.   The fourth characteristic of Japan Theory is that it tends to grow out of the author's own experience in foreign countries, or his own encounters with foreigners in Japan. Doi Takeo and others are quick to inform their readers that their books originated in some kind of international exchange or culture shock. The degree to which the author has an international or a "truly Japanese" self-image becomes a serious issue when the Japanese try to evaluate his work. For example, "Prof. Tanaka is too international to understand us," some might say. Others will retort, "But Mr. Yamada has no international experience, so how can *he* say anything about Japan's uniqueness?"

One suspects that Japan Theory is aimed primarily at a reading public with some international experience—from the seasoned world traveller to the young salaryman fresh from a five day JAL-PAK tour of Honolulu, Los Angeles and San Francisco. It is significant to remember that the boom in Japan Theories in the 1960s and 1970s coincided with a period of growing trade rivalries with the West and unprecedented contacts with other peoples. The shock of encountering unfamiliar values and world views, coupled with a growing pride in Japan's own economic tour de force, seems to have provided the greatest stimulus for pondering anew the old question: Who am I and who are my people? This, at least, I would allege as the primary factor in the burgeoning of this by no means new genre in these decades.

V.   Taken collectively, Japan Theories seem to play a number of roles. I have already suggested that they can function as an agent of social control reinforcing the norms of the society (or the values of the particular author). Another function is self-defense. The symbolic defense, justification or legitimation of a society is, of course, one of the major roles of a "civil religion", a point not to be forgotten when we later examine Japan Theory as a secularization of civil religious sentiments of the prewar period.

The defensive function of Japan Theory emerges rather clearly in books and articles which use feminine and maternal images to describe Japan and the Japanese. For example, Kawai Hayao in his book *The Pathology of Japan's Maternal Society* draws a contrast between maternal and paternal principles, a mixture of which, the author believes, constitutes the psychological foundation of all societies (Kawai, 1976). In a maternal society like Japan the individuals of the society are treated like children on a mother's lap. All of these citizen-children are regarded equally as belonging to the Social Mother regardless of their own individual achievements. All participate in the same "unity with the Mother" and share the same place (*ba*) on her lap. Among these children, social relations are governed by an ethic of place (*ba no rinri*), a locative morality in which each surrenders his claim to justice in order to preserve the subtle equilibrium of the group. For example, the guilty party in a traffic accident will visit the victim's home to apologize. The latter, however, customarily will not demand reparations because this would upset the ba. In paternal societies (i.e., the West), children must prove themselves to their father on the basis of their own merits and achievements. That is, the father does not accept his own children until they have performed adequately and rightly. This, of course, makes for a highly disciplined, strict society (Kawai, 1976).[3] From this contrast, Kawai concludes that the Japanese are an example of Jung's archetype of the "eternal child," a mythological lad enshrined forever upon the lap of the Eternal Feminine or Great Mother. The political consequence of this organic model of society is, as one might expect, profoundly conservative. Kawai follows Nakane in describing Japan as a highly unified, consensual society. It is a society in which serious reforms or rebellion are ultimately futile. Reformer and rebel alike inevitably slip back into the Great Mother's lap. Thus the locative ethic seems to fuse the ambitions of the eternal child (a symbol of the limitless possibilities open to all in this society regardless of their ability) with a passive acceptance of existing relationships of power, wealth and prestige. Finally, Kawai argues, because different principles govern Japanese society, one cannot measure Japanese maturity by Western psychological standards. Given the maternal foundations of the Japanese psyche, the periodic return to the Great Mother's womb by the Japanese adult therefore does not count against his maturity.

Okonogi Keigo has extended the mythological foundations of this psychological portrait of the Japanese in his study of the decline of the highly regimented Japanese work ethic. Building on Erik Erikson's notion of the "adolescent moratorium," Okonogi points out that in traditional societies adults allowed young people a period of time during which they could acquire the necessary skills and habits for maturity. During this time they were expected to remain single and defer to the power and status of their elders. After completing his apprenticeship, a young man would choose a wife, find a job and assume his various social responsibilities. Today, however, young people find the moratorium period too comfortable to leave. Furthermore, "Moratorium Man" has moved beyond adolescence and has become the modal personality of the society.

Moratorium Man is characterized by an inability to join institutions of any kind. All of his roles are temporary and therefore not expressive of his true self. His life style is therefore hypothetical, hedonistic, and self-centered. In his never ending search for novelty, Moratorium Man is practically identical with Protean Man described by Robert Jay Lifton (1976; see especially "Self" where the author makes excellent use of a Japanese example). Okonogi traces the development of Moratorium Man to various historical influences: the rising demand for educational credentials in technological societies, the diffusion of authority in modern corporations, the shifting of personnel from place to place, upward social mobility, consumerism, and (originally) the Occupation of Japan by the United States. The society which gives rise to this kind of national character is not one split between haves and have-nots, right and left, but between those who display a "host mentality" and those with a "guest mentality," i.e., joiners and non-joiners. Those who have committed themselves to the bureaucratic, competitive structures of modern society have become the protectors of society as a whole. The others—students, members of the service professions, the unemployed, the retired, and even many who *seem* to take part in social institutions—are, in fact, comfortably alienated Moratorium Men dependent upon the more responsible members of society for their protection and nurture.

While Moratorium Men can be found in all advanced industrial societies, Okonogi's theory of the Ajase complex seems to apply best to Japan's "maternal" society. The Ajase complex was originally put forth in the 1930s as a Japanese alternative to the Oedipus complex by the psychologist Furusawa Heisaku. A devout member of the Pure Land sect, Furusawa developed his theory in order to "internationalize" his own experience as a Buddhist and as a Japanese (Okonogi, 1978: 252). Without going into detail, the so-called Ajase complex, derived from a Buddhist legend about the Indian prince Ajase (Ajātaśatru), has to do with the mother-child relationship rather than the father-child axis which Freud had stressed in his Oedipus complex. The Ajase complex begins with the idealization of the mother and results in disillusionment and even acts of violence against her. The mother, for her part, endures the child's misbehavior. Thanks to her acceptance or forgiveness (*yurushi*) the rebellious child is reconciled, and the primordial unity between mother and child is restored. Thus, while the Western conscience is formed by the fear of the father's wrath (specifically his threat of castration), the Japanese conscience is molded by the mother's yurushi. Unlike Freud who tried to deduce universal psychological mechanisms from the myth of Oedipus, Okonogi—like Doi in his description of *amae* and Kawai in his treatment of the "eternal child"—is looking for something uniquely Japanese.[4] The masochism Freud thought was an illness is regarded by the Japanese as a primary virtue. It is precisely this masochism and the yurushi growing out of it that make possible the sense of oneness (*ittaikan*) which pervades Japanese society.

Like Kawai Hayao, Okonogi sees the obvious danger faced by a maternal moratorium society surrounded by an alert, competitive, and potentially hostile international community. In such a society, who will be mature enough to negotiate with foreigners who have not been narcotized in the same way? Who will take responsibility for things if everyone regards himself as a "guest" living at the expense of the country? To meet this challenge, Kawai calls for the strengthening of paternal principles. Okonogi, however, believes that because the Moratorium has its roots in child-rearing, it is something very human and therefore of great value. The democracy and pacifism of postwar Japan are predicated upon it. From this he concludes that state and society alike should be remolded to fit Moratorium Man. At the same time, he warns that the Establishment (bureaucrats, industrial and labor leaders, and politicians of all stripes) are ready to launch an "anti-moratorium" movement, for example, by rearming the country and instituting a military draft. This path must be avoided at all costs, he insists. The weaknesses of Moratorium Man must be overcome from within, not by hostile movements from without. Ominously, he warns that if international conditions (that is, the Occupation of Japan) could initiate the moratorium, new developments on the international horizon could possibly bring it to an end.

Lacking the professional credentials to analyze these theories in any greater detail, I will simply say that I feel that there is probably something to the theories of amae, the maternal society, Moratorium Man and the Ajase complex. I am not sure, however, whether this something has yet been expressed in a way that will pass muster as empirical psychology.[5] Call it femininity or what you will, a number of writers have pointed out the delicacy, softness, and passivity that so often characterize the Japanese. One thinks, for example, of Kamishima Jirō's emphasis on the "soft rule" tradition in government, of Motoori Norinaga's delineation of the intuitive nature of the Japanese people, of Robert Bellah's analysis of the feminine aspect of the emperor, and the novelist Endō Shūsaku's feminine portrayal of Christ in his novel *A Life of Jesus*.

Deferring therefore to those who are better able to judge these matters, I would like to return to the problem of the relationship between the national identity which emerges in this psychological version of Japan Theory and the international scene. It is here that, once again we catch a glimpse of the defensive use of the Theory. For example, Okonogi Keigo cites the words of a middle-aged Japanese woman who was taken as a hostage in the hijacking of a Japanese airliner in Dacca in 1977. "I just felt sorry for those kids [i.e., the terrorist hijackers]," she said. "Aren't they really pitiful, running around trying to escape but having no place to go? I wondered if it would be wrong just to forgive them [*yurushite yaru*]" (Okonogi, 1978: 206–208. See also 303ff.). Okonogi then cites with approval an article by Yamamoto Shichihei (Isaiah Ben-Dasan) who concludes that this woman's generous attitude represents the traditional Japanese way of overcoming confrontation. Quoting Kawai Hayao, Okonogi points out that while the Germans think first of abstract principles (i.e., "giving in to terrorist demands is *wrong*"), the Japanese approach emphasizes forgiveness and the importance of human life.

This scenario warms up a very old chestnut. In effect, it takes us back to the contrast drawn by Motoori Norinaga between the abstract, masculine principles of the Confucian classics and the intuitive, feminine spirit of the Japanese and their "*natural* goodness." On the other hand, its contemporary meaning emerges when we think about the international context of the hijack. Around 1977 Japan was being roundly criticized by other countries for giving in too easily to the demands of hijackers. Western countries which were trying to take more stringent measures against airborne piracy felt their efforts were being undercut by Japan's shilly-shally response to the problem. In the face of such criticism, Japan Theory seemed to say, "We have compromised with the hijackers because compromise and *yurushi* is part of our national character."

The hijacking affair and the reaction of the Theorists to it are good examples of the important role national image-making plays in international relations. Japan Theory is increasingly playing a role in the media, explaining and justifying Japanese attitudes and behavior to Westerners who, unfortunately, still believe that the Japanese are inscrutable unless their actions are explained in terms of some equally inscrutable psychology. Again, the function of the Theory is largely defensive.

Not long ago a young American, to protest the slaughter of dolphins by Japanese fishermen, went to Japan and cut the nets which the fishermen had laid for the dolphins. When the American was apprehended by Japanese authorities and brought to court, the case drew widespread interest among the Japanese people. An article in the *Japan Times* by a professor at Gakushūin University attacked what the author called "dolphinism" (Koyama, 1980: 12). Dophinism, the professor pointed out, is just one more Western "ism" designed to force an abstraction down other peoples' throats. Thus, he compared dolphinism with the crusades of the Middle Ages and other Western acts of violence. In fact, he says, Western history has been marked by continual violence—largely due to the excitement over "isms" (such as dolphinism)—whereas the Japanese "have lived peacefully in a Far East island country beyond the conflicts of other races, enjoying the beauties of nature." To the Japanese, "the history of Europe appears to be a history of " 'ism'-dictated killing." What is significant in this reaction to the dolphin affair is the way in which the Theorist justifies Japanese reactions to international events by generating sets of highly stereotyped, emotional images of Japan *versus* the West.[6]

Another example of the function of Japan Theory in international affairs comes from the pages of *Newsweek* (February 4, 1980). In 1979, problems in Iran and Afghanistan began to dominate the headlines. At that time, the American government was pressuring Japan and other allied nations to take concrete action against the Khomeini regime in Iran and against the Soviets for their invasion of Afghanistan. In particular, the United States wanted its allies to join in a program of economic reprisals. Caught between diplomatic obligations and self-interest, Japan, like France and Germany, initially seemed to waver. In a highly critical article, Japan's indecisive attitude was explained, or rather justified, by Nakane Chie of Tokyo University as follows: "The Japanese way of thinking depends on the situation rather than on principle. We Japanese have no principles. Some people think we hide our intentions, but we have no intentions to hide."[7] If Japan's indecisiveness was resented in America, one can easily imagine how Americans responded to this kind of statement. Here was a highly respected Japanese anthropologist saying that the Japanese were dragging their feet because they had "no principles." Furthermore, Nakane's catchy, media-oriented way of stating her case also represented the Japanese as totally inhuman. At least, in America and other Western countries, people without principles, or even intentions, hardly qualify as human beings. This is a good example of the danger of oversimplifing national characteristics. But there is something more to be learned from this article. The same issue of *Newsweek* also discussed the reluctance of France and Germany to follow the American lead against Iran and the Soviet Union. These countries too were hesitant to offend oil-rich Iran and weapons-rich Russia. But *Newsweek* explained the German and French reactions in simple geopolitical terms. And no German or French professor appeared to justify the response of his country in terms of "national character."

Japan Theory also seems to be on the defensive when it seeks to explain or justify the unending diplomatic ineptitude of the Japanese government. Often, diplomatic and political waffling is excused as merely a quirk in the national character. It has been said, for example, that the furor over whether to characterize Japan's relations with the United States as an "alliance" is simply a matter of distinguishing between *tatemae* and *honne,* one of the stock elements in Japan Theories of all stripes.[8] The same conceptual dichotomy is said to explain the fuss over whether or not nuclear-armed American vessels entering Japanese ports are in violation of Japan's three nuclear principles (Murata, 1981: 14). Likewise, in 1982 when South Korea and the People's Republic of China protested the whitewashing of Japan's wartime atrocities in public school textbooks recently approved by the Department of Education, a member of the textbook screening committee justified the revision of the textbooks on the grounds that the "national character" encourages the use of "soft language." A few months earlier when operatives from Hitachi and Mitsubishi were arrested in California for industrial espionage against IBM, the Japanese media immediately launched a massive editorial campaign on behalf of the defendants. Pictures of the Japanese engineers being led away in handcuffs by FBI agents filled the newspapers. The FBI itself was vilified in articles which zeroed in on its domestic surveillance of protesters during the Vietnam War. A highly respected financial paper, influenced perhaps by a TV program in which Franklin D. Roosevelt virtually caused the Japanese to bomb Pearl Harbor, suggested that the FBI caused the Japanese industrial spies to break American law. Another newspaper suggested that IBM was such a greedy giant that it deserved to have its secrets stolen—shades of Hop 'o my Thumb or Jack and the Beanstalk here!

The crowning argument for the defense, however, came from Murata Kiyoaki, editor of the *Japan Times* (July 2, 1982). The spy incident, Murata declares, was simply a case of innocent Japanese engineers falling into a trap set for them by the Americans. In a tour de force of legal reasoning, he tries to prove that IBM property was neither stolen nor lost. The crux of his argument, however, is that the Japanese defendants should be exculpated because of the "uniqueness of their culture." This line of thought I found odd indeed. After all, the FBI had entered the case only *after* IBM reported that vital information had been stolen. The Japanese defendants volunteered to the undercover agents that they had *already* obtained secret IBM materials and wanted more. The agent, in turn, repeatedly informed them that obtaining this information would be illegal. The Japanese nevertheless pushed ahead and knowingly purchased the materials. Now, what all of this has to do with "culture" is rather difficult to see. Such appeals to "national character" and "culture" seem to be little more than defensive ploys aimed at avoiding responsibility for past and present wrongdoing while, simultaneously, keeping the official policy of "building up the country through technology" (*gijutsu rikkoku*) on line at any cost.

Even the Japanese "work ethic" has a defensive edge. Not only do the Japanese regard themselves as hardworking (*kinben*); allegations that other nations are not so kinben are often used to justify existing trade imbalances.[9] At home, however, the work ethic functions to make industriousness next to not godliness, but patriotism. That is, if the Theory describes the Japanese as hardworking, then, indirectly, it is criticizing the not-so-kinben for being "un-Japanese." The work ethic itself is not primarily spontaneous, nor, as anyone familiar with Japanese universities will readily testify, is the "average Japanese" likely to toil very diligently in institutions designed for low productivity. On the contrary, given the right institutional setting, the Japanese can be the most unrelenting "goof-offs" imaginable. The work ethic actually has its origin not among the people but among their rulers and industrial bosses. It can be traced back to the preachments of daimyos, landlords and Confucian moralists of the Tokugawa period, the Imperial Rescript on Education (1890), the Boshin Rescript (1908), the creation and ideological use of the Ninomiya Sontoku legend (see Naramoto, 1971), and continues to be promoted today in the "spiritual education" programs sponsored by Japanese industry. Like the less successful preachments of Presidents Nixon and Reagan on the same subject, the officially promoted kinben-ness of Japan might better be called a work *ideology* than a work ethic. It inspires the work of others and legitimates accumulations of capital already in place.

One more defensive use of Japan Theory needs to be mentioned, namely that of language. Since this has been described recently by Roy Miller, I shall only touch on it here. Miller has shown in abundant detail how the Japanese have come to regard their language as

> ... somehow or other unique among all the languages of the world. This is the basic myth, and all the other guises that the myth assumes, depending upon time, place, and context of particular circumstance, are simply reworkings of this same, unchanging theme. From this essential claim of absolute uniqueness, for example, it is only a short step to simultaneous claims to the effect that the Japanese language is exceptionally difficult in comparison with all other languages; or that the Japanese language possesses a kind of spirit or soul that sets it apart from all other languages, which do not possess such a spiritual entity; or that the Japanese language is somehow purer, and has been less involved in the course of its history with that normal process of language change and language mixture that has been the common

fate of all other known human languages; or that the Japanese language is endowed with a distinctive character or special inner nature that makes it possible for Japanese society to use it for a variety of supralinguistic or nonverbal communication not enjoyed by any other society . . . (1982: 10–11).

While all else seems to be changing in Japanese language, here the line must be drawn. Language, if nothing else, is still purely Japanese. Miller shows how language, or rather "the myth of Nihongo," serves as a kind of cultural barricade protecting the integrity of Japanese cultural identity.

While the use of feminine and maternal images by some Japan Theorists suggests that the Theory itself is playing a merely defensive symbolic role, recent talk in Japan about the need for "internationalism," "internationalization," and "international men," implies the birth of a more aggressive posture vis-á-vis the rest of the world. Today "internationalization" (*kokusaika*) and "international exchange" (*kokusai kōryū*) are among the most lively buzzwords in the vocabulary of the country's business, educational and political elites. Exactly what is meant by these words is rather obscure, a fact that seems to give their users a feeling of self-assurance or even creativity. Yamamoto Mitsuru, professor of international politics at Hosei University, points out that "internationalization" is merely nationalism in mufti (1981: 10–17).[10] While the traditional Japanese businessman used to "smile, smoke and remain silent" (the three S's) during his unavoidable encounters with foreigners—and here one thinks of Prime Minister Suzuki's own performance at the economic summit held in Ottawa in 1981—the "international" Japanese is expected to take on foreigners in a more aggressive way. He is the kind of person who can say no to American demands; he can, with self-assurance, refuse demands for aid from Korea, China or other Third World countries; and he can drive hard bargains even with the Russians. He may still prefer dining with other Japanese (*tatemeshi*) to socializing with foreigners (*yokomeshi*), but he is able to function, and negotiate, in a natural way in both settings. The kind of internationalization promoted by the government may be a bit more complicated. While government, like business, naturally has a vested interest in securing a steady supply of hard-nosed negotiators, it would also like to project a more conciliatory self-image. "Internationalization" is therefore made to imply a new spirit of responsibility (for example, at the United Nations) and cooperation (for example, in negotiations over import and export policies). By creating the image of a country now firmly committed to "free" or "open" trade principles, the government seems to be trying to ward off reprisals by Western countries for its restrictive import policies and aggressive export campaign.

Finally, I would like to suggest that the blitz of books dealing with the essence of Japanese culture and society is, in reality, a groping for a new national self-identity in the face of increasing contact, competition and friction with Western countries. Looked at historically, many of the values and self-images of prewar Japan continue to flourish in this literature of the postwar period. One thinks, for example, of the high premium placed on consensus, unity, harmony, paternalism (or hierarchy), asceticism, loyalty, flexibility, efficiency, and so on. In the civil religion of prewar Japan these values were securely grafted into the emperor system and the Way of the Warrior (*bushidō*) and were therefore suffused with the religious and patriotic emotionalism of that period of history. With the defeat of Japan in 1945, this civil religion was radically secularized. If in Japan nothing succeeds like success, nothing fails like failure. When Japan lost the war, the emperor and the other Shinto deities were thought to have let the country down. During the war as many as 72 percent claimed to "believe in the *kami* and Buddha." By 1947, a survey found that only 6.8 percent of the population claimed to be Shintoists (Davis, 1980: 266).

In prewar ideology, such as the National Morality Movement (*kokumin dōtoku undō*) led by Inoue Tetsujirō and others, much was made of the national characteristics which set the Japanese off from the rest of the world (Davis, 1976: 5–40). But in the civil religious atmosphere of the emperor system, the national character of the people (*kokumin*) was always grounded in the mystery of the ineffable National Essence (*kokutai*)—just as the people were racially, or mythologically, derived from the sacred ancestors of the imperial household. In today's more secular atmosphere, kokumin has replaced kokutai as the focal point of Japan Theory. The essence of Japaneseness is seldom explained in religious terms, or even in terms of the imperial family. When religion is introduced in the Theory at all, it is to bring home the overall uniqueness of Japanese society. Religious customs are simply one example, among many, of the incomparable Spirit of Japan (*Yamato damashii*). Nevertheless, it is significant that Isaiah Ben-Dasan could sum up the nature of Japaneseness as a kind of religion (*Nihonkyō*) (Ben-Dasan, 1975).

Many of the functions of the civil religion of pre-1945 Japan—the generation of national purpose, symbolic self-defense, value-consensus, etc.—are now being assumed by the symbols, values and imagery produced by the literature of Japan Theory. To be sure there are also significant differences. Militarism, for example, is still largely taboo in the Theory, the Way of the Warrior yielding to the Way of the "international" salaryman. Authors are now free to explore the gentler side of the Japanese personality and to worry, publicly, about its darker aspects (e.g., violence in schools and in homes and the decline of self-discipline and loyalty). Produced by authors working under competitive conditions of a free publishing market rather than by scholars directly in the employ of the state, Japan Theory is anything but a unified movement. The self-images we see emerging in it are not the finished products of a new ideology, but an ongoing search for a new national identity by a people whose economic enterprise has recouped what generals, gods and a divine emperor previously lost. Although I have described Japan Theory as a secularization of a civil religion, because secularization itself is not inevitably a one-way or irreversible process, it is conceivable that Japan Theory, under new historical circumstances, will give birth to a new religious self-understanding, or perhaps even to a new civil religion.[11] I would even predict that the death and funeral of the now reigning emperor will make many Japanese realize that they still harbor many deep, but long-forgotten civil religious emotions.

NOTES

1. For my general understanding of Japan Theory, I am much indebted to Professor Harumi Befu (see his contribution to this volume) and to a paper by Professors Ross Mouer and Yoshio Sugimoto (1979).
2. For a highly critical assessment of Nakane's approach see Mouer and Sugimoto (1979), p. 21, Table 5.
3. The difficulty with Kawai's Jungian perspective is that it is completely ahistorical. Sexual roles, especially in modern societies, are anything but static. For example, Carl Degler discusses the decline of patriarchy and the liberalization of the American family from the Revolution to the present (*At Odds: Women and the Family in America,* Oxford, 1980). Also, Christopher Lasch describes the transformation of fatherly and motherly roles within the family (*The Culture of Narcissism: American*

Life in an Age of Diminishing Expectations, Norton, 1979). Thus it is difficult enough to get a firm picture of what is happening to sexual roles in modern society. It is doubly difficult—and hazardous—to abstract, stereotype, dehistoricize sexual identities and then assign them as labels for entire societies. Hence the fundamental problem of calling Japanese society "feminine" or "maternal."

4. I must confess that I find it odd that to find the quintessence of the Japanese psyche these writers turn to an Indian legend. Also, those parts of the Ajase story dealing with the tensions between the father and his son are passed over in silence. Before the birth of the prince, a fortune teller announced that Ajase would cause his father to come to grief some day. The father, King Bimbisara, therefore tried to kill the boy. When he grew up, Ajase revenged himself by putting his father under house arrest until he died. Furusawa and Okonogi in their search for an independent mythological foundation for the allegedly unique Japanese psyche have seen fit to "repress" this part of the legend, perhaps because it suggests the Oedipus complex itself.

5. Throughout this book Okonogi displays considerable misunderstanding of Western family customs and morality. In his discussion of the psychological roots of Western morality, he naively relies on a literal reading of Freud. That is, morality in the West is grounded in absolute commands, taboos and the fear of punishment—i.e., castration (see p. 210). He pictures the Western family as living in a home where parents erotically kiss and embrace before their children and where mothers (unable to control their lust) sleep with their husbands and not with their children (which is the custom in Japan). Such domestic egocentrism and lust leads, he believes, to the spread of pornography, child abuse, and a rising divorce rate (see p. 221ff). In Japan, on the other hand, because of the trans-sexual unity of the family, such a sexualization of parental roles would be extremely threatening to the child. The mother who is seen as a woman by her children would be regarded as their betrayer. I cite these passages not for their profundity but as examples of the way in which stereotypes of the customs of other nations are used in Japan Theory to build a positive national self-image.

6. The peacefulness of Japan as contrasted with the violence of the rest of the world is one of the more potent self-images found in Japan Theory and harks back to prewar literature of a similar nature, e.g., the contrast between the unbroken imperial lineage of Japan and the turbulent dynastic history of China. Some Theorists have tried to explain away Japan's militarism as the result of a misguided introduction of *Western* machismo (cf. Kamishima Jirō's contrast between "hard" and "soft" rule in *Jōmin no seijigaku* [Tokyo: Dentō to Gendaisha, 1972: 5–8] and also his contribution to this volume).

7. By way of contrast, I might point to the words of Kobayashi Koji, the president of Nippon Electric Company. Speaking in 1971 when the trade war between Japan and the United States was just beginning, Kobayashi declared: "While the Americans, by and large, take a pragmatic way of thinking and think in terms of power relations, the Japanese tend to emphasize morality and principles" (*The Japan Times,* Sept. 13, 1971: 11). Questions of moral bloat aside, we notice that the image Kobayashi has of the Japanese is just the opposite of Nakane's.

8. Tatemae refers to a principle, or ideological window dressing, used to smooth over one's real intentions or opinions (honne).

9. Japan Theory deals with the problem of trade imbalance almost exclusively in terms of cultural tension—and therefore does nothing to help solve, or concep-

tualize, the problem. Some have alleged that the real cause of trade friction is the West's own racism, especially its fear of the yellow peril (see Ōuchi Tsutomu, "Bōeki masatsu o umu kihon kōzō wa nani ka?" *Ekonomisuto,* May 4 and 11, 1982, vol. 60, no. 19: 12). Others have suggested that the best way to relieve those tensions is to export Japanese culture so that foreign countries will "understand" Japan and accept her imports in the spirit of yurushi. But clearly, no *Bildungsblitz* is going to have this effect. Economic and diplomatic dilemmas are not going to go away simply by shrouding them in the cultural mists of Noh drama and the tea ceremony.

10. Paradoxically, the nationalism which lies behind Japan Theory may explain why so many Theories begin and end with *humorous* episodes and anecdotes. Humor not only sells books, it is also a way of deflecting the antagonistic reaction nationalism inevitably generates among those not included in the "tribe," or among those critical of tribalism. In a similar vein, Daniel Bell astutely points out that "most definitions of national character, because of the aggressiveness of the subject, begin with a joke" (*The Winding Passage: Essays and Sociological Journeys, 1960–1980.* New York: Basic Books, 1980: 176, note 12).

11. I have argued in this paper that Japan Theory is the heir to the prewar civil religion, not that it is a civil religion itself. Nevertheless, in a secular age such literature plays some of the roles of traditional religion. Among the most important of these is spiritual guidance and the establishing of personal and collective identities.

REFERENCES

Ben-Dasan, Isaiah
    1975   *Nihonkyō ni tsuite* (On Japan's civil religion). Tokyo: Bungei Shunjū.
Chesterton, Gilbert K.
    1904   *The Napoleon of Notting Hill.* John Lane.
Davis, Winston
    1976   "The Civil Theology of Inoue Tetsujirō." *Japanese Journal of Religious Studies,* 3 (1): 5–40.
    1980   "The Secularization of Japanese Religion: Measuring the Myth and the Reality." In Frank E. Reynolds and Theodore M. Ludwig (eds.), *Transitions and Transformations in the History of Religions: Essays in Honor of Joseph M. Kitagawa.* Leiden: E. J. Brill.
Hayashi Chikio et al. (eds.)
    1975   *Nihonjin no kokuminsei* (The national character of the Japanese). Tokyo: Tōkei Sūri Kenkyūjo Kokuminsei Chōsa Iinkai.
Kawai Hayao
    1976   *Bosei shakai Nihon no byōri* (The pathology of Japan as a 'maternal' society). Tokyo: Chūō Kōronsha.
Koyama Ken'ichi
    1980   "Dolphinism: Ragtag Remnant of 'Imperial Isms.'" *The Japan Times* (April 20), p. 12.
Lifton, Robert J.
    1976   *Boundaries.* New York: Touchstone.

Miller, Roy A.
   1982   *Japan's Modern Myth: Language and Beyond.* New York and Tokyo: Weatherhill.
Mouer, Ross, and Yoshio Sugimoto
   1979   "Some Questions Concerning Commonly Accepted Stereotypes of Japanese Society." Canberra: Australia-Japan Economic Relations Research Project. Research paper no. 64. The Australian National University.
Murata Kiyoaki
   1981   "The Japanese Duality: *Tatemae* and *Honne* May Help Understanding of Nuclear Furor." *The Japan Times* (June 5), p. 14.
Naramoto Tatsuya
   1971   *Ninomiya Sontoku* (Sontoku Ninomiya). Tokyo: Iwanami Shoten.
Nomura Sōgō Kenkyūjo
   1978   *Nihonjinron* (Japan theory). NRI Refarensu No. 2. Kamakura.
Okonogi Keigo
   1978   *Moratoriamu ningen no jidai* (The age of man in moratorium). Tokyo: Chūō Kōronsha.
Yamamoto Mitsuru
   1981   "Nihon ga kokusai shakai de ikiru jōken" (Prerequisites for Japan's survival in international society). *Economisuto* (January 20).
Yasuda Saburō
   1980   "Nihon shakairon no tenbō" (Perspectives on the theory of Japanese society). *Gendai Shakaigaku,* 13, 7 (1): 3–14.

INTERNATIONALIZATION OF JAPAN
AND NIHON BUNKARON

Harumi Befu

THE MEANING OF THE INTERNATIONALIZATION OF JAPAN
Japan's position in the international scene has become increasingly
visible and important in the last ten years or so. The 1960s were the
economic "take-off" period for Japan. The double-digit economic
growth of the 1960s enabled Japan to catch up with the West. The
Johnny-come-lately was admired for its sprinting speed of economic
recovery after the war. Still, in the 1960s Japan was merely a latecomer
trying to catch up with the West. In the 1970s, however, Japan was no
longer behind the West, but had caught up with Western industrial
powers and even surpassed most of them. In order to achieve this
economic position in the world, Japan has had to develop numerous
modus operandi toward countries around the world. These modus operandi are best summed up in the concept of internationalization.

The process Japanese call internationalization (*kokusaika*) is in fact
not one but numerous and varied. I do not know how old the Japanese
term is, but it has come into vogue only in the last ten years or so.
Since it is a popular term rather than a technical one, it never was properly "introduced" with anything like a definition. To discover its
meaning, then, it is necessary to analyze the use of the term *kokusaika*
and related terms such as *kokusaisei* (internationality), *kokusaikan*
(international sense), *kokusaijin* (internationalist), and *kokusai-kōryu*
(international exchange) in the context in which they are used. These
terms, being of popular usage, are mostly found in newspapers and
popular magazines. By analyzing their usages in context, then, we can
make inferences as to the meanings suggested by them. The features,
or definitions, set forth below may not all be regarded as definitions in

the strict technical sense of "definition." But they are all processes implied by common usages of the term.

Western Impact on Japan

While it might be farfetched to speak of internationalization taking place in Japan in the nineteenth century, Western impact on Japan ever since the middle of the last century cannot be ignored in considering internationalization processes. Internationalization during the past decade was indeed directly built on the experience of adopting and adapting to foreign, especially Western, culture in the broadest sense. It is worthwhile to remind ourselves that from industrial technology to social institutions and material aspects like clothing, building and food, Western impact on the everyday life of the Japanese was pervasive and profound even before World War II. With the defeat in the last war and the military occupation by the Allied Powers, the impact of American culture in the postwar era began to have a visibility all its own in a way never seen before the war.

Acceleration of the diffusion of western culture into Japan continues to this day. But this same process of westernization is now often called "internationalization," the new appellation giving the process the prestige the term "westernization" once had. Even though internationalization implies involvement with non-Western cultures, as a process, it is hardly an evenly keeled involvement with all parts of the world, East and West, North and South, but is an elliptical affair predominantly pointed toward the West, as Western cultures remain, as it has been for the past one hundred years, Japan's reference groups.

Internationalization is of course not merely a quantitative increase of what had gone on in the past: the quantum jump which we call internationalization was made possible on the foundation of the massive and profound prior Western culture diffusion into Japan. This is not to imply that westernization ended as internationalization began. Western influence upon Japan continues to the present, but has acquired a new dimension as it is perceived as a part of the internationalizing process. Internationalization as a concept gradually and imperceptibly began to occupy a place in Japanese cultural development in the late 1960s and early 1970s. Thus the same process of westernization which has characterized Japan earlier is now perceived as part of its internationalization today.

Foreigners in Japan
Along with increasing technological, institutional, cultural and other impacts from the West, the foreign population residing or visiting Japan has increased in the last 20 years. The number of registered aliens increased relatively slowly from about 599,000 in 1950 to 767,000 in 1978. But the number of foreigners entering and exiting Japan multiplied phenomenally from roughly 145,000 in 1960, the earliest year in which the *Japan Statistical Yearbook* reports for this category, to over 1,000,000 in 1978.[1]

Of all the foreigners residing in Japan, only a small minority (about 5% or 39,000 in 1978) are from Europe and North America, areas of the world associated with Japan's westernization, and ultimately, with its internationalization. The vast majority of foreigners in Japan are Asiatics, among whom Koreans (659,000) by far predominate, constituting 86% of all foreign residents in 1978. This observation by and large holds true not only of present day Japan but throughout the postwar period, or as long as Koreans have been classified legally as aliens. Figures for foreigners entering and leaving Japan in a given year show a much larger proportion of Westerners (524,000 or 52% of all foreigners) entering Japan in 1978. Still in all, Asiatics constitute 41% of the total. Yet, the focus of Japan's internationalization lies in the West as that of "modernization" did in the past. This increase in the number of foreigners, especially Westerners, in Japan is one manifestation of Japan's internationalization.

Foreign Investment in Japan
Most foreign residents from Europe and America are in Japan for business reasons. Temporary visitors also come to Japan for the same reasons. Increase in these classes of foreigners to a considerable measure reflects increase in foreign investment. In 1955 a mere $52.2 million was invested in Japan by foreign concerns; in 1978 annual investment increased to $20.25 *billion*. Some of this investment no doubt is merely a matter of foreigners buying Japanese stocks, with negligible direct impact on social and cultural arrangements. At the same time, one finds a variety of foreign businesses being established or conducted in Japan, where Japanese are coming into direct contact with foreigners and foreign business institutions. Here, Japan's internationalization is necessarily involved in social and cultural impact.

Liberalization of Trade Policy

I take the liberty of including this definition of internationalization directly from Johnson's contribution in this volume. Increase in foreign investment in Japan is in part a product of the gradual liberalization of the Japanese government's trade policy. In the thirty-year period from 1949, when the Foreign Exchange and Foreign Trade Control Law was first enacted, to 1980, when it was last revised, the law went through numerous revisions. Also, within the guidelines of the law, Japan's trade policy, administered by the Ministry of International Trade and Industry, has been liberalized in the intervening years, such that both foreign investment in Japan and importation of foreign products to Japan have become easier, and increased in volume. This liberalization process is, as Johnson notes, internationaliation of the Japanese economy.

Japanese Investment Abroad

While all these internationalization processes are taking place on the domestic front, internationalization has been proceeding abroad as well. One such process is Japanese investment abroad, which increased from $159.4 million in 1965 to almost $4.6 billion in 1978—an almost thirtyfold increase in the short thirteen years. Like foreign investment in Japan, some of this is merely a matter of buying shares in the stock market with little impact beyond the financial. On the other hand, there are numerous business ventures abroad, where Japanese business institutions, technical know-how and personnel are "exported" to foreign countries and where some form of adaptation or accommodation to the local scene is necessitated, whether in terms of legal rights, resource demands or cultural customs.

Some firms, typically those employing Japanese nationals almost exclusively, have made minimal concession to local social and cultural requirements, the few local hires having to adapt to the essentially Japanese style of management. Some other Japanese business firms abroad, on the other hand, have gone all the way in adopting the local system of management (Kinugasa, 1979; Murayama, 1979).

As Japan's economic success has become unmistakable around the world, the search for keys to success has led many foreign concerns to look, justifiably or not, upon Japanese managerial style as the (or an) answer. Many scholars in business administration and social science fields have speculated on and researched specifics of the Japanese management style which is presumably responsible for Japan's economic success, and produced a plethora of reports and recommendations (Denison and Chung, 1976; Dore, 1973, 1979; Hazama, 1974; Naylor, 1980; Norbury and Bownas, 1980; Ouchi, 1981). The mystique attached to Japanese management style by foreign business concerns hungry for profit has led them to apply some aspect or other of Japanese management. One ironic example is the adoption of the "quality control circle" (QCC) in the United States, which was originally exported to Japan from America. Thus internationalization of Japanese business management has two distinct aspects: first, adaptation by Japanese business abroad to the local scene, and second, adoption of certain Japanese business practices by foreign businesses.

Japan's internationalization is also seen in the exporting of Japanese technical know-how, especially to developing countries through training for students from these countries. In 1975, for example, Tokyo University had 360 students from Asia, the Near East, Oceania and Africa, constituting 79.5% of all foreign students. The proportion of students from these parts of the world at Keio University was about the same (74.8%) that year (Kwansei Gakuin [ed.], 1977: 162). Students from these developing countries are overcoming language barriers and cultural problems, and enrolling in Japanese colleges and technical schools in increasing numbers. These students return to their respective countries and serve as teachers to their compatriots, thus promoting Japan's technical internationalization.

Foreign Language Competence

In order to accomplish the variety of internationalization processes discussed above, such as adopting Western technology, working in a multinational firm in Tokyo, and taking on an overseas business assignment, it is imperative to acquire minimal foreign language competence. For the other internationalization processes, too, such as travelling or studying abroad, or understanding foreign cultures (discussed below), being able to use foreign languages for communication is essential. Millions of Japanese study English and other foreign languages in school, on the job, in English-speaking societies, and privately. The phenomenon of so many Japanese spending so much time, energy and financial resources—in tuition, reference and text books, audiovisual aids, etc., is a potent manifestation of Japan's internationalization.

Association with Foreigners

Learning to speak a foreign language, however, is only a prelude to using it to read or associate with foreigners. It is especially in having direct contact with foreigners that Japanese are supposed to manifest their internationality. With increasing numbers of foreigners coming to and residing in Japan, there are more opportunities for Japanese to have contact with them.

But to be an internationalist in the true sense of the word in associating with foreigners, a Japanese is not supposed to interact with them as a traditional Japanese would—full of smiles, deference, purported ambiguity of expression, etc. Instead, he is supposed to be forthright (*shitatakana*) in asserting his position, expressing his opinion and "holding his own" vis-á-vis foreigners, especially Westerners.

Understanding Foreign Cultures

In order to develop one's ability to associate with foreigners as an internationalist, it is imperative to understand foreign cultures. To meet this goal, Japanese students receive in school a heavy dose of world history, geography, and worldwide "current events." Media are replete with news from abroad.

But understanding foreign cultures takes a quantum jump when they are directly experienced. Japanese are obtaining such experiences as they are assigned overseas by their companies, as they go abroad as dependents of such businessmen, as they study in a foreign country, and even as they travel abroad as tourists. After staying in a foreign culture for a period of time, Japanese begin to understand the cultural background of locals they have to associate with. Though this process is a slow one and is incomplete for most sojourners unless they spend many years in a given country, still in all it is the best way to gain the degree of cultural relativity necessary in associating with foreigners. As a Japanese begins to develop this understanding of foreign cultures, he is said to have acquired an international perspective.

This process is probably least complete for tourists, especially those who travel in large groups and who are abroad only a short time. For many, effects of short-term trips are anything but positive in internationalizing Japanese. Nevertheless, it cannot be denied that the experience has an internationalizing impact at least to some extent on the outlook of tourists. In 1960 only 119,000 Japanese left the country, whereas 18 years later 3,525,000 Japanese went abroad, most of them (about 80 percent) tourists. Small internationalizing effects multiplied by millions every year cannot but have some impact upon Japanese in broadening their cultural horizons.

Status of Foreign Faculty

One effective way in which to learn foreign languages, understand foreign cultures, and associate with foreigners takes place rather naturally on university campuses where foreign teachers are employed. While their services are thus invaluable for Japan's internationalization, foreigners teaching at Japanese universities, especially government schools, face discrimination in terms of promotion, raise, and participation in university governance.

Reischauer has pointedly accused Japanese of legally barring foreign faculty from becoming regular professors at government universities (1977: 421). Even without Reischauer's accusation, this problem has of late become an increasingly important social issue. A number of meetings, conferences and symposia have been held and much ink has been spilled on this topic. (See Hidaka and So [ed.], 1980, for a recent discussion of this issue from a variety of perspectives.)

Japanese universities are gradually coming around to providing equal status to foreigners. Also, legislative bills have been introduced in the Diet to effect this change "in view of," as one of the bills extolls, "the international nature (*kokusaisei*) of education and research at universities." Although contents of the bills may be less than ideal and in fact controversial to some, changes toward internationalization of universities is, albeit slowly, taking place.

Naturalization

Along with equalization of the status of foreign faculty, easing of the naturalization law (Civil Code No. 147) is an area in which internationalization is being urged. Currently it is extremely difficult for foreigners to become naturalized in Japan. Many foreigners have repeatedly voiced their complaints, and comparing Japan with some other countries in which naturalization is easier, criticized Japanese law.

So far, the Japanese government has not faced up to this issue in a positive manner. But public sentiment, though perhaps not representing a majority view, has been strongly expressed in favor of liberalizing Japan's naturalization law in line with that of "advanced" Western nations.

Japanese Language Instruction

With economic success and the rising reputation of Japan and things Japanese, with Japanese investment abroad increasing and technical and managerial know-how being studied by foreigners and exported abroad, the need to give Japanese language instruction has increased. Japanese language is taught to countless numbers of foreigners in Japan, for whom the need is obvious. Abroad it is taught not only to the small number aspiring to be Japan specialists, but also to the many more who need the language for business or conversational purposes. In Australia, Japanese language instruction is widespread at the high school level, there being proportionately more high school students taking up Japanese than in any other foreign country.

Enhancement of Cultural Understanding of Japan

As it is not sufficient simply to acquire minimum competence in a foreign language if one is to understand the culture which the language represents, it is not enough merely to teach language to foreigners if Japan is to expect their understanding of the Japanese way of thinking and acting. As Japan has moved into the international scene in trade and politics, accusations have been levelled against Japan whenever the situation is unfavorable to a foreign protagonist. Japanese have often perceived this accusation as being based on misunderstanding and insisted on it as such. Rectification of this misunderstanding, or "de-mystification" of the proverbial inscrutability of the Japanese, is thought to lead to a better relationship between Japan and the rest of the world.

Foreign language publications coming out of Japan are full of articles of a Japanological genre in an effort to internationalize Japan. Such publications include dailies, weeklies, monthlies (such as the *Japan Times, Japan Times Weekly,* and *East*) and monographs on Japan in foreign languages. Internationalization of Japanese colleges and universities is often gauged on the basis of how many foreign students they take in and how well their curriculum meets their needs (Kwansei Gakuin [ed.], 1977: 153–187).

Of late, Japan has taken an increasingly active role in providing materials to promote proper understanding of Japan to countries around the world. Dissemination of materials on Japan, the dispatching abroad of scholars and other experts on one aspect of Japan or another, the sending exhibits and performing arts overseas are some of the major activities in which the Japan Foundation and other Japanese government agencies and organizations have put so much effort.

Contribution to World Order

In *The Japanese,* which is otherwise replete with warm and appreciative appraisal of Japan and its people, Edwin O. Reischauer chastised Japanese for not doing their share of contributing toward world peace and order. Says Reischauer: "They [the Japanese] have developed enough skills to handle specific economic and other relations with the outside world but not to make a contribution to the solving of world problems that is commensurate with their size and skills. . . . Japan in its own interest needs to do better. The world faces grave problems, ranging from technical matters of global ecology and resources to complex problems of world trade and international tensions. Japan, with its great potentialities, should be attempting to maximize its contribution to the solution of these problems" (Reischauer, 1977: 419–420). Internationalism is here conceived of as ability and willingness to help solve global problems not directly or necessarily affecting Japan's national interest, such as increasing a favorable balance of trade.

The way in which Japan has contributed most toward these goals is in monetary contributions toward world or regional organizations, such as the United Nations, the United Nations University, the World Bank or Asia Development Bank. Even then, in the mid-1970s the Japanese government's contributions to these organizations was only a small portion of the total budget for international programs, the remainder being for those activities in which Japan's national interest was directly involved. What is more important than monetary contributions to impersonal organizations is qualitative considerations. In this respect the Japanese Overseas Youth Corps (the Japanese Peace Corps) casts a bright albeit small light in an otherwise dark expanse of Japan's unfulfilled international responsibility.

These definitions of internationalization are necessarily loose. As custom is king, however, these usages each are enthroned with legitimacy of their own. Up to now, terms such as "westernization" (*seiōka*), "modernization" (*kindaika*), and "liberalization" (*jiyūka*) have long been used as labels for many of these processes, and they are still current. However, the fashionable term to gloss all these processes nowadays is "internationalization."

A characteristic of the above definitions is that the defining processes are assumed to be at once processes of internationalization as defined and also often to promote the internationalization process in some other sense in which the term is defined. To take an example, successful operation of Japanese business overseas requires, and also promotes, learning of the language of the local area and goes hand in hand with experiential learning of the foreign culture concerned. Also, for business success, it is important to promote local goodwill through such activities as demonstration of performing and other arts. This is not to argue that language learning, *experiential* learning of the local culture, or promotion of Japanese arts abroad should be seen solely as servants of economic needs. Certainly noneconomic internationalization processes have their independent existence. But it is difficult to deny the relative primacy of economic internationalization.

THE CONSEQUENCE OF INTERNATIONALIZATION: NATIONALISM

While internationalization proceeds on all fronts, each process reinforcing and interacting with others, the very processes of internationalization which are supposedly making Japanese more cosmopolitan have the unexpected effect of making Japanese more nationalistic. It is this point which is the essence of the argument of this paper. Let us now turn our attention to this issue to see how internationalization promotes "anti-internationalization."

Enhancement of Contrast

Foreign language instruction. Increasing foreign language competence is an urgent need in an internationalizing Japan. English instruction, which is in the regular school curriculum and is taught to millions of students in Japan, is of course designed to meet this need. The numerical extent of English instruction is obvious to everyone: no other foreign language is taught in Japan to anywhere near as many Japanese in and out of school as English. In spite of this numerical predominance and decades of instruction going back to the Meiji period, the ineffectiveness of English teaching is as lamentable as proverbial. After years of lessons, drills, and card-flashing, most Japanese students are unable to communicate with native English speakers beyond the most elementary greetings. An important, though of course unintended, consequence is that the hardship experienced in learning English and other foreign languages impresses Japanese of the unfathomable gap between the Japanese language and foreign languages they study; it thereby convinces them of the separateness of Japanese from others. Thus, while learning foreign languages undoubtedly brings Japanese close to foreign languages and cultures, at the same time it helps them to recognize the helpless gap between the two. It is as if ineptitude of foreign language instruction and learning is maintained (though, needless to say, unconsciously) for the very purpose of convincing millions of Japanese of their separateness from foreigners.

"Gaijin" syndrome. What is true of language learning is also true of association with foreign residents in Japan. Here I would like to focus on the *gaijin* syndrome as a poignant expression of the separateness which Japanese are trying to assert. Among the several Japanese terms referring to foreigners (such as *gaikokujin, gaijin, ketō* and *ijin*), *gaijin* probably is the most frequently used in contemporary Japan. Seemingly neutral, and meaning "outsiders" and denoting people of all foreign countries in one sense, in another and more popular sense it refers more specifically to Caucasians. (One does not see Japanese children pointing to Koreans, saying "Gaijin, gaijin!") Foreigners in Japan are foreigners no matter how many generations they have lived in Japan, no matter how well they speak the language, and no matter how well they have adapted to Japanese culture. The term "gaijin" is a label forever attached to all Caucasians, and symbolizes their permanent outside status. "Once a gaijin, always a gaijin" is the unalterable principle which Japanese assume and force upon gaijin, whether they like it or not.

It is one thing, in the minds of Japanese, to take on features of Western culture; it is entirely another to obliterate their racial identity by admitting foreigners into the category of Japanese. Maintenance of uniqueness and distinctness as a social group seems to become all the more critical as the Japanese culture becomes inundated with foreign elements. Setting gaijin immutably apart is a way of maintaining Japanese identity. In turn, the stubbornly maintained separation between themselves and others allows Japanese to import and incorporate foreign cultural elements at will, since the latter process does not threaten their racial identity.

Take for example an average salaryman's daily routine. In the morning he is as likely to get out of a Western style bed as out of *futon*. Removing his pajamas he dresses in dark suit, possibly designed by Pierre Cardin, has his breakfast consisting of ham and eggs, bread and butter with coffee as he reads the morning newspaper, printed with a computer originally invented in the West, but using a system of writing adopted from the Chinese. He then dashes out to catch the commuter train, unless he is driving his "my-car." Arriving at his office which is in a ferroconcrete building, he sits at his desk all day; and if he works for a trading company, he may spend his day importing grains from the United States or meat from Australia. After work, he is likely to stop by at a favorite bar with his work mates for a shot of whiskey or two as they discuss how the Tokyo Giants are doing in the baseball league. On the train home he might read in the evening paper about the continual growth in the Japanese auto industry and in general how Japan is Number One in the world. Upon his return home, he would have his dinner of mini-steak, considering the cost of beef as he listens to his favorite Beethoven piece either on the radio or on the stereo set. Before retiring he would go to the family altar to thank the deity imported from India via China and Korea that he is 100 percent Japanese.

What is it that makes him so sure that he is 100 percent Japanese and no less, in spite of the fact that his daily life is replete with things, ideas, and institutions of obvious foreign origin? It is indeed because the question of being a Japanese is an Aristotelian matter of "you either are or are not," excluding any middle ground.

This absolute exclusion of foreigners is rooted in the Japanese definition of themselves as a people of one race and one culture. Let us set aside the issue of whether or not on scientific grounds Japanese are or are not in fact of one race or one culture. Rather, the matter of concern here is the conviction which unshakably holds the mass of racial unity and cultural homogeneity of the Japanese. Moreover, the conviction goes further and leads to the belief that ultimately the unique essence of

Japanese culture is transmitted genetically. Because, the belief goes, Japanese are racially one, the derivative culture is also unitary. In this belief, of course, infusion of Chinese and Western culture represents something other than alteration of the essential core of Japanese culture, though it may have penetrated beyond the surface.

I suspect this genetic definition of Japanese culture is at the root of the Japanese inability to admit foreigners into the rank and file of Japanese and at the basis of their adamant exclusion of foreigners from the category of people called Japanese. Use of the term "gaijin" by Japanese, especially by children as they point at foreigners, infuriates some, as letters sent from time to time by foreign readers to editors of English-language newspapers demonstrate. This infuriation very often comes from a foreigner who desires to be admitted into the Japanese fold and be considered a Japanese. Such a foreigner represents the type, usually a long resident of Japan and possibly with an intention of permanent or semi-permanent residence, who has mastered the language at least reasonably well and internalized the *modus vivendi* of Japanese. Many of them come from a culture such as the United States where foreigners and immigrants are readily incorporated in the category of locals. When their desire to be recognized as Japanese— when so to speak, their application for citizenship—is rejected they become furious. What they do not realize is that in the eyes of Japanese, they have not ceased to be gaijin one iota simply by acquiring linguistic and cultural skills of Japanese. Instead they simply are moved from the category of plain gaijin to its subcategory of *henna gaijin*.

I do not doubt to some extent the term is used pejoratively, especially when voiced by children. But the meaning of an act or a word is often in the eyes of the beholder. Once dissatisfaction is fixed in a foreigner's mind because of his permanent exclusion from the category into which he wishes to be included, the label of gaijin he is trying to rid himself of will necessarily sound pejorative when thrusted upon him against his will. Here is a classic case of mutual misunderstanding: a foreigner's wishful thinking is that internationalization obliterates the line between him and the Japanese, whereas for the Japanese internationalization compels them to draw a sharper line than ever before between themselves and outsiders.

Living abroad. Residing abroad for a period of time forces one to accomplish several internationalization processes at once: learning a foreign language, associating with foreigners, experientially absorbing foreign culture, possibly teaching Japanese to the locals, and showing what Japanese culture is like, thus serving in effect as a private "ambassador." The longer one stays, of course, the more one can accomplish these objectives of internationalization, and in fact we see evidence of this virtually wherever Japanese go in the world.

At the same time, however, foreign residence has a widespread effect of solidifying Japanese into their own ghettos and allowing them to turn their backs to the host culture. This is particularly true in areas where a large Japanese population resides, such as New York and Los Angeles. In these cities, Japanese tend to live in close proximity to one another, organize associations and clubs among themselves, associate only with other Japanese, and send their children to a Japanese school. Husbands may have to deal with locals at work, but here too if the office they work in is staffed by a fair number of fellow Japanese, they may need to associate with locals only to a minimal degree. Their wives might spend days or weeks without speaking the local language and without having social contact with locals.

As the most patriotic Americans often turn out to be those living abroad, many overseas Japanese strengthen their belief in the superiority of the Japanese and their culture as they encounter foreign culture and experience difficulty in local adjustment, intercultural communication, and mutual understanding. The end result of many Japanese living abroad is to return to Japan with renewed conviction of the deep gulf between their own culture and the foreign culture. At the very least, they are forced to ask themselves what it means to be Japanese and what constitutes their cultural identity. At worst, they return to Japan with antipathy toward the foreign culture they experienced. This is especially true when Japanese reside in areas of the world outside Western Europe and North America—in countries which are at the lower end of the totem pole of country-ranking which the Japanese are fond of engaging in.

Overseas children and their re-entry problem. Overseas experience takes on an entirely different dimension for children who accompany longtime sojourner parents. In many ways these children are or should be the best agents of internationalization. Their youth makes language learning enviously easy. Since playing with friends at school and in the neighborhood is the stuff of their life, they cannot help but learn local culture. Their impressionable age, adaptability to different cultural environments, as well as susceptibility to peer pressure from local friends make them ideal for internalizing as well as appreciating local culture.

Ironically it is this very adaptability which worries their parents. In the parents' eyes children are engaged in a zero-sum game: the more adapted to the local (foreign) culture, the less "Japanese" they will become, and the less capable they will be of fitting back into Japanese culture after their return home.[2] Since their sojourn is viewed as temporary and their life in Japan permanent, losing "Japaneseness" and being handicapped in readjustment upon returning home are generally regarded as a liability to be avoided. Not the least important among the readjustment problems is that of catching up with other Japanese children in the competition of college entrance examinations. But there are other problems, such as Japanese language learning, establishing friendship, and acquiring comfortable bodily comportment. To minimize these problems of readjustment, parents send their children to a Japanese school while abroad, if there is one, rather than to a local school. But this option is available only to those in a small number of large urban centers around the world where enough Japanese are concentrated to justify the expense of maintaining such a school. Elsewhere, Japanese communities abroad have set up Saturday schools, which parents complain of as woefully inadequate.[3]

As parents tend to form their own ghettos within the local culture, children also tend to stay within it. At worst, their contact with locals and their experience with local culture is limited to the bare minimum, restricted by and large to an impersonal level such as marketing. In extreme cases, which are not at all uncommon, parents simply leave their children back in Japan in order to avoid the problem, in effect, depriving them of the opportunity to be internationalized. In sum, the overall tendency is for the education of Japanese children overseas to counter the lofty goal of creating a person "rich in internationality." In Ebuchi's observation (1978: 5–6), internationalization and "Japanization" of overseas children are contradictory goals inimical to one another. In this battle of internationalization pitted against Japanization, it is clear which way the majority of parents are oriented: their efforts are directed toward keeping their children as Japanese as possible, with the conviction that, if left alone, the children would become too internationalized and too un-Japanese in the parents' eyes.

Parents who live in an area where a Japanese school is not available are forced to send their children to a local school, which is a common practice for those sojourning in "advanced" parts of the world—meaning Western Europe and North America. For those in less "advanced" countries, such as in Southeast Asia, the tendency is to send children to an international school, if there is one, at considerable personal expense. Whether sending them to a local school or to an international school, these are regarded as decidedly secondary and poorer alternatives to sending them to a Japanese school. If the sojourn becomes lengthy, parents in these areas are resigned to the fact that their children will suffer adjustment problems upon re-entry to Japan. Some of them even give up the hope of their children eventually entering a Japanese university, and allow them to pursue their college education abroad. This, of course, virtually eliminates preferred employment opportunities for them in Japan.

Once children with overseas experience return to Japan, a host of problems are waiting for them. First of all, immediately upon returning, their identity is questioned. While overseas, no matter how acculturated, they are always considered by locals as Japanese. They are veritable little ambassadors abroad. They have no question as to their identity as Japanese. But once back in Japan their foreign mannerisms, their foreign ways of thinking and behaving, etc., not only quickly draw the attention of other Japanese but their criticism as well, precisely because Japanese conceive of their culture in monolithic and homogeneous terms (Murase, 1978b: 12) and have little tolerance for cultural diversity. Also, as some returnees have confided, if they manifest some even mildly deviant behavior, this is immediately interpreted as an undesirable consequence of foreign experience, even though another person with no foreign experience might manifest the same degree of deviancy without drawing similar criticism. In short, foreign experience as such becomes a stigma to many returnees.

To cope with this problem returnees must be "de-internationalized." They quickly learn to readjust and readapt to the Japanese scene. Conformity to Japanese norms is the major guiding principle in this coping process. For those who are responsible for facilitating this process, such as teachers, the task is frequently described as "peeling off foreignness" (*gaikoku hagashi*), "redyeing" (*somenaoshi*), or "scrubbing off foreign experience with a brush."

From the point of view of self-identity, too, as Anne Murase has commented, the multicultural individual has inner problems to deal with. Multicultural experience at once gives him an opportunity for cognitive flexibility. But the same multicultural experience is also a potential source of confusion and mental chaos when opposing or contradictory values of different cultures are internalized (Murase 1978a: 16). Whether or not this multicultural experience can be turned into positive energy in later life will depend in great part on what the surrounding social system will demand. The social system may encourage the individual to use the multicultural experience as a positive asset by rewarding him for the experience. On the other hand, it may discourage him from playing a "cosmopolitan" role. The Japanese social system clearly is of the latter type. One saving grace of the Japanese system is that it is clear and unambiguous in defining the type of person it desires, thus leaving little room for internal confusion and chaos in the identity of the individual. But the same social system demands those who have developed multicultural cognitive flexibility to revert back to the Japanese mono-cultural mode of cognitive style and poses difficulty to those who are unwilling to make this readjustment.

To sum up this section on overseas children and their re-entry problems, these children are best suited for internationalization and are ideal candidates for shouldering a Japan which in the next generation has to play a major role in the international scene. But they are in fact stifled in the process of becoming internationalized—by their parents, by the education system the parents accept, and by the society which is intolerant of internationalism.

Japanese language. If learning English is a formidable task which impresses the Japanese with its difficulty, having foreigners speak and understand Japanese presents an even greater challenge in the perception of Japanese. While an increasing number of foreigners are learning to speak the language, thus contributing toward internationalization of Japanese, most Japanese have a deep-seated belief that foreigners' Japanese language competence and comprehension are and will forever be less than complete. On this issue I can do no better than to cite and quote from Roy Andrew Miller's *Japanese Language in Contemporary Japan* (1977). The fundamental reason, Miller argues, why foreigners are not thought to be able to master the language lies in the "indescribable," "inevitable" and "illusive" nature believed by Japanese to be inherent in the spirit of Japanese language (*kotodama*). Miller demonstrates that speaking Japanese—for Japanese—is a Jamesian mystical experience: "ineffable, neotic, and yet totally transient" (Miller, 1977: 40). It is this inexplicable mysteriousness of the language which makes Japanese declare, "There is no way foreigners can comprehend Japanese" (*Gaikokujin niwa nihongo ga wakaru hazu ga nai*). Toyama goes so far as to declare that the reason Japanese flatteringly praise foreigners even for speaking faltering Japanese is that they are confident that foreigners can never speak Japanese properly anyway (Toyama, 1975: 23).

This outright dismissal by Japanese of foreigners' ability for the acquisition of Japanese does not deter the latter from continuing their efforts to master the language. The reward for all the hard work is often not commensurate with the effort, however. Miller (1977: 77) presents us with a priceless quote from Basil Hall Chamberlain (1850–1935): "Seeing that you speak Japanese, they [Japanese] will wag their heads and smile condescendingly, and admit to each other that you are really quite intelligent—much as we might do in the presence of a learned pig or an ape of somewhat unusual attainments." As Miller bemuses, if a bit sarcastically, few modern students of Japanese language need to update or revise this 70-year-old remark of Chamberlain's. What makes it worse is that the more fluent a foreigner becomes in Japanese, the less regard he is granted by natives. Hence Miller's "law of inverse returns," wherein "the better you get at the language, the less credit you are given for your accomplishments: the more fluently you speak it, the less your hard won skills will do for you in making friends and favorably impressing people, but by the same token the less you can do with the language, the more you will be praised and encouraged by Japanese society in general and your friends in particular" (Miller, 1977: 78).

Miller's analysis is that this law of inverse return is premised upon the Japanese need to define "sociolinguistic territorial integrity" (Miller, 1977: 82). "Genuine fluency in Japanese by foreigners living and working in Japan," Miller argues, "provides overt evidence of large-scale, long-lasting and extremely serious invasion of sociolinguistic territorial interests that are to be defended. To speak Japanese with a foreigner is to admit defeat in this battle over territorial invasion" (Miller, 1977: 82). The question of sociolinguistic integrity is inextricably tied in with the Japanese belief that Japanese language, culture, and race are one, a point to which we shall return later.

The conclusion one draws from this analysis of the meaning Japanese attach to their language is that it allows Japanese to draw an indubitable line between themselves and foreigners. Drawing a heavy and clear line is all the more important as more and more foreigners learn Japanese, many speaking it fluently, and threaten to violate "sociolinguistic integrity" of the Japanese. Thus while linguistic internationalization proceeds as foreigners learn Japanese, at the same time Japanese culture builds its defense against "linguistic invasion."

In this regard it is highly interesting that the Japanese which foreigners learn is call *Nihongo,* as Roy Andrew Miller once remarked at a lecture at Stanford University, whereas Japanese children study *kokugo,* not *Nihongo.* For example, in reference to studying, say, Japanese classics, one would not ask a school child in Japan "do you have homework in *Nihongo*?" as one might ask an American school child, "Do you have homework in English?" The question would be as nonsensical as if one were to ask an American male, "What size blouse do you wear?" The proper way to ask would be: "Do you have homework in kokugo?" It is instructive in this respect that Toyama, in his article "Nihongo kokusaika no jōken" (Prerequisites for Internationalization of the Japanese Language), refers to *Nihongo* in the title, since internationalization of Japanese means teaching the language to foreigners. In the text Toyama uses *kokugo* when referring to the Japanese which Japanese students study, and switches to *Nihongo* when speaking of foreigners' Japanese (Toyama, 1975).

In other words, at least in certain contexts, *Nihongo* denotes a separate psychological and semantic domain from *kokugo.* To be sure, in other contexts, Nihongo means Japanese spoken by Japanese, as in *Nihongo no keitō* (history of Japanese). The important point is that Japanese do separate the same language conceptually into two types, one belonging to themselves and the other belonging to foreigners.

Assertation of Cultural Autonomy
Transition from assertation of cultural separateness to declaration of cultural autonomy is as natural as it is imperceptible. Especially in language use, the distinctiveness of Japanese—the fact that it is the

native tongue of only one ethnic group called Japanese—expresses both separateness and autonomy. As Japanese culture is "exported"—in performing arts, exhibits and the like—again, these are not only a way to disseminate knowledge about Japan but also to assert throughout the world the uniqueness of Japanese culture and proclaim her cultural autonomy. Need to assert cultural independence is felt at home as well. With the inundation of Western culture in Japan, reaction to what is felt to be excessive adoption of Western culture is poignantly expressed by Honda Katsuichi, who is well known for his many best sellers on foreign cultures which he studied by adopting the anthropological participant observation technique. A seasoned observer of foreign culture and, thus, a well internationalized journalist, Honda criticizes in an article in the *Asahi Shimbun* (February 25, 1980) the confusion Japanese are guilty of concerning westernization and modernization. He laments excessive use of European loanwords. He chastises the Japanese for not following Japanese convention but rather writing surname first when writing a foreigner's name in Japanese transliteration, as in "Regan Ronarudo." Honda regards all this as colonialization of Japanese culture and likens it to the fate of the vanishing Ainu culture. In short, the internationalist Honda is decrying for cultural independence of Japan.

National Interest

A sub-theme in this assertation of cultural autonomy is protection of national interest, in particular, economic interest. Internationalization after all, means, among other things, trade liberalization, expansion of Japanese investment abroad, exportation of Japanese technology and managerial know-how, all of which are directly relevant to Japan's economic well-being.

As mentioned above already, the theme of economic interest is a dominant one in the concept of internationalization and is at the basis of other themes of the concept. As Yamamoto has pointed out (Yamamoto, 1981: 11), the oft-heard exhortation to produce a tough-minded internationalist (*shitatakana kokusaijin*) among Japanese turns out to mean that Japanese should be tough and assertive negotiators in international trade who can deal with aggressive Western negotiators on an equal basis.

Yamamoto notes that this notion of national interest as the underlying basis of Japan's internationalization sharply contrasts with that used in the European Economic Community, where internationalization means to relativize erstwhile absolute national sovereignty and to create an organization for deliberation and decision making which transcends nationality (Yamamoto, 1981: 11). It is precisely because national interest is at stake and is at the bottom of many of Japan's internationalization processes that these processes produce effects creating separateness between Japan and the rest of the world and asserting cultural autonomy—effects which can be best summarized as "nationalistic."

Bunkaron

The field of writing which is variously known as *Nihon bunkaron* (theory of Japanese culture), *Nihonjinron* (theory of Japanese national character), *Nihon shakairon* (theory of Japanese society), or simply *Nihonron* (theory about Japan) constitutes a genre familiar to any Japanese. "Theory" here does not mean "scientific theory" in any rigorous sense of the term, but refers to a loose aggregation of ideas which purports to explain or account for certain characteristics of Japanese culture, society, or national character.

While these terms each denote different concepts, one dealing with Japanese culture, one dealing with the Japanese national character, one with Japanese society, etc., in reality no such clear-cut conceptual distinction is made. A partially annotated bibliography in this genre titled *Nihonjinron* (Nomura Research Institute, 1978), for example, includes books (like Nakane's *Tate shakai no ningen kankei,* 1967) which clearly belong to the category of shakairon and Isaiah Ben-Dasan's *Nihonjin to Yudayajin* (1970), which is definitely a contribution in the field of bunkaron. In addition, many books in this genre, such as Hamaguchi Eshun's *"Nihon rashisa" no saihakken* (1977), span social, cultural and psychological dimensions, defying neat categorization. For these reasons it is a futile exercise to try to distinguish among these subfields. Instead they will be treated together, and here, for the sake of convenience the term "Nihon bunkaron" will be adopted to encompass the whole field.

It should be pointed out at the onset that bunkaron is not by and large an academic field comparable to, say, "theory of bureaucracy" or "dissonance theory." To be sure a few writings in this genre qualify as straightforward academic treatises (e.g., Murakami, Kumon and Satō, 1979). But the vast majority of the writings are meant to impress the lay public rather than fellow academicians.

As such, writings of the bunkaron type comprise an industry whose producers are intellectuals and its consumers the mass. Since the literature of bunkaron is thus a mass consumer-oriented product, writers must try to please the mass, who are the final judge for success or failure of the product. Criteria of evaluation, thus, are vastly different from those for purely academic work, where methodology of verification, logic of argument, etc., are the ultimate criteria. In Nihon bunkaron, the criterion is, rather, how well the product is received by the mass, for whom canons of scholarly procedure are of little concern.

The boom in Nihon bunkaron must be seen in the light of Japan's internationalization (Reischauer, 1977: 409). A complete tally of publications in this field is impossible, given the nebulousness of its definition. Nomura Research Institute's aforementioned bibliography lists 698 monographs published in the 32-year period from 1946 to 1978. If articles from periodicals such as *Chūō Kōron* and *Bungei Shunjū* are added, the number will become staggering.

Although concern for Japan's cultural identity, which Nihon bunkaron is all about, had existed from the Meiji or even before (Minami, 1976: 1980), it was at that time a worry of only a small number of intellectuals. The mass was by and large oblivious to this concern. With the increasing internationalization of Japan, however, at present no Japanese can escape being affected by its impact, in fact the majority are directly involved in the process. This problem of cultural identity ultimately arises from the psychological insecurity of Japanese. In the words of the editor of *Japan Interpreter*:

> Psychologically, a Japanese tends to be insecure, uncertain of his ego-identity unless he can clearly define his relationship with others around him, his relative position in the community or the group(s) he belongs to. This tendency not only leads the individual to focus attention on what others think of him—his "appearance" —but also creates a national hypersensitivity about international reputation and image. The Japanese preference for ranking and hierarchies is closely related to this particular psychological pattern and their social structure that has sustained it" (*Japan Interpreter* [ed.], 1973: 157)

Need for a secure cultural identity through identification of unique Japanese characteristics, then, has become a concern for the mass. The boom in Nihon bunkaron is a response to this need by the mass. For the objective of Nihon bunkaron, if there is one, is to provide the mass with a treatise which assures them of Japan's separateness and autonomy by spelling out how Japanese culture, society, and people are unique. It is worthy of note in this regard that around 1970 when Japan's internationalization "took off," the number of books in the genre of Nihon bunkaron also "took off" from about 20 a year to double that number. Using 1960 as the index, by 1977 annual publications of books in this genre increased fivefold (Nomura Research Institute, 1978: 3).

There is no need to review in detail the supposedly unique features of Japanese culture, society, and national character claimed in Nihon bunkaron. Only a few of the more popular themes relevant to internationalization will be briefly summarized here.

Homogeneity

That Japanese are a homogeneous people racially and culturally is a very popular idea, expressed as *tan'itsu, dōshitsu, tōshitsu, junsui*, and the like. For example Nakane's *Tate shakai no ningen kankei* is subtitled *Tan'itsu shakai no riron* (Theory of a Homogeneous Society), while Masuda Yoshiro titles his book *Junsui bunka no jōken* (Conditions of a Pure Culture). This homogeneity implies that the substance of Japanese culture is homogeneous, that it is not made up of elements of different cultural or ethnic origins. Regional variations in cultural practices from Aomori to Okinawa are not considered an invalidation of this thesis. Nor are the vast class differences observed in the feudal days—from the genteel nobility in Kyoto through the humorless confucian warriors and hedonistic, fun-loving townspeople to ignoble peasants—of any particular concern for defenders of the homogeneity thesis. For ultimately this homogeneity has to do, not with overt behavior or manifest customs, but with some fundamental premises about the culture and the people such as those I shall discuss in the next section.

Homogeneity, in a similar sense, also applies to language and race. That the Japanese language is a unique language spoken by all Japanese and only by Japanese is a claim which plays a crucial role in the thesis of cultural homogeneity since much of the essential character of Japanese culture is to be found in the semantic contents of the language and must be at any rate expressed though the language and can presumably be expressed only thus. Racial homogeneity of the Japanese people has mythological validation tracing Japanese people back to their ancestral Sun Goddess. While this myth may be regarded askance in contemporary Japan, the conviction that there is something genetic which unifies all Japanese is firmly entrenched. Belief in "Japanese blood" being carried among the Japanese is common place. The expression *Nihonjin no chi ga nagareteiru* has the primary meaning of "Japanese blood" circulating through the body in the ordinary, physiological sense and also the implied but crucial meaning of "Japanese" blood streaming through generations, a necessary condition for the belief in genetic transmission of culture and language. For "blood" in this context carries more than red and white corpuscles and other biological substances; it carries spiritual substance making up the basis of Japanese culture.

The notion of racial homogeneity also implies that the collective identity of Japanese is "racial historical" (*ketsuenshi-teki*), according to Kimura (1973: 12), who writes a piece on Nihon bunkaron from the perspective of psycho-pathology of the Japanese. "It is an identity," Kimura tells us, "which exists prior to the individual Japanese—an identity out of which each Japanese is born" (1973: 13). This "priority" does not refer to temporal order but to ontological order, i.e., to the foundation of existence. It has to do with the basis of realization of who one is. It is for this reason that not only foreigners are forever foreigners, excluded from the fold of Japanese, but even those of partial Japanese descent are regarded as less than full Japanese in the social and cultural sense (Mushakōji, 1980).

Biological and phenotypic similarity between Japanese and neighboring peoples such as Koreans, Chinese, and Southeast Asians is not sufficient evidence to destroy the supposed racial integrity of the Japanese even though genetic traits, such as blood groups systems, form a quantitative gradation from surrounding areas to Japan, and genetic differences between Japanese and neighboring groups are merely statistical. For the racial purity of the Japanese is presumably defined by genetic continuity through generations. Japanese would make sure to point out in this connection that stretching as far back in history as they can document—at least 2,000 years—there has not been any large scale migration of outsiders to Japan. They are likely to call your attention with ill-concealed pride that there are still pockets of Korean potters in Kyushu whose ancestors were brought to Japan 400 years ago at the time of Toyotomi Hideyoshi's Korean campaign and that they are still kept separate from Japanese.

A further meaning of homogeneity to be noted is the unity of race, language, and culture: linguistic and culture homogeneity is assumed to be maintained because of the homogeneity of race (Miller, 1977: ch. 6). Implied in this meaning is the further assumption that certain core traits of Japanese language and culture are genetically transmitted (Hayashida, 1976). It is no wonder in this context, as was pointed out to me by Robert J. Smith (personal communication), that even an eminent anthropologist like Ishida Eiichiro would argue in his *Japanese Culture* (1974) for the inception of the Japanese language to coincide with the appearance of the Japanese people. Ambiguity of the meaning of the term *Nihon minzoku* (Japanese people) is significant here. *Minzoku* is often translated as "race" by Japanese writers; but it also means an ethnic group possessing a distinct culture. The dictionary definition given in *Kōjien* clearly specifies that race, culture, and language are all defining criteria of the term.

It is this genetic base of Japanese language and culture which closes all doors to foreigners who might wish to become or be considered Japanese. Lack of this genetic base for foreigners precludes any possibility of acquiring Japanese culture or language as Japanese do; they are regarded as unable to acquire the essential core of Japanese sociolinguistic competence, even though they may be able to practice the culture and speak the language at a more superficial level. To the slightest linguistic error foreigners make, Japanese are fond of remarking (in their presence!) "That goes to show how difficult Japanese language is!" as if to imply that the difficulty is totally insurmountable for foreigners.

The relative difficulty of becoming a naturalized Japanese citizen according to the present civil code may also be interpreted as a legal expression of the ethos of the culture which rejects non-Japanese as lacking the potential of becoming culturally full-fledged Japanese. Interestingly, according to a recent opinion survey only 28 percent of Japanese living in the largest cities (and hence those presumably most internationalized) are willing to allow foreigners to settle in Japan or be naturalized, compared with 41 percent of those living in smaller cities and 35 percent of those in rural areas expressing the same view (*Japan*. Sōrifu Tōkeikyoku, 1981). While the reversal of the trend between small cities and rural areas is puzzling, it is as though the more internationalized Japanese become, the more they shun foreigners. Also, the Japanese unwillingness to dilute racial and cultural homogeneity is probably implicit in their reluctance to accept the boat people of Southeast Asia on a permanent basis and also their nonacceptance of foreign immigrants as a way of solving the labor shortage problem.

This same genetic theory of language transmission, which is at the basis of the assumed inability of foreigners to acquire competence in Japanese, also assumes that Japanese-Americans should be able to speak Japanese without learning it.[4] The utter amazement nearing bewilderment which Japanese manifest to Japanese-Americans travelling or staying in Japan who cannot speak the language is a testimony to the strength of this belief. By the same token when Japanese-Americans learn to speak the language, the Japanese are not as charitable with their praise as they might be for Caucasians learning the language, since for Japanese-Americans linguistic competence is implicitly assumed to be "in the genes" and need only be given an opportunity for its "phenotypic" expression.

A possibly related phenomenon often observed in Japan should be mentioned. American born and raised *nisei* and *sansei* living in Japan are often turned down in their applications for positions to teach English. The common excuse is that students prefer Caucasion teachers. This in itself is of course a blatant expression of reverse racism—a conviction that a white man has something to teach simply because he is white and that a yellow man is not qualified to teach about the white man's culture simply because he is yellow. Behind this reasoning there may well be a genetic assumption as to the Japanese-American's linguistic and cultural competence, namely that his biological background stigmatizes him and casts doubt concerning the authoritativeness of his credentials as a teacher of matters Western and his ability to speak English. Probably because this assumption is widespread though implicit, private English language schools would not jeopardize their reputations by hiring a Japanese-American.

Armed with this genetic theory, or racist theory as Reischauer would put it (1977: 47), and the theory of unity of race, language, and culture, Japanese have a secure line of defense in maintaining their separateness and distinctness even in the face of an onslaught of foreign cultural diffusion.

Minimum Essence of Japanese Culture

The genetically based Japanese language and culture have certain irreducible essences which define their uniqueness. Japansee cultural philosophers have explicated ad nauseum such esthetic concepts as *iki, wabi, sabi,* and *mono no aware.* The personal character of the Japanese is epitomized by theorists of Nihon bunkaron in such concepts as *kokoro, seishin,* and *tamashii.* Through sharing of these and other essential and unique characteristics Japanese claim to possess certain uncanny, non-verbal abilities to communicate with one another, often expressed as *ishin denshin* (from mind to mind) or *haragei* (belly-art) (Kunihiro, 1976: 270–73). Foreigners, lacking in this ability, are said to be hindered in communicating with Japanese.

The group orientation of the Japanese is also said to be a unique Japanese social institution, with its predominantly hierarchical alignment of members, bonded by the psychological glue of *amae,* woven together by the social threads of *on* and *giri* in a particularistic relationship. This group structure is said to provide a model for all kinds of concrete organizations in Japan—from bureaucracy and school clubs to schools of tea ceremony and organized crime. The miraculous success of Japanese business is attributed by scores of Japanese management specialists and Western scholars from Abegglen on down the line to the uniquely Japanese managerial system, which is in turn characterized in terms of Japanese groupism (Abegglen, 1958; Ballon, 1980; Brown, 1966; Dore, 1973; Hazama, 1971; Inuta, 1977; Iwata, 1978; Ouchi, 1981; Rohlen, 1974; Tsuda, 1977; Urabe, 1978).

This is not the place to elaborate on these Japanese concepts. Suffice it to note that these are a sampling of traits which define the uniqueness of Japanese culture and which according to Japanese claim make Japanese culture difficult or impossible for foreigners to understand (Katō, 1962). It is interesting that while this claim is often made by Japanese, it is seldom conceded by foreigners, especially those who are specialists in Japanese studies.[5] Be that as it may, these are some of the essential traits of the homogeneous culture which the Japanese claim is so unique.

Claim of Uniqueness

That Japanese culture is unique no one doubts. After all, every culture in the world is unique in its form and content. Thus when Japanese claim uniqueness of their culture, in fact they are not saying anything special, different, or new about their culture. However, there is something different, special and possibly unique in the vehemence with which they make a point of the uniqueness of their culture. This claim to uniqueness is of course a byproduct of the first two claims; that is, their uniqueness lies in the claimed homogeneity of their culture, with all that implies, and in the possession of certain irreducible essences. The question is why do Japanese have to proclaim their uniqueness so vociferously? The answer to this question should be obvious by now. The internationalization of Japan has brought about Japan's identity crisis on a massive scale. The claim to uniqueness is an answer to this crisis.

This claim to uniqueness has a Western bias as does the Japanese concept of internationalization. The exercise of enumerating unique Japanese features is of course aided by a comparative method, which allows Japanese to see what is different about the Japanese in contrast to other cultures. In this comparison, other cultures to be compared with Japan are predominantly Western. This is understandable in light of the fact that acculturative impact is by and large provided by the West and consequently the threat to Japan's cultural identity also comes from the same direction.

Thus when Japanese claim a trait to be "uniquely Japanese," in many cases it merely means that the trait is present in Japan and absent in the West, ignoring the possibility of its presence in any of the several hundred other cultures not examined. Its possible presence in some obscure culture in Africa or the Amazon jungle, however, is totally irrelevant from the point of view of what Nihon bunkaron is supposed to accomplish, namely to assert cultural autonomy from those cultures which are violating the cultural territorial integrity. Insofar as an unknown African or Amazon tribe is no threat to cultural integrity of the Japanese, they can be safely ignored.

Positive Valuation

The history of Nihon bunkaron goes back to the early Meiji, or perhaps even before. As long as Japan has had some awareness of foreign countries, such as China, Portugal, or Spain, from the Edo period and earlier, Japanese were compelled to produce some sort of Nihon bunkaron, though of course it did not have such a label then. From one historic period to another, the dominant features selected to characterize Japan's uniqueness have varied, though I have no space here to go into this question. Moreover, the dominant valuation attached to views of Japan also varied in history from positive to negative. Again, there is no space here for a systematic review of this pendulum swing back and forth even from the late Tokugawa. Suffice it to mention the near-total negative valuation given to Japanese culture in the postwar era of defeat, devastation, and hopelessness which is still fresh in our memory. "Feudalistic vestige" (*hōken isei*) and "premodern" (*zen-kindai-teki*) were the epithetic terms widely invoked in those days in reference to such values as *on* and *giri* and to the whole of traditional social structure.

In short, in bad times, Japanese blame their history, their culture, and themselves for all the wrong around them. By the same token, in good times, they credit their culture, social structure, and themselves for their success. Indeed, the same values and the whole traditional social structure, which were blamed for causing the war and the attendant misery, are now credited by Japanese as the very secret of their current economic success.

Internationalization is a concrete manifestation of Japan's success on the world scene. Assertion of cultural autonomy and national identity, resulting as a reaction to the very process of internationalization, then, must retain and incorporate Japan's pride in this success. It is for this reason that the definition of the national image is asserted with positive valuation.

CONCLUSION: FROM KOKUSAIKA TO KOKUSUIKA

The internationalization of Japan is first and foremost an economic matter, and secondarily it refers to processes which result from and/or facilitate economic internationalization. This is not to deny that other, non-economic processes of internationalization have independent roles entirely apart from or unrelated to the economic. However, in

terms of relative weighting, the primacy of economic internationalization cannot be denied, and it serves Japan's drive to achieve economic eminence and even dominance in the world. In short, the
goal of Japan's internationalization is to enhance and protect Japan's
national interest, and this is most prominently expressed in economic
terms.

I have argued in this paper that the very processes of Japan's internationalization induce its separateness from the rest of the world and
cause Japan to assert its cultural autonomy. Thus the more Japan becomes internationalized (kokusaika), the more nationalistic (*kokusuika*)
Japan becomes (Yamamoto, 1981: 15). Internationalism and nationalism are supposedly antithetical to one another. Yet in the Japanese case,
one leads directly to the other. I wonder if the current conservative
move and mood in Japan may not be riding the tide of nationalism
resulting from internationalization and cashing in on the reverse-
internationalism to promote the conservative cause.

Offhand, internationalism may seem like a process which inevitably
leads to cosmopolitalism. Funk and Wagnalls' *New Standard Dictionary
of the English Language* (1963: 591) defines "cosmopolitan" as follows:

1. Common to all the world; not limited to any region of the
   physical world or to any department of the world of thought.
2. Free from local attachments and prejudices, equally at home in
   all parts of the world; unprejudiced.
3. Having or exhibiting cosmopolitan character.

Some Japanese writers in fact apparently have in mind cosmopolitanism as the ideal and result of internationalism. For example, Kurihara
has advocated a meaning of "internationalization" in which universal
humanism transcends nationalistic interests and boundaries (1972: 294–
95). De Vera's conception echoes Kurihara's: "Internationalism is a
value-laden term that denotes an ideology. We take it here as the attitude of those who believe in the solidarity of the human race and the
possibility of a world-community, and who are striving to bring it
about" (De Vera, 1976: 2–3).

Mingling with peoples around the world, learning foreign languages,
working shoulder to shoulder with foreigners, living abroad next door
to locals, absorbing foreign cultures, teaching foreigners Japanese and
showing what Japan is like—in short doing what internationalization

implies seems like a textbook recipe for creating a cosmopolitan individual.

Yet, as we have seen, results have been the opposite. Instead of freeing Japanese from local attachment (to Japan) and prejudices against foreigners in Japan or against locals abroad, Japanese experience with foreigners at home and in foreign countries seems to renew their attachment to their fatherland and even awaken their prejudices against locals or foreigners (such as Southeast Asians) to whom their sense of prejudice in the past was at best merely dormant. Instead of leading directly by the surest and shortest road to the cosmopolitan world, internationalization, at least for Japan, leads to the opposite world, as if each internationalization process is a U-turn, returning to renewed nationalism.

It behooves us to remind ourselves of this juxtaposition of positive and negative aspects of internationalization. On the one hand, processes of internationalization—from trade liberalization through language learning to spreading knowledge about Japan worldwide—are eminently laudable. No one needs to feel ashamed or guilty about blowing the bugle of internationalization in this sense. On the other hand, nationalistic consequences of the process are less than 100 percent commendable. What is problematic about the concept of internationalization is that it is both a statement of facts and also a moral imperative, a slogan. It is a fact that Japan is internationalizing in the various ways outlined above. But the term, as I have mentioned, has a prestige connotation: to internationalize is fashionable and good, and not to do so or to resist doing so is a sign of the backwardness of a country bumpkin.

In the 1950s "democratization" (*minshuka*) was the symbol of modernity, until the symbol became tired and worn out. Then it was replaced in the 1960s by "modernization" (kindaika) as a new symbol and torchlight to guide the people. As the latter symbol also lost its novelty and luster, "internationalization" took over to serve as the new symbol of morality and to guide people into a new era.

What is sinister about internationalization is the unintended consequence of this laudable process: namely the abovementioned "U-turn anti-internationalism." Japan can continue on the road of neonationalism (kokusuika) with impunity since it happens as Japan flies the banner of internationalism (kokusaika). Thus the two processes are as inextricably inseparable as the two Japanese terms for them are barely distinguishable.

As Umesao (1975) has pointed out, the concept of internationalism assumes nations, national boundaries, and national interests. As long as we accept this assumption, we are not likely to have "one world," a cosmopolitan world, and we should not expect to have one. This is not to say that cultural differences need to be obliterated to achieve this goal. The unique aspects of different cultures certainly may remain; the world would be dull without them. However, defending political and economic interests of one group at the expense of another is another matter. Speaking of uniqueness, the two-pronged effects of Japan's internationalization may not be so unique. It may in fact be commonplace around the world. One may even venture to suggest that neo-nationalism in the guise of internationalization is one of the root problems of the contemporary world.

NOTES

1. These figures on foreign residents, visitors entering and exiting Japan, Japanese leaving and returning to Japan, foreign investments in Japan and Japanese investment abroad are taken from *Japan Statistical Yearbook,* 1978 and 1979.
2. A study by a Kyoto University group on overseas returnees does in fact show that the time needed for readjustment in Japan is a negative function of the length of sojourn, fluency with foreign language learned abroad, the number of local friends, and whether the returnee went to a Japanese school, an international school, or a local school. This study also shows, however, that variation in the adjustment time is mostly within the first year, and that by the end of the first year of their return, most returnees, regardless of these variables, do achieve a similar degree of adjustment (Kyoto University School of Education, Department of Comparative Education, 1978).
3. Ostensibly, establishment of Japanese schools overseas is justified on the basis of academic needs; namely, that children must be given as far as possible an education comparable to that back home, so that upon return they will have minimal problems in academic adjustment, as Katō Kōji of the National Institute for Educational Research rationalizes (1978: 21). However, if we take into consideration the fact that within a year, even those who attended a local school attain readjustment, one wonders whether all the expense and effort poured into establishment and maintenance of Japanese schools abroad are justified even on academic grounds (Kyoto University School of Education, Department of Comparative Education, 1978: 45).
4. When I was in Japan in 1978–79 with my high-school age daughter, her Japanese friend could not comprehend that in the United States there are people called *nisei* and *sansei,* of full Japanese biological extraction, who cannot speak or understand Japanese. When she visited us in the United States after our return home, we invited my sansei nephew, whose Japanese vocabulary can be counted on one hand,

to meet this girl. Only then was she convinced—most reluctantly—that Japanese genes do not automatically confer Japanese language competence.

5. It is curious in this respect that Isaiah Ben-Dasan, that erudite Jewish scholar of Japanese history and thought, plainly admits his inability to attain complete understanding of the Japanese language (1970: 49–95), which makes one think he perhaps is not the foreigner he claims to be, but is a Japanese as many suspect.

REFERENCES

Abegglen, James C.
　1958　*The Japanese Factory*. Glencoe: Free Press.
Ballon, Robert J.
　1980　*Nihongata bijinesu no kenkyū* (A Study of Japanese Managerial Style). Tokyo: Prejidento.
Ben-Dasan, Isaiah
　1970　*Nihonjin to Yudayajin*. Tokyo: Yamamoto Shoten.
Brown, William
　1966　"Japanese Management: The Cultural Background." *Monumenta Nipponica,* 21: 47–60.
Denison, Edward F., and William F. Chung
　1976　*How Japan's Economy Grew So Fast*. Washington, D.C.: Brookings Institute.
De Vera, Jose M.
　1976　"Internationalization of the University." *PHP* (September): 2–11.
Dore, Ronald P.
　1973　*British Factory, Japanese Factory*. Berkeley: University of California Press.
　1979　"Industrial Relations in Japan and Elsewhere." In A. Craig (ed.), *Japan, a Comparative View*. Princeton: Princeton University Press.
Ebuchi Kazukimi
　1978　"Nihonjin no ibunka eno tekiō to kyōiku" (Education and Adjustment of Japanese to Foreign Culture). In Kyoto University School of Education, Department of Comparative Education (ed.), *Zaigai kikoku shijo no tekiō kyōiku no jōken ni kansuru sōgōteki kenkyū: Kenkyū kirokushū II*
Hamaguchi Eshun
　1977　*"Nihon rashisa" no saihakken* (Rediscovery of "Japaneseness"). Tokyo: Nihon Keizai Shimbunsha.
Hayashida, Cullen T.
　1976　*Identity, Race and the Blood Ideology of Japan*. University of Washington doctoral dissertation.
Hazama Hiroshi
　1971　*Nihonteki keiei* (Japanese Style Management). Tokyo: Nihon Keizai Shimbunsha.
　1974　"The Samurai and Modern Enterprises." *East* 10: 10–12.
Hidaka Rokurō, and So Yong-dal
　1980　*Daigaku no kokusaika to gaikokujin kyōin* (Internationalization of the University and Foreign Instructors). Tokyo: Daisan Bummeisha.
Inuta Mitsuru
　1977　*Shūdan shugi no kōzō* (The Structure of Groupism). Tokyo: Sangyō

Nōritsu Tanki Daigaku Press.

Ishida Eiichirō
1974 *Japanese Culture*. Tokyo: University of Tokyo Press.

Iwata Ryushi
1978 *Gendai Nihon no keiei fūdo* (The Environment of Management in Modern Japan). Tokyo: Nihon Keizai Shimbunsha.

Japan, Prime Minister's Office. Statistics Bureau
1978, 1979 *Japan Statistical Yearbook*. Tokyo: Japan Statistics Association.

Japan. Sōrifu Tōkeikyoku
1981 "Gaikokujin no nyūkoku to zairyū" (Immigration and Residence of Foreigners). Japan Sōrifu Kōhōshitsu (ed.), *Yoron Chōsa*, 13 (1).

Japan Interpreter (ed.)
1973 "Why the Search for Identity." *Japan Interpreter*, 8: 153–58.

Katō Kōji
1978 " 'Kaigai shijo no tekiō ni kansuru chōsa' no igi o kangaeru" (The Significance of "The Study of Adjustment of Overseas Chidren"). In Kyoto University School of Education, Department of Comparative Education (ed.), *Zaigai kikoku shijo no tekiō kyōiku no jōken ni kansuru sōgōteki kenkyū: Kenkyū kiroku II*

Katō, Shūichi
1962 "Nihonjin no gaikokukan" (Japanese Views of Foreign Countries). *Shisō*, no. 458: 1–12.

Kimura Bin
1973 *Hito to hito tono aida* (Between One Person and Another). Tokyo: Kobundo.

Kinugasa Yosuke
1979 *Nihon kigyō no kokusaika senryaku* (Strategies of Internationalization of Japanese Enterprises). Tokyo: Nihon Keizai Shimbunsha.

Kunihiro Masao
1976 "The Japanese Language and Intercultural Communication." *Japan Interpreter*, 10: 267–82.

Kurihara Akira
1972 "The International Sense of the Japanese." *Japan Interpreter*, 7: 293–301.

Kwansei Gakuin. Kōhō Iinkai (ed.)
1977 *Kokusai kōryū to daigaku* (International Exchange and the University). Nishinomiya: Kwansei Gakuin.

Kyoto University School of Education, Department of Comparative Education
1978 *Zaigai kikoku shijo no tekiō ni kansuru chōsa: Kaigai kikoku shijo kyōiku kenkyū III* (A Study on Adjustment of Returnee Children: Research on the Education of Overseas Returnee Children *III*).

Masuda Yoshiro
1967 *Junsui bunka no jōken* (Conditions of a Pure Culture). Tokyo: Kōdansha.

Miller, Roy Andrew
1977 *The Japanese Language in Contemporary Japan: Some Sociolinguistic Observations*. Washington, D.C.: American Enterprise Institute for Public Policy Research and Stanford: Hoover Institution.

Minami Hiroshi
1976 "The Introspection Boom: Whither the National Character." *Japan Interpreter*, 8: 159–84.

1980 *"Nihonjinron no keifu"* (The Genealogy of Theories About Japanese People). Tokyo: Kōdansha.

Murakami Yasusuke, Kumon Shunpei, and Satō Seizaburō
1979 *Bummei to shiteno ie shakai* (The *ie* Society as a Civilization). Tokyo: Chūō Kōronsha.

Murase, Anne E.
1978a "The Problems of Japanese Returning Students." *International Education and Cultural Exchange,* 13: 10–14.
1978b "Education for the Multicultural Child." *The Five Seasons,* 1.

Murayama Motofusa
1979 *Keiei kaigai itenron* (Overseas Expansion of Business). Tokyo: Soseisha.

Mushakōji Kinhide
1980 *Chikyū jidai no kokusai kankaku* (International Sense in the Global Age). Tokyo: TBS Britannica.

Nakane Chie
1967 *Tate shakai no ningen kankei: Tan'itsu shakai no riron* (Human Relations in a Vertical Society: A Theory of a Homogeneous Society). Tokyo: Kōdansha.

Naylor, Martyn
1980 "Japan's Unique Group Dynamism." In Paul Norbury and Geoffrey Bownas (eds.), *Business in Japan.* Boulder, Colorado: Westview Press.

Nomura Research Institute (ed.)
1978 *Nihonjinron* (reference no. 2)

Norbury, Paul, and Geoffrey Bownas
1980 *Business in Japan.* Boulder, Colorado: Westview Press.

Ouchi, William G.
1981 *Theory Z: How American Business Can Meet the Japanese Challenge.* Reading, Mass.: Addison-Wesley.

Reischauer, Edwin O.
1977 *The Japanese.* Cambridge: Harvard University Press.

Rohlen, Thomas P.
1974 *For Harmony and Strength.* Berkeley: University of California Press.

Toyama Shigehiko
1975 "Nihongo kokusaika no jōken" (Prerequisites for Internationalization of the Japanese Language). *Kokusai Kōryū,* no. 5: 19–29.

Tsuda Masumi
1977 *Nihonteki keiei no riron* (Theory of Japanese Style Management). Tokyo: Chūō Keizaisha.

Umesao Tadao
1975 "Nihonjin no kokusaisei o tou" (I Question the Internationality of Japanese). *Ushio,* no. 191: 107–115.

Urabe Kuniyoshi
1978 *Nihonteki keiei o kangaeru* (Thoughts About Japanese Style Management). Tokyo: Chūō Keizaisha.

Yamamoto Mitsuru
1981 "Nihon ga kokusai shakai de ikiru jōken" (Prerequisites for Japan's Survival in International Society). *Ekonomisuto* (January 2): 10–16.

INTERNATIONALIZATION
AS AN IDEOLOGY
IN JAPANESE SOCIETY

Ross E. Mouer
Yoshio Sugimoto

"Internationalism" in Japan

Tokyo is one of the world's greatest cities. It has first-class museums, offers a rich variety of national cuisines, and constantly draws the world's top performers. Tokyo has also become a repository for information from every corner of the world. In short, it is cosmopolitan. Since rejoining the international community in the early 1950s, Japan has been active in the United Nations and its various agencies, the OECD, the Club of Rome, the Trilateral Commission, the International Labor Organization, the World Bank, GATT and the International Monetary Fund. Japanese have also been enthusiastic members of Rotary International, the International Boy Scouts, the Lions, the Experiment in International Living and other similar bodies. The zeal with which English and other foreign languages are studied is unparalleled in the world. The number of titles translated into English by the Japanese themselves is also no small accomplishment. It would be difficult to criticize the Japanese for not being international.

At the same time, however, the alleged failure of the Japanese to internationalize is commonly discussed in the Japanese media, often with lament and sometimes with vexation. The Japanese are constantly prodding themselves to be more international. It would seem reasonable, therefore, that we ask why so much self-doubt is expressed about Japan's internationalization when Japan already appears to be so internationalized. There are, no doubt, several reasons.

Internationalization is a multivarious process. Societies may be international in some regards but not in others. While few societies have been as open as Japanese society to foreign ideas, the knowledge many

Japanese have of the outside world is qualitatively quite limited. As such, it is not really as formidable as it seems when we think only of the quantity of information and the number of titles imported into Japan. Although many Japanese are very sensitive to comparisons with "the West," there has been a tendency to view the West as a monolith. Moreover, the massive amounts of data or factual information on foreign societies collected in Tokyo have not necessarily produced an understanding of the societies studied.

On the other hand, from the viewpoint of social engineering, such "factual" information has assisted Japanese businessmen intent upon knowing about functional or mechanical relationships in order to exploit or manipulate foreign economies. Further, it is not unusual for an idealized notion of the West to be used as an ideological concept. Whether it is the desire of management to raise productivity, the goal of unions in the public sector to regain the right to strike, or the objective of leaders in the various anti-pollution movements to embarrass the government, appeals to something international or to some ideal believed to have been actually attained in the West are commonly used to mobilize large numbers of Japanese.

In recent years, "internationalism" and "the age of internationalization" have come into vogue in the Japanese vocabulary. Although the idea of "being international" has positive connotations for most Japanese, the term hides more than it reveals. It has served as a convenient euphemism for talking about foreign policy while really avoiding a number of major issues which divide the Japanese. Most discussions of "internationalization" in Japan focus on activities rather than on ends. In leading discussions on internationalization in several major Japanese cities in 1980 and 1981, it was fairly easy to establish that nearly every person present thought that "internationalization" was a positive thing which they as individuals supported. However, when asked what "internationalization" meant to them, about ten items frequently received mention. They ranged from studying English to learning about foreign cultures and are essentially the items (definitions) mentioned in Befu's contribution to this volume. Once the list was compiled, participants were further asked to indicate whether the definitions referred to means or to ends. Nearly all the participants saw each item listed as representing some kind of instrumental activity. Internationalization was seen as being a number of steps or strategies to achieve an undefined goal. The experiment was repeated with other formats using different cross sections of the Japanese population. The results were invariably the same: "internationalization" (*kokusaika*), "becoming international" (*kokusaijin ni naru koto*), "internationalism" (*kokusai shugi*) or even the "age of internationalism" (*kokusaika no jidai*) were positively evaluated and then defined as activities rather than as situations which were to be attained. In other words, "internationalization" was not conceived as a process producing a clearly defined state of affairs different from some present arrangement. Perhaps in most languages "internationalism" is an ambiguous term which generates vague notions of something good. Nevertheless, because the term is frequently used to justify various kinds of behavior in Japan, it might be useful to examine its usage and the goals it implies.

The term "internationalization" seems to be commonly used in Japanese to imply two conflicting goals. As Yamamoto (1981) has observed, "internationalism" is often used to mean the smooth promotion of "Japan's national interests." In this context, the term has come to mean the achievement of Japan's economic goals overseas without rocking the boat in international waters. It has meant the sending of smiling performers in the traditional arts as unofficial ambassadors to calm the "locals" and to distract attention from economic difficulties or from charges that Japan's multinational enterprises (MNEs) are exploiting the local economy. In the "cultural understanding game," Japan is portrayed as a country with a culture so unique that economic conflicts of interest abroad can always be dismissed either as cultural misunderstanding or as ethnocentrism on the part of foreign negotiators. Accordingly, the responsibility for conflict resolution is shifted to the foreigner who is advised that his salvation lies not in learning economic facts about Japanese firms or in looking at their balance sheets, but in endlessly running the gauntlet of petty customs—from bowing to knowing all the nuances of "*amae*" or "*sō desu ne*." In many cases, the "learn-from-Japan campaign" can also be understood in this light. In our minds, this usage of "internationalism" is associated primarily with the establishment: members of the Liberal Democratic Party, the business community and certain conservative labor leaders.

"Internationalization" is also used to imply more idealistic goals. Given the general disillusionment with nationalism which was widespread following defeat in 1945, the word's idealistic connotations were reinforced by the socialist movement which emerged during the Occupation. The strong commitment of many Japanese to the idea of peace, their concern about nuclear weapons and their demonstrations against the security treaty with the United States are legend. However, when asked for a more concrete definition of their goals, those sympathetic to this type of internationalism tend to gravitate in one of two directions: either to make vague references to international brotherhood and goodwill among nations or to outline the way in which some form of world government might be encouraged.

The ordinary citizen may not consciously distinguish clearly between these two usages of "internationalization" which imply very different goals. Yet the word seems to be manipulated as an ideological symbol by at least two groups in Japanese society. One is a committed elite with a solid grasp of the realpolitik and the realities of Western imperialism in Asia earlier this century. Its members generally accept the nation-state system and subscribe to the first set of goals mentioned above. The second group consists of those who are wary not so much of nationalism as of the present political arrangements and the present conservative regime in Japan. This group of persons tends to subscribe to the second set of goals mentioned above. To be sure, there is also a sizeable stratum of persons interested only in "getting along" and in promoting their own self-interest. They are fairly apathetic; indeed, they are even alienated by the constant efforts of the others to use the concept of "internationalism" as an ideological tool. While this third grouping could be crucial in determining the future direction of Japanese politics, it represents a segment of society which is open to a give-and-take form of interaction with foreign governments, firms and individuals based on the notion of comparative advantage and the idea of protecting their own limited interests. A swing to the right in their support could bring in a reactionary government; a swing to the left could bring in a more reformist coalition government. If there is a key to how Japan will internationalize in the future, it may very well lie in our understanding of this stratum.

There is today in Japan a considerable debate on the "internationalization of Japan." Part of the discussion is focused on identifying the consequences or ramifications of certain "inevitable" changes. In the past many Japanese have seen the national goal as being one of catching up or as national survival itself. Now that Japan is a front-runner and in a position where its ability to influence the survival of other countries is recognized, it is increasingly playing a leadership role. Moreover, the international environment, including America's role in the world, has changed. Accordingly, Japan can no longer depend upon America to lead the way; rather it must now begin to plot its own course. In democracies where different images and ideologies are free to compete, public opinion is an important force influencing the formation of foreign policy. For this reason, Japan's future will be shaped in part by the way in which Japanese perceive of their internationalization and the goals they associate with that process. However, as in any democracy, to the extent that the goals remain implicit and are not explicitly debated, they are decided not openly by public debate but by a mixture of elected and self-appointed decision makers. The decisions of these decision makers as to what the goals should be and the public's acceptance of those decisions will in turn be shaped by the way in which the outside world is perceived by the leadership and by the electorate.

In this paper we argue that the present ambiguity with regard to goals cannot be understood apart from the self-images which Japanese have of themselves. These images, we argue, serve as a mirror for looking not only at themselves but also at the world around them. Our view is that Japanese perceptions and public opinion on many of the issues related to internationalization are not firm. Cynics and apologists alike have tended to regard Japanese indecision as an expression of typically Japanese "situational ethics" or even as the internalization on a grand national scale of the values associated with opportunism. Such irresolution can also be interpreted as being evidence of a certain fluidity in Japanese society. There seems to be room for debate, and many Japanese want to be in a position to effect and to choose Japan's foreign policy. If we accept David Apter's definition of "modernity" as an attitude which values the ability to choose (Apter, 1965: 9–11), many Japanese would seem to be quite modern with regard to their views on how Japan's international relations ought to be conducted.

The next section of this paper gives a brief discussion of Japanese sensitivity to foreign ideas. As perceptions, Japanese images of the outside world influence public opinion on foreign policy issues; as ideology, they are used to mobilize Japanese on domestic issues. The section concludes with the suggestion that politicization of the term "internationalization" is linked to Japanese self-perceptions and the production of a large body of pseudo-social scientific literature often referred to as "*Nihonjinron*". In the third section we delineate the major features of Nihonjinron. In the final two sections we consider the significance of these perceptions for Japanese seeking to function outside Japan and for Japanese and non-Japanese seeking to understand Japanese society.

The "International" in Japanese Political Culture

Some time ago Kunihiro Masao (1979) coined the word "inter-domestic" to refer to the way in which essentially domestic matters in one society often have ramifications which markedly affect the essentially domestic affairs of another society. In his view, "inter-domestication" is a global phenomenon. Perhaps, the political use of terms like "internationalization" within the Japanese context may have made it easier for a Japanese to perceive this trend. Still, the significance of Kunihiro's new term lies less in its descriptive value and more in the way it illustrates how such words are used to encourage a certain course of action: because the international situation is "inter-domestic," Japanese must do "X, Y and Z." This kind of moralizing is also a feature of Nakane's analysis (1972) of the difficulties faced by the Japanese in Southeast Asia and can be found in the political messages of Doi (1971).

Japanese concern with the international is also characterized by frequent and extensive use of international comparisons to justify a behavioral choice. One might argue that, to some extent, this is inevitable given Japan's great dependence on foreign resources and its reliance on the goodwill of other nations in the pursuit of its economic goals. Although others have discussed propositions concerning Japan's dependence (Hollerman, 1967; Kojima, 1971), our interest here is not in the actual extent of Japanese dependence as measured according to some universal standard; it is in the perception that many Japanese have of their nation and their society as being dependent on external developments. This view can be seen in Document 1.

In Australia a fairly strong sense of dependence is felt, as well as even fear, perhaps, with regard to Asia, as reflected in past notions of the Yellow Peril and in the now elapsed "White Australia Policy."

DOCUMENT 1

ON JAPAN'S NEED TO EXPORT TO SURVIVE

...In the Tokugawa Period, Japan was self-sufficient,...and there was no need to think about the outside world. However, shortly after entering the second half of the nineteenth century, the country was opened up and exposed to the threat of imperialism from every direction. The country was thereby forced to assert its own independence.

...As one can easily understand by considering the Russo-Japanese War, a country without artillery and warships could very easily end up being a colony without realizing it.

However, Japan could not produce the necessary iron ore domestically. ...Even today there is no change in that basic fact. For this reason,... all the raw materials not available domestically had to be imported. Assurance of these imports was the major precondition for maintaining economic independence....

...Given this situation, it was only natural that Japan had to export in order to import. In other words, from the beginning of Meiji, throughout the prewar period and even in the postwar period Japan has had to earn foreign exchange in order to import.

Before the war, Japan's trade balance was always in the red. Even in the textbooks for primary school it was written that we must cut back on imports and use domestically produced goods. The image of Japan's economy held by prewar Japanese with regard to the balance of payments ...was one of chronic deficits. The fact that Japan could never become economically independent as long as it remained in the red was posed as a fundamental problem (for all Japanese).

Today Japan's trade balance is clearly in the black, and by the end of 1970 foreign exchange reserves totalled about four million dollars. When the Government published its Socio-Economic Development Plan in 1967, the plan included the warning that foreign exchange reserves equalling two billion dollars must be obtained. Even as late as 1967 the accumulation of such reserves was regarded as a tremendous task. Without considerable care Japan's economy has been directed by that fear.

Nihon Rōdō Kyōkai (Japan Institute of Labor), ed., 1971: 6–8.

Nevertheless this anxiety is not verbalized to the extent that it is in Japan. Why this concern appears to be so important for so many Japanese would certainly make an interesting study in intellectual history. One part of that history, it seems to us, must deal with the extent to which images are not created with a view to understanding better the policy choices which do exist in the "inter-domestic age," but to mobilizing people to support one ideological position or another within the domestic political arena. A number of case studies clearly show how essentially domestic events in Japan have a tendency to become "internationalized."

This can be seen in the anti-pollution movement of the early 1970s. In five rather well researched cases—Minamata Disease,[1] Ashio Copper Mine Pollution,[2] Yokkaichi Asthma,[3] the Fuji City Paper Companies,[4] and the Tokyo Garbage War[5]—parties to the disputes frequently referred to the situation outside Japan in order to promote their own position inside Japan. The anti-whaling groups, the Muskie Law, the stationing of Japanese pollution victims outside the United Nations Conference on the Environment in Stockholm in June 1972, and the shepherding of tourists to pollution-hit areas in Japan: all served to bring international pressure to bear on the Japanese government. In response, the government sought to diffuse criticism by "out-internationalizing" the "internationalizers." It offered to sponsor international gatherings; as the situation required, it either cited international averages in an attempt to soften the demands of the pollution victims, or, with equal skill, it sought to show how Japan was different from the rest of the world when the victims tried to use the notion of international standards to support their case. In the early stages, the victims would seem to profit from international exposure. However, that momentum was difficult to maintain, and the initiative was often lost in the latter stages to the government and to big business. Satellite communications and the electronic media certainly facilitated, on a global scale, the use of inter-domestic symbols.

Beginning with *Kutabare GNP* (Down with GNP!) which occupied a full page in the Sunday edition of the *Asahi Shimbun* (Asahi Newspaper) from May to September 1970, the media launched a movement to criticize GNP. This campaign became the rallying cry for the onslaught against GNP growthmanship. In the barrage of publications which followed,[6] foreign opinions were important. For example, considerable attention was given in March 1972 to the Club of Rome Report, *Limits to Growth*.[7] A similar or even greater stir was created in 1973 by the widely read report of the OECD on Japan's labor force policies. The report recommended that the Japanese government rethink its priorities, particularly with reference to the trade-off between continuing high economic growth rates and improved welfare for the labor force.[8] The speed with which these reports were translated into Japanese and published is amazing. The same can be said for the

OECD report on the Japanese system of education, which also underlined the connection with high economic growth rates. What foreigners were saying did seem to make a difference.

Two themes appeared regularly in this campaign. One was the idea that the Japanese had become obsessed with catching up to the West and with GNP growthmanship at any cost. The futility of doing so was underlined by reference to the fact that Japan had fallen short of the "Western" ideal (e.g., the "Western" standard of living) in many ways despite the all-out efforts of the conservative leadership. The issue was not so much the question of whether or not to catch up, but the question of what catching up meant. The criticism was that GNP growthmanship as promoted by the LDP had given people a false sense of catching up. It was pointed out that actually the people had been deceived. Some argued that Japan had fallen behind, particularly in terms of the quality of life. The second theme was a nebulous concern for world ecology. It arose perhaps not so much out of a respect for nature and the notion of "Mother Earth" as out of a systems overview and functionalist assessment of the prospects facing "Spaceship Earth" and Japan's share of the world's finite resources.

Another area where essentially domestic issues have been internationalized is in labor-management relations. Attempts to involve the ILO in the right-to-strike issue and the strategy of arguing for shorter hours of work in the 1960s by referring to the shorter hours worked abroad provide good examples. In the latter case, it is interesting to note that the goal was not shorter hours of work but rather a reapportionment of the work between the standard workweek and overtime so as to increase take-home pay.

As per capita GNP rose to the levels achieved in other countries, management too shifted its arguments. In the early 1960s, it claimed that longer hours of work were appropriate in a poor country like Japan. In the late 1970s, it attempted to show that Japan did not work excessively long hours (*Nihon Keizai Shimbun,* morning issue in early January 1981). In other words, by using a different definition of hours of work to suit its own convenience, management could still use international comparisons as the trump card in dealing with labor. Management also used these comparisons as a device to consolidate public opinion within Japan. Various attempts were made to weaken the class consciousness of Japanese by emphasizing how Japan as a society was being criticized unfairly by jealous trading partners.

Finally, in looking for the motivation behind the government's move to support shorter hours of work in the early 1970s, the presence of international pressure was again important.[9] Newspapers cited an endless number of foreign opinions saying that the Japanese worked too hard.[10] Survey teams were sent overseas and various study teams made international comparisons.[11] Editorials on leisure almost invariably started with some kind of international comparison. The word "workaholic" was imported from the United States as though it had been concocted especially for the Japanese.[12]

The appeal to a convenient overseas standard can also be seen in labor's campaign for higher wages. Within the somewhat successful framework developed for the annual spring wage offensive, unions pushed for wages on a par with those in Europe (*Yōroppa nami chingin*) during the 1960s. Once that goal had been achieved, the union movement was quick to shift its demands to having a distribution of GNP on a par with that found in Europe (*Yōroppa nami bumpairitsu*). Accordingly, during the early 1970s we see a great clamor about "life cycle needs." At the same time, the government was quick to respond by importing "quality-of-life indicators" which it could manipulate with its massive array of statistics. Foreign ideas are again introduced to mobilize Japanese around domestic political issues and to control the vocabulary with which such issues are discussed. This jostling for positions can also be seen in the discussion of an incomes policy in the early 1970s.

The point to be made here is that the institutionalized concern with knowing about other societies is not necessarily motivated by a desire to understand other cultures. Rather, there is an instrumental concern with supporting a political (or ideological) position at home, with developing stable export markets and with obtaining reliable sources of raw materials and certain other necessary goods abroad. Finally, this use of foreign ideas to promote ideological positions can be seen not only on the part of the government, but also within the labor and socialist movements themselves. This does not mean that no Japanese see a value in understanding other cultures, but suggests that the efforts of those who do need to be seen in relation to the ideological thrust of the main political actors.

It is in this context that the recent boom in the literature emphasizing

276

Japanese uniqueness needs to be carefully studied. The literature is variously referred to as *Nihonjinron, shinfūdoron, Nihon bunkaron, Nihon shakairon, Nihonkyō* or simply *Nihonron*. This literature is of considerable interest to us in terms of understanding Japanese society and assessing the possibilities for increased Japanese participation in the international community (either in its present form or in some future form). The way in which many Japanese themselves perceive their situation and the choices they have will in no small measure define the situation and the choices available. In other words, perceptions often yield self-fulfilling prophecies. One might simply dismiss the literature and its images of Japanese society as popular culture except for the heavy involvement of the academic community and of the political and business establishment in promoting such images not only at home but abroad as well. In this regard, three points deserve mention. First are the interesting similarities with the intellectual underpinnings of prewar Japanese nationalism as found in *Nihon shinkokuron, Yamato damashii* or *Jōiron*. The second concerns the extent to which the view of Japanese society as an integrated whole tends to serve the interests of the elites. The way in which self-fulfilling prophecies work needs little elaboration. Acceptance of such views of Japanese society encourages Japanese to accept the status quo. Acceptance abroad will discourage well-meaning foreigners who might otherwise accept an invitation to "interfere" in Japan's domestic affairs. It may well be no accident that the Japanese Foreign Ministry chooses actively to promote this view of Japan abroad. Finally, it is important to note how explanations of this view have been used as a convenient negotiating tactic by Japanese in their dealings overseas. If the Japanese are seen by foreigners as being inscrutable and if Japanese decision making is seen as a unique process which foreigners cannot understand, on the one hand, and if the doctrine of "cultural relativisism" is then used to defend one's own way of doing things, on the other, a tremendous barrier is placed in the way of the foreigner's understanding of and involvement in the activities of his or her Japanese counterparts. A mystique is created in which Japan is hidden in mist. In such misty surroundings it is obviously easier for Japanese to parry the approaches of foreign negotiators.

The holistic view of Japanese society as a unique entity is not new. Kawamura (1980b) has traced its development back to the idea of *wakon kansai* (Chinese learning with the Japanese spirit) in the eighteenth century. Befu (1982) has suggested that the Meiji Restoration was accompanied by numerous developments which resulted in "the West" becoming the reference group for many Japanese. He has also pointed out that defeat in World War II served to focus Japanese attention even more narrowly on the United States. The more pathological aspects of the psychology of catching up while maintaining one's cultural integrity are well described in the work of Franz Fanon and, more recently, Goulet (1971) and Naipaul (1980). As Befu has written (1982: 190):

> It is quite natural, then, for the group model of Japanese society, as it came to be formulated in the postwar years, to incorporate features of Japanese society which stood out in contrast to American society. Moreover, as a folk model, it was important for the group model to incorporate overt and covert contrasts with the culture which had come to play such a salient role in the everyday life of the Japanese.

There are now a good number of reasons for doubting the validity of this "folk model" and these have been spelled out elsewhere (Sugimoto and Mouer, 1979a, 1980a and 1980b; Befu, 1982). They include various methodological shortcomings, contrary empirical findings and certain unanswered questions from the perspective of a sociology of knowledge. Our interest here, however, is not with whether this folk model of Japanese society is correct, but rather with considering some of the implications of its widespread acceptance among the Japanese for Japanese society in terms of the current concern with "internationalization."[13] Before doing that, however, we wish briefly to describe what we are referring to with terms such as "the folk model," "the group model," "the model in the Nihonjinron literature" or "the holistic model of Japanese society."

The Holistic Model of Japanese Society

Although there is no one model of Japanese society in the Nihonjinron literature, its various descriptions and explanations of Japanese society seem to share a number of common properties. While the commonly held image of Japan and Japanese society seem to be characterized by a number of paradoxes, there also seems to have emerged out of the emphasis on the cultural inevitability of Japan's modernization a coherent picture of Japanese society and culture as a holistic entity. This emphasis seems to have focused attention on those characteristics believed to be unique to Japanese society. The holistic theory also has attached considerable importance to Japanese values or thought patterns as the major independent variables explaining Japanese development, a transition which is assumed to have occurred in a more or less voluntaristic fashion. Herman Kahn (1970), Nakane Chie (1970), Doi Takeo (1971), Ezra Vogel (1979), Edwin Reischauer (1977) and a large number of others have painted a picture of Japanese society which leads us to believe that it is exceptionally well integrated. They have argued that more than people in other similarly industrialized societies the Japanese are group-oriented and regulated by norms placing a value on consensus and loyalty.

Elsewhere we have summarized the composite image of Japan which emerges from these scholars (Sugimoto and Mouer, 1979a, 1979b and 1979c). First, the Japanese are seen as being group-oriented. Self-interest for most Japanese is defined as belonging to some group. Second, Japanese groups are characterized by harmonious interpersonal relationships among their members. Third, the strongest bonds of solidarity and loyalty occur among those in "vertically" or hierarchically structured positions within the same organization. Fourth, in the "vertically structured" group Japanese are easily mobilized to achieve their group's goals. Fifth, cultural, linguistic and social homogeneity give Japanese a particularly strong sense of belonging to the same society. Sixth, Japanese society is closed to outsiders both culturally and structurally. Seventh, the informal level of social organization is relatively more important in Japan.

In more concrete terms, these features are seen within the framework of the labor market as being consistent with (1) lower levels of dispute activity, (2) lower labor turnover and lifetime employment, (3) group decision making from the bottom up and the Japanese system of *ringisho* (formal memoranda requiring the signatures of all involved before action is taken), (4) company unions, (5) greater social equality in terms of the distribution of income and wage differentials, (6) a greater sense of national identity, and (7) lower levels of alienation. As these illustrations suggest, the world of work and industrial relations is one place where these kinds of images have been most readily associated with concrete examples.

To summarize, the predominant image of Japan is characterized by two main themes. First, Japanese society is seen in terms of paradoxes: Japanese society is seen, often by the same individuals, as simultaneously being harmonious yet exploitative, efficient yet inefficient, open yet closed, traditional or quaint yet modern, clean yet dirty. From this perspective, the major task is to find a logic which ties together all the opposites. Second, and partially in answer to this need perhaps, certain isolated aspects are lifted out to form a "coherent" image of Japanese society as a holistic entity such as "Japan Inc.".

At the same time, it should be noted that there is a second view of Japanese society which emphasizes conflict. This perspective is characterized by the efforts of its adherents to understand social realities in Japan by taking specific groups—and particularly classes in the Marxist sense—as the major behavioral unit and by considering how inequalities in the distribution of wealth and power are related to conflicts of interest. This conflict-oriented approach, which in the broadest sense subsumes the Marxist viewpoint, focuses its attention on the causes, structure and dynamics of social class. The theoretical propositions associated with this approach can also be enumerated. First, conflict is endemic to Japanese society. Second, divisions in Japanese society run parallel to the lines of inequality. Third, reward inconsistency (or Lenski's status inconsistency) is the exception; consistency, the rule. Fourth, individuals are concerned with self-interest. Group affiliation is defined in terms of self-interest. Fifth, the way in which inequalities are structured will depend upon the ways in which interests are defined and the ways in which the means of production are owned. Sixth, the opportunity for individual Japanese to articulate their interests or to express their values varies directly with their access to positions of authority.

These two competing views of Japanese society seem to surface in several other settings. One is the debate on convergence and divergence. The first position tends to be associated with the emphasis on Japan's cultural uniqueness while the second seems to highlight aspects seen as being more universalistic. The debate has a long history in Japan, having come to the fore at least since the eighteenth century. As Kawamura (1980a) has observed, the phrase "wakon kansai" (Japanese spirit with Chinese learning) and its derivative *"wakon yōsai"* (Japanese spirit with Western learning) indicate this concern with whether Japan

TABLE 1

THE DISTRIBUTION OF THE CONFLICT AND HOLISTIC TRADITIONS
IN THE ENGLISH AND JAPANESE LITERATURE ON JAPANESE SOCIETY

		Model of Japanese Society	
		Conflict Model	**Holistic Model**
Language in which the literature on Japanese society appears	**English**	Almost non-existent although a small trickle in the 1970s	Monopolistic position since the end of the war
	Japanese	A long and established tradition among a minority and receiving some support from anti-establishment groups	A long and established tradition occupying a very dominant position in the media and receiving support from business and government circles

can in fact import foreign technologies without also importing all the associated cultural baggage and the social adjustments or changes such importation seems to imply.

Questions from the viewpoint of the sociology of knowledge are also raised. Although perspectives emphasizing conflict are held by a decided minority in Japan, they do have a healthy existence in Japan whereas such perspectives are almost totally nonexistent in the English-language literature on Japan.[14] Accordingly, the distribution of perspectives seems to be along the lines shown in Table 1. In this regard, those who tend to propagate the view of Japanese society as a holistic entity tend also to think of internationalism according to the first decision given above. Those associated with the emphasis on conflict in Japanese society tend to identify with the second usage. Parallels can perhaps be drawn with Mannheims' notion of "ideology and utopia." As an "ideology" (ideology type I) to promote self-fulfilling prophecies, the view which pushes for consensus perhaps sees national unity as an important element affecting the ability of the nation state to maximize national interest in the international arena. As a "utopian vision" (ideology type II) to change things, the view which seeks to expose the exploitative aspects of Japanese society and their link with the social structure perhaps sees as a viable solution social transformation (or social revolution) imposed as part of a worldwide transformation. It is from this perspective that the notion of a world system has some attraction.

False Images and International Isolation: Some Consequences

In spite of having a fairly good grasp of the raw facts (e.g., reams of statistical data) concerning other societies, as long as the images the Japanese have of themselves are ideologically colored and are consciously created by Japanese leaders as self-fulfilling prophecies, the understanding which many Japanese have of other cultures may be seriously limited. Serving as a kind of looking glass not only for viewing themselves but also others, Nihonjinron will likely transpose ideological distortions created for domestic politics onto the images which many Japanese have of the outside world. In the context of Japan's increasing interaction with the world economy and the international political situation, and the concern of some Japanese with becoming international citizens in a way which would facilitate the free movement of individuals into and out of Japan, it seems to us that the ability to see the outside world without these ideological lenses and to assess more accurately realities outside Japan becomes an increasingly important asset.

Before considering more fully the implications of a moratorium on Nihonjinron, we wish to consider briefly several ways in which the methodological shortcomings in Nihonjinron shape the perception of the outside world held by many Japanese. Most outstanding are the various sampling biases contained in Nihonjinron. Even when presented primarily as a description of "the Japanese," Nihonjinron is implicitly comparative. The initial problem is one of clearly defining the concepts used to describe Japanese society. This is not done in Nihonjinron. The problem of sampling is also crucial to deriving accurate descriptions of a society as large, as complex and as varied as Japanese society. Most Nihonjinron includes no mention of sampling procedures. When the descriptive concepts are not defined, and comparative adjectives (such as "tall" or "short") are used instead of absolute units of measurement (such as centimeters), the problems of sampling are multiplied. They pose a problem not only with regard to obtaining a representative picture of Japanese society but also with regard to obtaining a fair picture of the other society or societies implicitly being compared.

As mentioned above, the West in general and the United States in particular are often cited as the major reference groups in much of the Nihonjinron literature. For a small minority caught up with the conflict perspective, the reference group may be the Soviet Union, China or some other society believed to have achieved a socialist state. To the extent that internationalism is a goal associated with the acquisition of a more cosmopolitan outlook, the almost exclusive concern with a very narrow range of societies undermines efforts to internationalize. This problem is further aggravated by the tendency to view the West as a monolith. More realistic appraisals of any one specific, real-life society are replaced by generalizations which fit no one society and which even in themselves are often fallacious or of dubious validity. This means that individuals are left to act without being aware of the full range of behavioral choices.

Images of the outside world presented to Japanese by the Nihonjin-ron literature are also shaped by the limited samples which are taken from any given society. Seldom are the readers of Nihonjinron shown the importance of considering both formal and informal groups in making comparisons. Few are taught to distinguish between the norms and the "actual behavior" in evaluating symbolic interaction. Whereas many Japanese frequently refer to the distinction between *honne* and *tatemae* in Japan, they fail to see the distinction abroad.[15] In comparing Japanese cultures and other cultures, the Nihonjinron literature does not help the Japanese to become more sensitive to the intricacies of translating back and forth between the *etic* and the *emic*.

Several simple examples from the Australian experience with Japan may serve to illustrate how misunderstandings are created by the lack of concern for rigorous comparison and by the excessive concern with ideology. Although disadvantaged in negotiations with their Japanese counterparts, Australian businessmen seem to find the stereotypes of Japanese society a convenient perspective for "bashing unions" or as a face-saving excuse to fallback on whenever they feel compelled to give way in negotiations. For example, in recent years Japanese busi-nessmen coming to Australia have often scorned Australia for its poor system of industrial relations. In negotiations the Japanese have all the statistics; figures from the Japanese minister of labor and the Australian Bureau of Statistics clearly show that Australian workers strike more frequently, a phenomenon which is interpreted as being consistent with an Australian culture emphasizing individualism and strong class consciousness. No mention is made of the fact that the two data collecting bodies use different definitions of strikes and collect data in different ways. No mention is made of the fact that it was not long ago that Japan had many strikes and that Australia had relatively few (see Sugimoto, 1977). No mention is made of the fact that national averages are deceiving; Australia's strikes happen largely in the mining sector (Chalmers, 1981). This is a sector which Japan does not now have but one which is characterized by higher levels of disputes in all societies, including Japanese society in the past if we recall the Miike strikes. Nevertheless, Japanese negotiators come to Australia full of cultural theories as to why Australia (with a "strike ethic") ought to sell at lower prices its resources to Japan (which is said to place a high cultural value on "stability").

Another example involving the notion of contract might also be mentioned. Several years ago the "sugar dispute" captured the headlines in Australia and Japan. Australia's first long-term contract had called for a stable supply of raw sugar to the Japanese refineries. However, when the world price dropped, stability was no longer a value to the Japanese; cheaper imports were. The Japanese made a good deal of publicity about the need for cultural understanding and their true intentions in negotiating agreements. It was suggested that in Japan the notion of contracts was underdeveloped or was tied to some sense of "amae" which allowed one party to "get out when the going got to be too rough." From that perspective it is incumbent on the other party to acquiesce magnanimously. Australians were accused of trying to impose their rigid contract-oriented interpretation of the agreement on the Japanese, and therefore of being ethnocentrically insensitive to the idea of cultural relativism and the notion of give-and-take (Marsh, 1979). More recently, however, when shipments of iron ore were delayed owing to industrial disputes in late 1980, Japanese executives representing Japanese steel interests came to Australia and released statements about the importance of stability and of honoring contracts (*The Australian,* 16 November 1980: 1). Meanwhile, the Australian press lamented the aggressiveness of the economic animals from Japan who seemed to have no sense of mateship or no human warmth when it came to economic dealings. The Japanese were obviously seen as being second to none when it came to materialistic instincts and rigid contracts. Taken together, these two examples illustrate how images are created and manipulated in order to obtain advantage in negotiating and in domestic politicking.

Perhaps the most serious shortcoming of Nihonjinron is the attitude toward other cultures which it often implants. As a folk model packaged to sell to the public, there is a great emphasis on the storytelling of interesting anecdotes chosen and arranged not so much for their truth value but rather for their entertainment value. While the arbitrariness with which such anecdotes and unique phrases in the Japanese language are chosen is another facet of the sampling problem,[16] it contributes to the idea that accuracy should be subordinated to enjoyment in the production of national stereotypes. There is also the ideological role of folk models, and one major characteristic of Nihonjinron is its moralizing.[17] Invariably the lessons are drawn both by the authors themselves and by those who use such models: "To meet international standards [e.g., to be like the West or to be like 'the United States'] the Japanese must do such and such" or "To avoid falling behind [like 'the West' has] Japan must not do this or that." In most cases, both the West and Japan are presented in an idealized though ambiguous form. Without a careful reading, it seems to us that the ideological message has changed over time as suggested in Table 2. The message derived from Nihonjinron is varied through space, depending upon the country in which it is expounded. The message has also changed through time, depending upon the value attached to Japan which in turn is linked to Japan's position in the world at a given time (Kawamura, 1980b). To the extent that Nihonjinron is characterized by moralizing, it tends to limit the options presented to the Japanese and to those who must deal with Japanese on official and nonofficial levels. It also tends to mobilize people to achieve national goals. This reinforces the ideal of competing nation states and limits the extent to which value is attached to cosmopolitanism and international understanding. The result is that only one type of internationalism is promoted.

This is not to argue that each society does not have its own national myths which are comparable to Nihonjinron. Nor do we wish to suggest that citizens should not be socialized to see the world as it is (i.e., as a collection of competing nation-states). We would, however, argue that people's lives are shaped and controlled by the stereotypes built into the national myths to which they are exposed. We would also argue that the decisions of political leaders and others in positions of authority are often based on such stereotypes, and particularly so

TABLE 2

		Audience	
		Japanese (Japanese-language literature)	**Westerners** (e.g. Americans and Australians) (English-language literature)
Society and culture to which superiority is attached	One's own	**STAY THE SAME** Strengthen the uniquely Japanese teachers (teach the West) (1970s)	**STAY THE SAME** Invite the Japanese over and help them to westernize their society to become a "fortress of Western democracy" (1950s and 1960s)
	The other	**CHANGE** Modernize Japan and work for economic growth (1950s–1970s)	**CHANGE** Learn respect for nature and spirituality (1950s and 1960s) Learn Japanese management style (late 1970s)

at junctures where a society is facing some kind of crisis, including the search for identity. From this perspective, a few comments may be made about the significance of Nihonjinron for understanding Japanese society today.

Internationalization and Japanese Society: An Australian Perspective Once Removed

In thinking about the "internationalization of Japanese society" from an Australian perspective, several sets of questions come to mind.[18] The first concerns the way in which "internationalism" or "internationalization" is used. Is the concept used basically to mobilize the Japanese people? If so, to what ends? Does internationalization lead to a world view in which Japanese hegemony is seen as being desirable, as in an expanded version of the Greater East Asian Co-Prosperity Sphere? Does internationalization imply, as in the sugar and steel trade, the manipulation of concepts such as "cultural relativism" to mean "do it my way"? Does it imply more gift editions of Nakane's *Japanese Society* from the Foreign Ministry and a steady stream of *PHP* philosophy on the importance of labor cooperating with management? Does it imply that, through the propagation of the Japanese national stereotypes, management and other conservative types in Australia and Singapore should have more ammunition against unions in order to maintain the status quo? Does it imply an attempt to keep employees in Japanese MNEs abroad better in line? The Japanese are sometimes portrayed in the Australian mind as running about in a great flurry of activity, intent on gathering data about the physical environment. They are seen as being intent upon manipulating, but without any interest either in explaining motivations or in understanding societies and their cultures. There are in Australia real anxieties concerning the meaning which those leading the private and public sectors in Japan give to a frequently used term like "internationalism."

A more academic concern relates to the level of consensus or the degree of voluntarism in Japanese society. For many non-Japanese there is something plastic or artificial about the images of Japanese groupism and harmony presented in the mass media and by Japanese leaders who visit Japan. When the lower level of strike activity in Japan in the late 1970s is presented as a cultural trait of Japanese society, an incredulous picture is created in the minds of many foreigners. Given their smattering of information about student riots, assassinations, the Red Army, the anti-pollution and anti-nuclear movements, the AMPO demonstrations, the struggle at Miike or the frustration of examination hell, they are confused by the sharply cut paradoxes. Rather than helping to bridge cultural differences, the Nihonjinron type of explanation often makes the cultural gap appear to be much wider than it actually is. Not infrequently the gulf is seen as being so wide that only the most fantastic assumptions about the Japanese pattern of culture can tie it all together.

Emphasis on the emotionalism of the Japanese and their paradoxical nature, as well as the use of words like "Japanology" (which, like "Kremlinology" or "Sinology," suggest that a certain mysticism is central to the description of the society concerned), tends to buttress the belief that intuition is the best key to understanding Japanese society. To be sure, intuition is one of the most valuable assets a social scientist can possess; however, intuition is not the major source of "scientific" verification in the social sciences. Moreover, intuition is useful only to the extent that the theory and conceptual framework upon which it tries to build are clearly defined and an effort is then made to build hypotheses from one's intuitive speculations which are capable of empirical verification.[19]

Many Japanese and many foreigners like to think that the cosmopolitanism, the information gathering on a global scale and the television coverage of overseas events have resulted in an imbalance in the flow of information, with the Japanese having come to know a good deal about the outside world and the outside world still knowing little about Japan. In much of Nihonjinron there is an assumption that Japan is so unique that the foreigner can never understand it. There is thus a tendency to believe that a small priestly class has a monopoly on understanding Japanese society and that they somehow have the intuitive insight necessary to make reliable pronouncements about the essence not only of Japanese society but of other societies as well. From an Australian viewpoint, we would suggest that the concern in Nihonjinron with generalizing from American (and, to a lesser extent, European) examples has given many Japanese a very limited knowledge of the world. Indeed, one could argue that Australians have a better understanding of the Japanese than do the Japanese of Australians, even though Australians may have less statistical information and fewer fancy data banks. To make the point, one need only consider the direction and volume of cultural exchange. Without going into an elaborate definition of "culture," let it suffice to say that we are talking about the realm of ideas and the feelings generated by a given social milieu. Here we might examine briefly material expressions, artistic expressions and intellectual expressions.

The first concerns the exchange of economic goods, the artifacts produced by economic activity. Australia imports various kinds of consumer durables that are used widely throughout Japanese society: cars, household appliances, tools, machinery and electronic computers. Australians have some idea about the kinds of products Japanese workers produce and Japanese consumers purchase. There is also a sizeable Japanese community in Australia. These Japanese are rather visible and easily distingusihed from other Asians. Finally, many Australians have eaten at a local Japanese restaurant. In the other direction, however, Japan imports largely raw materials from Australia. The materials are

288

processed and never really seen in their original form by Japanese consumers, although they may have eaten Australian beef. Moreover, the imported materials are mined from rural Australia whereas most Australians live in large cities and do not relate to the materials or to the processes by which they are extracted. Japanese images of Australia are of kangaroos and koalas, sheep stations and the vast outback which few Australians have seen or experienced (Atsumi, 1978). There are no Australian restaurants in Japan. The few Australian businessmen in Japan are not conspicuous as Australians.

In the area of art, the Japanese government and other organizations are constantly dispatching to Australia *kabuki* troupes, arrangers of flowers, masters of tea ceremony, *jūdō* experts and some professional *go* players. It is basically elitist or upper-middle class culture, but it comes in a steady stream. From Australia there is very little, if any, flow of performers to Japan.

Finally, in the realm of the intellectual climate there are lacunae on both sides, although Australians have access to a large number of books about Japan in English and a large number of Japanese novels in translation. The percentage of secondary school students studying Japanese as a second language is second only to the figures for Korea. Japanese films and television programs are frequently shown in Australia. Few Australian novels are translated into Japanese; few Japanese schools teach the Australian version of English; few, if any, Australian films or television programs are shown in Japan.

The absorption of Australian culture is not the acid test of internationalism. However, in the case of Japan its absence suggests that the concern of many Japanese with foreign ideas and international culture has been narrowly focused. We suspect that a closer examination of longitudinal data will also show that Japan's interest in Australia (in terms of coverage in the mass media, for example) is largely a function of its economic inroads into the Australian economy and its need for economic information. One again wonders whether "internationalization" in Japan means simply the acquisition of more information to facilitate further the penetration of the Australian economy.

In many of the discussions on Japanese society in comparative perspective, the debate on convergence and divergence is frequently mentioned. Without going into the details of that debate, we simply wish to state that the concern with Japanese values is a core issue. From the point of view of those concerned with economic development, the question of the need to mobilize masses as opposed to simply directing or leading a spontaneously motivated population is of considerable interest. From the point of view of moving into the post-industrial era, the apparently lower crime rates, lower levels of alienation, the lower levels of industrial unrest, the attention given to corporate welfarism and the generally high level of purposive activity also draw considerable interest. From either angle, there is concern with the trade-off between voluntarism and control, spontaneity and coercion. Nihonjinron tends to minimize the importance of control and coercion. At the same time, it places cultural blinders on many Japanese and leads them to think they are so unique that they could not possibly survive overseas. In discussing civil rights in the Soviet Union one commonly cited piece of evidence used to argue their absence and the presence of coercive controls is the way in which the Soviet government obstructs the emigration of those unhappy with the system. Although Japan is one of the great postwar democracies, it seems to us that the official and nonofficial support given to Nihonjinron by the government, business leaders and management, conservative politicians and the mass media serves to create psychological barriers which are equally effective in preventing migration. It is from this perspective that the recent interest in internationalism holds a certain significance for those studying Japanese society. It is only when all Japanese feel comfortable in moving internationally and in accepting immigrants into Japanese society that we can discuss in a meaningful way the extent to which Japanese society is characterized by uniquely high levels of social consensus.

Internationalism in this context is not the only index or even the ultimate index of how open a society is. It is but one index. As an index, however, it draws our attention to restrictions on the issuance of passports and foreign exchange which in the past tended to limit the ability of Japanese to travel abroad. It makes us more aware of the air fares charged to Japanese travelling out of Japan which are considerably higher than those charged to foreigners flying the same routes to Japan from other countries. It makes us more sensitive to the folk models which build cultural and psychological barriers to leaving Japan. It underlines the fact that citizenship requirements deny Japanese citizenship to the children of Japanese women married to non-Japanese men. It scores the reluctance of the Japanese government to accept refugees or to permit non-Japanese to be employed in tenured tracks at national universities. While internationalism or even openness are not the only criteria for judging societies, such concepts are not irrelevant when seeking to explain social behavior in terms of social values. Indeed, they throw considerable light on the question concerning voluntarism and control, spontaneity and coercion, democracy and totalitarianism, nationalism and militarism, values and ideology. And, after all, this is the key question in much of the debate on Japan's uniqueness.

NOTES

1. In the footnotes the following abbreviations have been used for newspapers:

AEN	*Asahi Evening News*
ASC	*Asahi Shimbun* (morning edition)
ASY	*Asahi Shimbun* (evening edition)
JT	*Japan Times*
SRN	*Shūkan Rōdō Nyusu*

Seet Ui Jun, *Kōgai no seijigaku* (The Politics of Pollution) (Tokyo: Sanseidō, July 1968); Ui Jun, *Kōgai genron* (A Theory on Pollution), vol. 1 (Tokyo: Aki Shobō, March 1971), pp. 3–188; "Researcher's Warning 2 Years Before Outbreak Ignored: Niigata Minamata Disease," *AEN* (March 1, 1971), p. 1; "Osen Rettō no Kyōfu Fuyasu: Daisan Minamatabyō no Hakken" (Increased Uneasiness in Polluted Japan: The Third Outbreak of Minamata Diesase), *ASC* (May 22, 1973), p. 3; "Nagai Kurō no Sue ni: Minamatabyō Kanja no Hoshō Kyōtei (The End of A Long Bitter Struggle: Minamata Victims Reach Agreement on Compensation), *ASC* (July 9, 1973), p. 3; "Minamata Victims May Attend Stockholders' Meeting," *JT* (March 7, 1972), p. 3; "Minamata Responsibility," *JT* (March 23, 1973), p. 16; "University Doctors Disagree on 'Minamata' Symptoms," *AEN* (August 7, 1973), p. 3; and Harada Masaumi, "Minamatabyō to Igaku no Setten: 'Kanja ni Manabe' ni Modotte" (Minamata Disease and Medicine: A Return to 'Listening to the Patients'), *ASY* (March 16, 1973), p. 7.

2. Hayashi Eidai, *Bōkyō: Kōdoku wa kiezu* (Homesickness: The Copper Poisoning that Won't Go Away) (Tokyo: Aki Shobō, April 1974); Uchimizu Mamoru (ed.), *Shiryō Ashio kōdoku jiken* (Research Materials on the Ashio Copper Poisoning Incident) (Tokyo: Aki Shobō, 1973); Matsuoka Nobuo, "Pollution Imperialism and People's Struggle," *AMPO*, no. 16: (March 1973), pp. 30–34; Tamura Norio, "Kōgai Kenkyū no Genten: Ashio Kōdoku" (The Beginnings of Pollution in Japan: Ashio Copper Poisoning), *ASY* (June 6, 1972), p. 5; Imata Yasushi, "Tanaka Shōzō and the Ashio Mine Poisoning), in *Shisō o aruku* (Back Through Intellectual History), ed. by the Asahi Shimbun (Tokyo: Asahi Shimbunsha, April 1974), pp. 135–56; and "Furukawa to Close Ashio Copper Mine," *JT* (November

2, 1972), p. 2. A similar case involves the Toroku Mine in Kyushu at which debilitating pollution was totally concealed from the public for more than fifty years. See Tanaka Tetsuya, *Toroku kōdoku jiken* (The Toroku Mine Poisoning Case) (Tokyo: Sanseidō, November 1973); "Kyushu Schoolteacher Bares Pollution Peril," *AEN* (February 4, 1972), p. 5; "New Pollution Case Exposed by Teacher at Nikkyōso Meeting," *AEN* (January 17, 1972), p. 3; and "No Indications Found of Arsenic Poisoning," *JT* (February 3, 1972), p. 3.

3. Tajiri Muneaki, *Yokkaichi shi no umi to tatakau* (Fighting Yokkaichi and the Sea of Death) (Tokyo: Iwanami Shoten, April 1972); "JCP's Ishibashi Charges Collusion: Tacit Gov't Approval of Polluter Attacked," *JT* (January 1, 1971), p. 1; "Gov't Unable to Refute Charge of Collusion in Yokkaichi Case," *JT* (January 30, 1971), p. 3; "Ishihara Sangyō Deal Described," *JT* (February 3, 1971), p. 2; "Ishihara Co. Charged with Polluting Port," *JT* (February 20, 1971), p. 2; "Firms Get Pollution Inspection," *JT* (August 26, 1972), p. 3; "Yokkaichi Plants Face Fuel Curb," *JT* (early 1972); "Industrial Pollution," *JT* (July 27, 1972), p. 4; "Pollution Victims Using 'Dangerous' Medicines," *JT* (April 14, 1972), p. 2; "Yokkaichi no Kōgai Zaidan wa Dekita ga" (The Yokkaichi Foundation for Pollution Victims is Established, but. . .), *ASC* (September 6, 1973), p. 5; "Five Years in Tajiri's Life," *AEN* (June 23, 1974), p. 4; and Tokushū: Yokkaichi Kōgai Soshō (Special Issue on the Yokkaichi Litigation), *Jurisuto*, no. 514 (September 10, 1972).

4. Okamoto Hideaki, "Industrialization: Environment and Anti-Pollution Movements A Case," *Japan Labor Bulletin*, vol. 11, no. 11 (November 1972), pp. 4–12; Koda Masahiko "Hedoro no Fuji: Kakushin Shisei to Taiketsu: Dominteki Jumin Undō ga Hajimatta" (Hedoro Sludge at Fuji: Coming to Grips with A Reformist City Government: Grassroots Citizens' Movement Begins), *Ekonomisuto*, vol. 49, no. 47 (November 9, 1971), pp. 80–84; "Paper Mills in Fuji to Idle Once a Month," *AEN* (March 25, 1971), p. 3; "Final Plan Worked Out to Rid Port of 320,000 Tons of Sludge: Shizuoka Prefecture Government," *AEN* (February 9, 1971), p. 3; "Prosecutors Won't Push Tagonoura Case," *JT* (April 13, 1971), p. 3; "Anti-Pollution Rally Held at Suruga Bay Against Paper Firms," *JT* (August 10, 1970), p. 3; "Fuji Citizens Squash Plant Building Project," *AEN* (October 30, 1971), p. 3; "Farmers, Paper Mill Still Locked in Dispute," *AEN* (July 10, 1971), p. 3, and "Gov't to Loan Yen to Dredge Port Sludge," *AEN* (August 12, 1970), p. 1.

5. Yorimoto Katsumi, *Gomi sensō: Chihō jichi no kunan to jikken* (The Garbage War: the Experience and Dilemma of Local Government) (Tokyo: Nihon Keizai Shimbunsha, January 1974); "Minobe Declares War on Garbage," *JT* (October 4, 1971), p. 2; "Garbage War," *AEN* (October 13, 1971), p. 4; "Tokyo's Garbage Problem," *JT* (November 28, 1971), p. 12; "The Garbage War," *JT* (May 27, 1973), p. 12; "Tokyo 'Garbage War' Spreading to Adjacent Prefecture," *JT* (June 12, 1973), p. 3; "Suginami Landowners Refuse to Sell Out in 'Garbage War,' " *JT* (November 6, 1973), p. 3; "Tokyo Gov't Suspends Collection of Garbage in Suginami Ward," *JT* (May 23, 1973), p. 3; "Kōtō Ward to Block Dumping by Suginami," *JT* (May 22, 1973), p. 2; "Rival Wards Face Second Garbage War," *JT* (May 19, 1973), p. 2.

6. For example, see Yano Seiya and Yamazaki Mitsuru, *Shōhisha binbō no tsuiseki: Nihonjin no yokkyū fuman wa doko kaka ka* (Looking at the Impoverished Japanese Consumer: Sources of Need Frustration in Japan) (Tokyo: Tōyō Keizai Shinpōsha, 1972). In the preface they write that dissatisfaction with the standard of living will become increasingly pronounced among the people as better statistics become

available. Other similar works include Itō Mitsuharu, *Seikatsu no naka no keizaigaku* (The Economics of Everyday Living) (Tokyo: Asahi Shimbunsha, 1972); and Yomiuri Shimbunsha (ed.), *Denaose keizai ōkoku: Nihon no kokumin mokuhyō o Kangaeru* (Rethink the Meaning of Being an Economic Power: Goals of the Japanese People) (Tokyo: Daiyamondosha, September 1971). These kinds of books have continued to be published even in the mid-1970s, as evidenced by Asahi Shimbun Keizai Bu (Asahi Newspaper, Economics Department), *Shin bimbō monogatari: Infure fukyō e no kokuhatsujō* (The New Poverty: An Indictment Against Stagflation) (Tokyo: Asahi Shimbunsha, May 1975). Finally, see the article of Maruyama Tsuneo, a reporter for the *Chūnichi Shimbun,* a large daily newspaper in Nagoya: "GNP Sekai Dai Nii no Anbaransu" (The Distortions Caused by Having the Second Largest GNP in the World), *Ushio*, no. 128: (September 1970), pp. 149–53.
7. For example, see "The 'Crisis of Mankind,' " *AEN* (March 25, 1972), p. 4; or "Kono Chikyū: 50 Nen Saki no Shigen Kokatsu" (This World: Resources Dried Up in Another 50 Years), *ASC* (May 4, 1972), p. 4. These are just two examples of the kinds of articles which flooded the Japanese press in 1972. Attention might also be given to the speed with which the original report, *The Limits of Growth: A Report for the Club of Rome's Project on the Predicament of Mankind,* prepared by Donella H. Meadows, Dennis L. Meadows, Jorgen Randers and William W. Behiens III (New York: Universe Books, March 1972) was translated into Japanese. Within two months a Japanese translation was on the market, translated under the supervision of Ōkita Saburō, *Seichō no genkai* (Tokyo: Daiyamondosha, May 1972). As this applies to energy resources in particular, it is important to note that the so-called oil shock in late 1973 served to maintain for several years the public interest in this issue.
8. The original report, which was one in the series of OECD national reviews of manpower and social policies in member countries, appeared as *Manpower Policies in Japan* (Paris: Organization for Economic Cooperation and Development, 1973). Even before the "official" English version appeared, a Japanese translation was published: Keizai Kyōryoku Kaihatsu Kikō (OECD) *OECD Tainichi rōdō hōkokusho* (The OECD Report on Labor in Japan), translated by Rōdō Shō (Ministry of Labor) (Tokyo: Nihon Rōdō Kyōkai, November 6, 1972). The report strongly suggested that Japan's rapid economic growth was in no small measure assisted by three institutions: lifetime employment (*shūshin koyō*), the seniority wage system (*nenkō joretsu chingin*), and the enterprise-based labor union (*kigyōbetsu kumiai*). In the view of the OECD investigations, particularly important on the negative side would seem to have been the dual structure which created "haves" and "have-nots" within the labor force and certain restrictions on the individual's freedom of movement.
9. See, for example, an even earlier editorial in the *Japan Times*:

> There are some excellent reasons why the nation's political and industrial leaders should urge adoption of the five-day week—a position they have but lately moved toward. Sensitive to foreign criticism that Japan is disrupting world economic balances, and particularly to charges of dumping, they recognize that measures must be taken to counter the image of cheap labor in this country. This pressing problem has given a sense of urgency that has not been seen before to the purpose of the five-day week ("The Five-Day Week", *JT* [April 3, 1971], p. 14).

10. See "ILO no Yūkyū Kyōiku Kyūka" (The ILO on Paid Educational Leave), *SRN* (March 13, 1972), p. 2 and *SRN* (April 2, 1973), p. 2 or "Ōshū Gokakoku no Tabi Kara" (A Visit to Five European Countries), *SRN* (November 13, 1972), p. 3. Similar articles can be found in the leading national papers.

11. On a survey by the Foreign Ministry, see "5-Day Workweek", *JT* (February 10, 1973), p. 14. In the fall of 1972 the Japan Institute of Labour also sent its team abroad. See "Shū Itsuka Sei no ato ni Kurumono" (After the Five-Day Workweek), *Nihon Rōdō Kyōkai Zasshi*, vol. 15, no. 4 (April 1973), pp. 2–16. Other examples are readily available.

12. See "Japanese Workaholics," *AEN* (July 28, 1973), p. 4; and "Japanese Are 'Workaholics,' " *AEN* (May 5, 1972), p. 4. The word was originally created to describe Americans.

13. Obviously, one's assessment of the validity of the "folk model" will influence how one evaluates the consequences of its widespread diffusion for Japanese society.

14. At the same time, as we have tried to point out (Mouer, 1978: 5–9; Sugimoto and Mouer, 1979a: 137; 1979d: 4–6; and 1980a: 3) and have often been reprimanded by historians such as Mason and Bolitho for not emphasizing more explicitly, consensus and integration are not the only aspects of Japanese society described in the English-language literature. For example, the peasant riots which occurred in the Tokugawa period, the brutality with which dissidents were repressed in the 1930s, postwar *ampo* demonstrations and the anti-pollution movements have been well documented. Nevertheless, it is our feeling that those writing about these events and other anti-establishmentarian themes in postwar Japan have not produced theories which predict why, when or how dissatisfaction ignites into mass protest in Japanese society. In other words, the literature on conflict has tended to recount particularistic events characterized by conflict without yet yielding a comprehensive or systematic view of Japanese society. Accordingly, those wishing to have an overview of Japanese society have had to turn for inspiration to the work of those emphasizing consensus.

We also feel that the absence of views on Japanese society which are linked to the conflict tradition is more pronounced in the English-language literature than in the Japanese-language literature. Ōhashi's *Nihon no kaikyū kōsei* (1971) and Horie's *Nihon no rōdōsha kaikyū* (1971) have no counterparts in English, although the work by Norman (1975) and Steven (1979) immediately come to mind. Moreover, there is a solid Marxist/socialist tradition in Japanese scholarship on Japanese society which is matched neither in volume nor in creative diversity by the small dribble which comes through from *AMPO, Rōnin* or the *Bulletin of Concerned Asian Scholars*. In this regard, we feel that the study of Japanese society outside Japan would benefit from theories which struck a better balance between these two streams. It is our impression that the holistic view of Japan is quite entrenched among leaders in business, government and the media, although this seems to be changing slightly in recent years, particularly in Australia. Nevertheless, the books by which Japanese are known abroad in the early 1980s seem to be those which are authored by Reischauer (1977), Vogel (1979), Ouchi (1981), and Pascale and Athos (1981).

15. On this point it is surprising to note the number of Japanese who believe that Westerners are so individualistic, that they never feel a need to hide their feelings and, consequently, that the distinction between honne and tatemae is unique to Japan and is of academic interest only outside Japan.

16. In Japanese, we have referred to these practices as *episōdo shugi* and *kotobashugi* (cf. Sugimoto and Mouer, 1979a).

17. To cite but one well-known example, we might consider the work of Nakane Chie. It seems to us that Nakane's work is characterized by a good deal of moralizing. This seems to be the underlying tone in chastising Japanese publishers for wasteful competition or Japanese farmers for growing too many cabbages in *Japanese Society* (p. 93). This element is even more pronounced in the first part of *Tekiō no jōken,* and one wonders whether the contrasts between Japan and other societies might be exaggerated in order to marshall the Japanese into line. This also would seem to be related to her idealized notions of the West which appear in her discussion of democracy in *Japanese Society* (pp. 148–49).

18. In mentioning "Australian perspectives," we do not pretend to speak for Australians. As a Japanese and an American who have spent roughly the last third of our adult lives working in the Australian context, we believe that we have gained a perspective somewhat different from that obtained earlier in Japan and the United States. While not fully acculturated in Australian society, we nonetheless feel intellectually stimulated and enriched by the years spent living there and wish to label the resultant perspective "Australian." If there is an Australian perspective on Japanese society which is distinct from the American or the Japanese perspective, it may be delineated by the greater awareness of authority relationships and institutional histories in the study of Japanese society. For a fuller exposition of these themes, see the volume edited by Mouer and Sugimoto (1980) which contains the papers given to a symposium on "Alternative Models for Understanding Japanese Society" held in conjunction with the first national conference of the Japanese Studies Association of Australia in May 1980.

19. In addition to these shortcomings, there is the way in which such an approach inevitably leads to a logical contradiction of the very comparative statements Nihonjinron sets out to "prove". The logical conclusion to the assertion that only Japanese or properly initiated Japanologists can understand Japan is that others cannot have more than superficial understanding of the societies they seek to compare in order to show Japan's uniqueness. To follow that line of reasoning further, we would also expect to find little of value in the classics by the German Marx on the French Revolution, by the French de Tocqueville on American society or by the Polish Malinowski on primitive societies. To insist that the major sources of sociological understanding must come from a member of the society in question tends to deny the possibility for comparative research.

REFERENCES

Apter, David
    1965   *The Politics of Modernization.* Chicago: University of Chicago Press.
Atsumi, Reiko
    1978   "Images of Australia and Australians as Reflected in the Japanese Mass Media." Paper presented at the Second National Conference of the Asian Studies Association of Australia (Sydney: The University of New South Wales, May 14–18).
Befu, Harumi
    1982   "Alternative Models: The Next Step." *Social Analysis,* 5/6 (December

1980): 188–93.

Chalmers, Norma
  1981 "Japanese Perspectives on Australian Industrial Relations." Paper no.
        16. Brisbane: Center for the Study of Australian-Asian Relations.

Doi Takeo
  1971 *Amae no kōzō* (The Structure of '*Amae*'). Tokyo: Kōbundō. Trans-
        lated into English by John Bester as *The Anatomy of Dependence*. Tokyo:
        Kodansha International, 1973.

Goulet, Denis
  1971 *The Cruel Choice: A New Concept in the Theory of Development*. Philadel-
        phia: Atheneum.

Hollerman, Leon
  1967 *Japan's Dependence on the World Economy: The Approach Toward Economic
        Liberalization*. Princeton: Princeton University Press.

Kahn, Herman
  1970 *The Emerging Japanese Superstate: Challenge and Response*. Englewood
        Cliffs: Prentice-Hall.

Kawamura, Nozomu
  1980a "Sociology and Society in Early Modern Japan." Monograph no. 6
        in Sociology Papers, Department of Sociology, La Trobe University,
        Bundoora, Victoria, Australia.
  1980b "The Historical Background of Arguments Emphasizing the Unique-
        ness of Japanese Society." *Social Analysis,* 5/6 (December): 44–62.

Kojima, Kiyoshi
  1971 *Japan and a Pacific Trade Area*. Berkeley: University of California Press.

Kunihiro Masao
  1979 "The Interdomestic Age." *PHP*, 10 (6) (June): 6–16 and 77–78.

Marsh, Robert
  1979 "The Australia-Japan Sugar Negotiations." Research paper no. 56
        (March). Canberra: Australia-Japan Economic Relations Research
        Project.

Mouer, Ross E.
  1978 "Conservative and Radical Approaches in the Literature on Japanese
        Society." A Paper presented to the Second National Conference of the
        Asian Studies Association of Australia (Sydney: The University of New
        South Wales, May 14–18).

Mouer, Ross E., and Yoshio Sugimoto (eds.)
  1980 *Japanese Society: Reappraisals and New Directions*. Published as a special
        issue of *Social Analysis,* 5/6 (December), Adelaide: University of Adelaide.

Naipaul, V. S.
  1980 "People Are Proud of Being Stupid." *Newsweek* (August 18): 38.

Nakane Chie
  1970 *Japanese Society*. Ringwood: Penguin Books.
  1972 *Tekiō no jōken* (The Conditions for Adapting [e.g., Internationalization]).
        Tokyo: Kōdansha.

Nihon Rōdō Kyōkai (Japan Institute of Labor) (ed.)
  1971 *70 nendai no chingin dōkō: Chingin yōkyū no mokuhyō o saguru* (The Direc-
        tion of Wages in the 1970s: The Decision on Wage Demands). Tokyo:
        Nihon Rōdō Kyōkai (March 30). Translated by the authors.

Norman, E. H.
   1975   *Origins of the Modern Japanese State: Selected Writings of E. H. Norman.*
           John W. Dower (ed.). New York: Pantheon Books.
Ouchi, William
   1981   *Theory Z.* Reading: Addison-Wesley.
Pascale, Richard T., and Anthony G. Athos
   1981   *The Art of Japanese Management.* New York: Simon and Schuster.
Reischauer, Edwin
   1977   *The Japanese.* Cambridge: Belknap Press.
Steven, Ron
   1979   "The Japanese Bourgeoisie." *The Bulletin of Concerned Asian Scholars,* 11
           (2) (April–June): 2–24.
Sugimoto, Yoshio
   1977   "Comparative Analysis of Industrial Conflict in Australia and Japan."
           In R. D. Walton (ed.), *Sharpening the Focus.* Brisbane: Griffith University.
Sugimoto, Yoshio, and Ross E. Mouer
   1979a "Kutabare Japanorijii—'Nihonjin Dōshitsuron' no Hōhōronteki
           Mondaiten" (The Limits of Theories Emphasizing the Homogeneous
           Nature of the Japanese: Some Comments on the Need for Analyzing
           the Dimensions of Inequality and Variance). *Gendai no Me,* 20 (6)
           (June): 134–45.
   1979b "A Discussion Paper on the Limits of Japanology as a Paradigm for
           Understanding Japanese Society." A Paper delivered to a seminar
           organized by the Australia-Japan Economic Relations Research Project
           (The Australian National University, Canberra, Australia) on Novem-
           ber 12, 1979.
   1979c "Japanology: A Methodological Deadend for Theories Assuming Uni-
           formity Among the Japanese." Griffith Translation Series, no. 2.
           Brisbane: School of Modern Asian Studies, Griffith University.
   1980a "Some Questions Concerning Commonly Accepted Stereotypes of
           Japanese Society." Research paper no. 64. Canberra: Australia-Japan
           Economic Relations Research Project.
   1980b "The Future of Japanese Studies: Philosophy, Journalism, Science or
           Art?" *Center News,* 4 (8) (March): 1–6.
   1980c "Reappraising Images of Japanese Society." *Social Analysis,* 5/6 (De-
           cember): 5–19.
   1982   *Nihonjin wa "Nihonteki" ka* (A Reconsideration of the Arguments about
           Japanese Society). Tokyo: Tōyō Keizai Shinpōsha.
Vogel, Ezra
   1979   *Japan as Number One: Lessons for America.* Cambridge: Harvard Uni-
           versity Press.
Yamamoto Mitsuru
   1981   "Nihon ga Kokusai Shakai de Ikiru Jōken" (Some Conditions for
           Japan to Survive as a Member of the International Community). *Ekono-
           misuto,* no. 2389 (January 13–20): 10–16.

INTERNATIONALIZATION
OF THE JAPANESE:
GROUP MODEL RECONSIDERED

Wagatsuma Hiroshi

The question to be addressed in this essay is whether or not the Japanese have recently become more "internationalized" and whether they will become more so in the future. The word "internationalization" can mean a variety of things. It can mean the flood of foreign commodities in Japan's domestic markets, frequent JAL-PAK tours through the European and American continents, or collective male expeditions into Southeast Asian nocturnal societies. It can also mean, at the governmental level, an increased awareness of economic and political interdependence among Japan and many other countries. It can mean, from the viewpoint of other nations, increased curiosity, if not knowledge and understanding, about Japan, which may even serve as a model of new economic growth. It can mean increased knowledge and understanding among the Japanese of other countries. I would think that in these aspects the Japanese have become internationalized to a great degree and this trend will continue in the future. However, when the word is used to mean an increased willingness, readiness and capability of meaningfully relating, interacting and working with people of different cultures in non-Japanese settings, and the question is asked if the Japanese have become and will continue to become internationalized, my answer is sadly negative. Most Japanese at present do not as yet seem ready to interact with foreigners with the same degree of ease and comfort with which they interact among themselves. It will be quite a while before the Japanese cultural norms and psychological tendencies change (if they ever change) and Japanese people become internationalized.

I would like to discuss the reasons for my negative answer. When

I mentioned "the Japanese cultural norms and psychological tendencies" the reader might very well interpret it to mean *group orientation*; that Japanese are so dependent on their group and bound by its norms that they cannot act on their own, dealing with more individually oriented people of different societies. To tell the truth, I do intend to make some statements about group orientation among the Japanese in reference to internationalization. My statements, however, need some footnotes.

In his excellent article, Befu pointed out the shortcomings, inadequacies and inaccuracies of the "group model" in the field of Japanese studies (Befu, 1980). The group model of Japanese society presupposes the existence of a nation which behaves like one harmonious family, and in which everybody is fundamentally dependent upon and deeply committed to his group. It is somehow assumed that all the Japanese, except for a few deviants and misfits, are selflessly oriented toward their group goals and loyal to their group causes. Befu points out that the group model overlooks the distinction between ideology and behavior. "Much of what the group model purports to account for is in the ideological realm of how the society ought to be and how human relationship should be" (Befu, 1980). In reality, however, Japanese society is ridden with all kinds of conflict and competition. Furthermore, in my opinion, the group model fails to differentiate among various levels of abstraction at which independent variables for the behavior that looks "group oriented" should be investigated and analyzed. The group model is "mono-causative," in the sense that it reduces to a single causal factor, such as dependency need (*amae*) or selfless subordination and loyalty among individuals, all the motivational factors behind apparently group oriented behavior. In reality, however, what looks like group oriented behavior (or any kind of behavior, for that matter) can be and often is motivated by a variety of individual needs. Devereaux quotes a Roman expression, "Si bis faciunt idem, non est idem" (if two people do the same thing, it is not necessarily the same thing) (Devereaux, 1961). Different Japanese individuals show so-called group oriented behavior, both willingly and unwillingly, for a variety of reasons—conformity to norms, sense of security, convenience, expediency, practicality, and very likely dependency in many cases—just like different German individuals once supported or presented no open resistance against the Nazi regime for a variety of reasons—fear, apathy, ignorance, greed, ambition, and perhaps, in some cases, "obsessive-compulsive," "sadomasochistic" or "authoritarian" tendencies. Not all Japanese show total emotional participation in group behavior, just as not all Germans were enthusiastic about Nazi ideology. Devereaux states that a variety of fuels, when thrown into the same furnace, can heat the same boiler. Parsons was of the same opinion when he stated that the same motives are not necessarily present in all individuals who are playing the same role. Concomitantly, the recurrent patterns of behavior required for institutional functioning may well have different meanings in different individuals (Parsons, 1949).

In his attempt to correct the inadequacies of the group model by combining it with social exchange theory, Befu states, "in many cases Japanese are loyal to their group *because it pays to be loyal*" (my emphasis). This statement should not be misconstrued to imply that in many cases Japanese consciously and deliberately remain loyal as long as it pays to be loyal and stop doing so as soon as it no longer pays. As Befu explains, the reward for an act (or a profit for a cost) is not only an instrumental gain but also an expressive gratification of emotional needs (which can be conscious or unconscious).

For those with a deep-seated need for dependence and security, going along with their group, rather than asserting themselves, "pays" because it gratifies their needs. Even for such people, going along with the group may at times entail frustration and irritation. Yet they will repress or suppress their resentment as long as it is more painful to loose the group support and sense of security as the consequence of expressing such resentment. Befu states, "social exchange theory claims not that what one does always brings pleasure, but that it is at least *less unpleasant than doing something else*" (my emphasis). Of great importance for our discussion is the continuing presence of the cultural norm that emphasizes the harmony and solidarity of the social group. For most people, it pays to be able to consider themselves as respectable societal members, observant and supportive of and compliant with their significant cultural norms, one of which in Japan is the group orientation.

Pointing out various, often unconscious, personal needs of the Hungarian Freedom Fighters of 1956, many of whom had explained their fight against the Russian tanks as their patriotic duty, Devereaux writes, ". . . both organized and spontaneous social movements and processes are possible not because all individuals who participate in them are identically (and 'sociologistically') motivated, but because a variety of authentically subjective motives may seek and find an ego-syntonic outlet in the same type of collective activity. This is equally true of spontaneous revolutionary movements and of extreme conformity" (Devereaux, 1961).

Even an individually "pathological" motive can be ego-syntonic (under the disguise of being "normal"), if the behavior motivated by such a need looks on the surface similar to a normative one. So-called pathological amae is a case in point. Since the publication of his best-selling book and its English translation, Doi's theory on dependency seems to have been misunderstood at times (Doi, 1970). Doi points out that when an infant's need for amae is well satisfied by its mother's (or surrogate's) nurturant behavior, the "basic trust" (Erikson, 1950) in its mother, and subsequently in the external world in general and in oneself, develops. The infant "trusts" its mother and does not panic when the mother temporarily disappears. When the basic need for amae is gratified the infant's ego becomes strengthened and it gradually tries to be independent of its mother (Doi, 1965). When, however, the infant's need for amae is not sufficiently gratified, the basic trust does not develop. The infant, with its need for amae frustrated may then try to "cling to" the mother in a desperate attempt to defend itself against separation anxiety. When such an infant grows to adulthood, with the need for amae continuously frustrated, the individual may "move toward people" as in Karen Horney's classification of neurotic orientations (Horney, 1945). Phenotypically, then, the individual's behavior may look like an ordinary dependent behavior. However, the motivational factors behind this seemingly amae behavior of such an individual, lacking the gratification of amae, the basic trust, and the strength of an independence-seeking ego, are *neurotic* in the sense that they are compulsive, insatiable and accompanied by incompatible and uncompromisable factors such as anger, resentment and fear. Thus, genotypically the "pathological" act of excessive dependence ("clinging") may very well contain elements of angry exploitation and untrusting manipulation of the others to whom the dependency is directed. In contrast with the case of such abnormal amae, an individual whose amae has been sufficiently gratified since early childhood basically trusts others and has no need to "cling to" them. Such a person is often described as *sunao-na* individual, upright and compliant, one of the ideal types of personality in Japanese society (DeVos and Wagatsuma, 1970). Such an individual can act independently when necessary and can also choose to be dependent (*amaeru*) on others when necessary. He can remain flexible, spontaneous and trusting. As long as the genotypically pathological act of excessive and compulsive dependence looks phenotypically similar to the normally dependent behavior, it can be interpreted, or misinterpreted, both by the actor and others, as a normal act and is therefore accepted. This is particularly the case with Japanese society in which cultural norms condone or even encourage dependence and interdependence among its members. A pathologically dependent individual may be able to maintain an illusion that he is quite normal because he is acting in accordance with the norm that emphasizes the value of group orientation.

In American society, in contrast with Japan, dependent behavior, normal or neurotic, receives strongly negative sanctions, while aggressive self-assertion and self-sufficiency are highly valued. In such a society, individuals "moving toward (excessively dependent upon) people" will quickly be singled out and labeled (by themselves and others) as neurotic or immature. On the other hand, those compulsively (and hence neurotically) moving against other people (aggressive, domineering and/or exploitative types) and/or those moving away from people (withdrawn and isolated) may be considered normal because their behavior seems in accordance with the cultural norms. In Japanese society, on the other hand, moving against and moving away from people (either normally or pathologically) may more quickly be deemed "deviant" and against the cultural norms (which do not encourage aggressive self-assertion and self-sufficient autonomy).

The second criticism Befu directed to the group model is that it is concerned with describing the internal structure of a group and subsequently fails to describe systematically how two different groups are related to one another. Befu states that in reality Japanese society is ridden with all kinds of conflict and competition. Needless to say, most of such conflict and competition is between and among social groups of various kinds. It is a widely known fact among the Japanese that a strong sense of competition, jealousy, and at times even vague un-focused animosity exists between neighboring prefectures, villages, towns, schools, bureaucratic branches, corporations, and families. It should further be mentioned that not infrequently competitiveness or even some degree of expressed negative feelings and criticisms are expected or encouraged by implicit norms among the in-group members. The group model is certainly inadequate if it assumes that the entire Japanese society is a harmonious whole. However, the model still applies to social groups of various sizes inside Japan. Also the model must incorporate the presence of tensions among such social groups.

As demonstrated by the functional analysis of institutionalized warfare or witch hunting among nonliterate people (Kluckhohn, 1944; Hallowell, 1938, 1940), in-group solidarity and out-group enmity are the two sides of the same psychodynamic coin. Aggressive and destructive tendencies that are generated but are not allowed to be expressed inside a social group are often directed outwardly and take the form either of hatred focused upon a specific scapegoat or of a diffuse sense of suspicion and animosity toward the outsiders. When aggressive self-assertion and confrontation are avoided among the members of a social group, they are deprived of the opportunities to "air" their pent-up tensions in a sublimated fashion. Consequently, it seems logical, or psycho-logical, to assume that the stronger the emphasis upon in-group harmony and solidarity, the more intense is the out-group enmity.

Japanese like to be among *kigokoro no shireta nakama,* those whose dispositions are well known to each other. Among the *kigokoro no shireta* friends and colleagues, Japanese can be relaxed, informal, frank and trusting. The group pressures on each individual member are expected to be very strong but often many Japanese feel that they need no extra efforts to make themselves "fit into" such a congenial group. In such a situation one feels that one is understood by others without verbally expressing and explaining oneself. Very often, what is really important for an individual's sense of security and belonging is not so much the actual fact of mutual understanding as the shared assumption of mutual understanding and acceptance. A Japan Airlines advertisement on Japanese language television in Southern California encourages the viewers (supposedly the Japanese business-

303

men and their families stationed in the United States) to invite their parents and relatives to America from Japan. Then it declares, "*kigokoro no shireta Nikkōki nara anshin desu*" (you can be sure of the safety of their trip on kigokoro no shireta JAL) as if the intimate acquaintanceship were the safeguard against hijacking or mechanical failure!

When a single person whose *kigokoro* is not equally known to others —somebody belonging to another company, a person from another village or prefecture, an alumna of another school—enters the scene, the atmosphere of the circle somehow becomes stiffened or chilled (*za ga shirakeru*). Japanese dislike to deal with *doko no uma no hone tomo wakaranu mono* (a horse bone whose origins nobody knows), a total stranger with no proper introduction or reliable sponsor, who is not even considered human!

Those Japanese who are strongly tied to their small groups— family, neighborhood, work or school groups—do not easily relate themselves to strangers nor do they find the casual acquaintanceship very meaningful or emotionally rewarding. Individuals A and B, friends of many years, walk along the street and along comes a third person C, who is an intimate acquaintance of A but does not know B at all. When this happens in American society, one can expect A to introduce B to C. If A begins to talk with C, without introducing B to C, B would feel slighted, ignored and offended. However, when these three individuals are Japanese, it often happens that A and C begin talking, while B turns around, as if socially disappearing from the A-C dyad. When their conversation ends and C walks away, A turns to B and apologizes for impoliteness ("*dōmo shitsurei itashimashita*"), *not* for failing to introduce B to C, but for causing B to wait until the conversation ended.

That casual acquaintanceship means very little to many Japanese has been demonstrated by the Asch experiment of conformity (Asch, 1946) conducted with Japanese subjects (Table 1). Both Frager and Sako found that the Japanese subjects were less inclined than the American subjects to go along with the (false) judgement of the laboratory group by giving up their own (accurate) judgement (Frager, 1970; Sako, 1975).

Compared with the individualistic Americans, the Japanese may indicate a greater degree of conformity to their group norms in reality. However, the "group" cannot be just any group. It has to be the group

304

TABLE 1

CONFORMITY BEHAVIOR IN "ASCH EXPERIMENTS"

Experimenter	Time	Place	Number of Subjects	Number of Non-Con-formists	Average Number of Conformity Behavior
Asch	1951	U.S.A.	50	13 (26%)	3.84
Frager	1966	Japan	128	34 (26.6%)	2.92
Sako	1975	Japan	22	11 (50%)	2.18

of very significant others. It seems that those people who happen to be sitting together in a psychological laboratory do not constitute for the subjects a group that is significant enough to elicit conformity. Badly needed are the experiments using a variety of categories of people, colleagues, classmates, family members to find out how the Japanese subjects behave toward them. I would hypothesize that the conformity behavior will increase when subjects are placed with the "real" group of significant others and face their (false) judgement. These results may be interpreted in the following way: American subjects demonstrated a sufficient tendency to relate themselves to a group of "strangers" in the laboratory so that the group exerted pressure to conform; but the Japanese did not relate to the same degree with the "strangers," who therefore did not constitute a significant group that can pressure the subjects. Here I am primarily interested in conformity as an indicator of the readiness of an individual to relate himself to people whom he has not known before. The results of other Asch experiments (Krech, Crutchfield and Ballachey, 1962) also indicate that the Americans are capable of relating themselves to the "strangers" more readily than the Japanese, although more experiments with the Japanese subjects are badly needed.

I have tried to argue for two points. First of all, the group model, when corrected and modified with multi-causal considerations, still works and is quite useful. In this regard, I am fully in agreement with Befu, although I have not, this time, tried to incorporate into my observation his idea about *seishin*. Secondly, inter-group conflict and competition should be the psychodynamic implication of the group model itself. All in all, in my opinion, most Japanese do remain "group oriented" (in their "eventual" overt behavior) and do not seem ready to relate themselves meaningfully to "outsiders" and "strangers." It is this last point that I think is crucial to the question of internationalization of the Japanese.

There are Japanese who are more individualistic or less group-oriented than others. There are also Japanese who remain in the group only because their "cost-profit" ratio slightly favors group conformity over individualistic self-assertion. These potentially individualistic Japanese, under different circumstances, such as an overseas assignment for businessmen, will and actually do demonstrate non-group oriented behavior. Many trading company employees, or *shōsha* men, are good examples. My next questions then would be: "Are there many such potentially individualistic Japanese today?" and "Can those Japanese, once their potentially individualistic behavioral tendencies are actualized, for example during overseas assignment, easily return to the previous group situations?" My answer to the first question is negative, although it is based on my impression, rather than any systematic empirical data. My answer to the second question is also negative, although here again empirical studies are urgently needed. I would assume that an individual cannot switch back and forth between individualistic and group orientations as a radio switches between AM and FM because a complicated cognitive, emotional and motivational cathexis is involved in each orientation.

There are an increasing number of Japanese children born and raised in foreign countries where their fathers' work has made it necessary for them to live for a prolonged period. Many of them grow up bilingual and bicultural, although circumstances vary depending upon their age and the length of their stay (Minoura, 1979). When they "return" to Japan, many of these children find it difficult to fit into group orientation. For example, many of them wonder why everybody has to wear the same school uniform and draw the picture of the same object in class.

Once a Japanese becomes too non-group oriented to comply with the major cultural norms, he/she will often have to find a place outside Japanese society. We may even speculate on the possible "polarization" of the Japanese into the group-oriented, non-internationalized majority and the individualistically oriented, internationalized minority. It would be tragic for the nation if such a minority were made to remain a group of "misfits" and if inter-group enmity developed between the majority and minority. It may be our task to look for some way in which such a minority can be functionally integrated into Japanese society, so that internationalized Japanese can play meaningful roles as "cultural brokers" (Wolf, 1956) in various parts of this society, which, whether it likes it or not, is increasingly exposed to international contacts.

REFERENCES

Asch, E. Solomon
    1946 "Studies of Independence and Conformity. A Minority of One Against a Unanimous Majority." *Psychological Monograph*, 70 (9).

Befu, Harumi
    1980 "The Group Model of Japanese Society and an Alternative." In C. M. S. Drake (ed.), *The Cultural Context: Essays in Honor of Edward Norbeck*. Rice University Studies, 66 (1).

Devereaux, George
    1961 "The Two Types of Modal Personality Models." In B. Kaplan (ed.), *Studying Personality Cross-Culturally*. Row, Peterson and Co.

DeVos, George, and Wagatsuma Hiroshi
    1970 "Status and Role Behavior in Changing Japan." In G. H. Seward and R. C. Williamson (eds.), *Sex and Roles in Changing Society*. New York: Random House.

Doi Takeo
    1965 *Seishin bunseki to seishin byōri* (Psychoanalysis and Psychopathology). Tokyo: Igaku Shoin.
    1970 *Amae no kōzō* (Structure of Dependence). Tokyo: Kōbundō.

Erikson, Erik H.
    1950 *Childhood and Society*. New York: W. W. Norton.

Frager, Robert
    1970 "Conformity and Anticonformity in Japan." *Journal of Personality and Social Psychology*, 15: 203–210.

Hallowell, Irvin
    1938 "Fear and Anxiety as Cultural and Individual Variables in a Primitive Society." *Journal of Social Psychology*, 9: 25–47.
    1940 "Aggression in Saulteaux Society." *Psychiatry*, 3: 395–407.

Horney, Karen
    1945 *Our Inner Conflicts—A Constructive Theory of Neurosis*. New York: W. W. Norton.

Kluckhohn, Clyde
    1944 *Navaho Witchcraft*. Papers of the Peabody Museum, Harvard University. Vol. 22 (2).

Krech, David, Robert Crutchfield, and E. L. Ballachey
    1962 *Individual in Society*. New York: McGraw Hill.

Minoura Yasuko
    1979 "Growing Up in Two Cultures: Socialization Experiences of the Children of Japanese Businessmen in Southern California." Unpublished Ph.D. dissertation, University of California, Los Angeles, Department of Anthropology.

Parsons, Talcott
   1949   *Essays in Sociological Theory*. New York: Free Press.
Sako Hidekazu
   1975   "Dōchō kōdō no jikken-bunka shinrigaku-teki kenkyū" (An Experi-
          mental-Cultural Psychological Study of Conformity Behavior). B.A.
          dissertation. University of Osaka, Department of Human Sciences.
Wolf, Eric R.
   1956   "Aspects of Group Relations in a Complex Society: Mexico." *American
          Anthropologist,* 58: 1065–1078.

定価2,900円
in Japan